Training Wheels

How a Brazilian Jiu-Jitsu Road Trip Jump-Started My Search for a Fulfilling Life

Valerie Worthington

DEDICATION

This book is dedicated to my parents; my sister and brother-in-law; and my niece and nephew. While I am solely responsible for the content of the book, each of you has contributed significantly to the content of my character. With apologies to Elizabeth Stone, your presence in my life means that every day, at any given time, my heart is running around outside my body in six different places.

CONTENTS

"I've been absolutely terrified every moment of my life—and I've never let it keep me from doing a single thing I wanted to do."

---Georgia O'Keeffe

FOREWARD

At my Pennington, New Jersey, high school, each graduating senior was immortalized in the yearbook with a black-and-white head shot and a self-selected quote or message underneath the photo to commemorate the milestone of graduation. When I was one of these hopeful seniors, one of the quotes I chose was, "She couldn't help thinking that there was a little more to life somewhere else," from the song *American Girl* by Tom Petty. At the time, the choice probably just reflected my snarky desire to escape the confines of small-town adolescence and go away to college. Where this book is concerned, though, the sentiment has more substantive meaning.

Of course, it implies the geographic journey, which frees and restricts us in ways that differ from those of a stationary routine, and which I have taken multiple times in many forms. However, it is also about the idea that there is more to life than I personally can live. I will not let that idea stop me from trying to experience as much as I possibly can, but I will use it as a reminder that there is always more.

The very next person I meet could be my next teacher, and the very next book I read, song I hear, or building I enter could provide clues to the next steps for me to take on my journey. My choices have not unlocked all the secrets of the universe for me, but over time I have become more

1

strategic about searching for keys.

In 2006, shortly before my 36th birthday, I ran away from home. The decision to do this placed an exclamation point at the end of a multi-year sentence of confusion, during which I had fumbled with questions of meaning, purpose, and fulfillment. Perhaps not surprisingly, I did not make much headway, particularly since at the time I was not even wording the questions as clearly as I am now. In that multi-year process of looking for *something*, though, I became increasingly sure that *it*, whatever it was, was elsewhere. So I started a new paragraph by going on a road trip that disentangled me from the familiar but ultimately wrong-for-me life I had built for myself in Chicago. Of course my personal baggage—my biases, fears, weaknesses, and quirks—insisted on coming along, backseat driving like the devil's GPS, and this made things interesting and sometimes terrible.

The road trip is nothing new. It was not even anything new to me, as when I was in college, I took a cross-country excursion with a friend. However, that trip was for a pre-set amount of time (the ten weeks of our junior fall quarter) and for a specific purpose (to assess the earning power of individual franchises in a chain of bowling alleys—a great story in itself). I was 20 years old, temporarily trying the realities and benefits of adulthood on for size. However, I was not expected to stay in adulthood until more years had elapsed and more youthful indiscretions had added dimension to my personality.

In contrast, the journey of 2006 was far less delineated and, as a result, far scarier. In this second scenario, more years *had* passed, and in those intervening years I had theoretically become a responsible adult with sensible life goals and sensible plans for attaining them. I had always been reasonably responsible, even from childhood, but theory and reality diverged once I moved toward the business about goals and plans.

I am also not the first to write about a road trip. Many have done this before me, but I am adding my story to the collection, precisely because it is mine, and it is what I have to offer. Perhaps it will add an unusual dimension to the "personal travelogue" genre because of its focal point: a martial art called Brazilian Jiu-Jitsu (BJJ) or submission grappling that I had been studying for about eight years by the time I decided to uproot myself.

At that point, jiu-jitsu was the only thing in my unsatisfying life that was not. So I followed the breadcrumb trail it created for me, hoping it would lead me toward something more fulfilling. My jiu-jitsu journey changed me forever and mostly for the better, thanks to my fair share of luck, support from my friends and family, and more fear and innocence lost than I wanted (though who wants any of that?). In fact, the previous sentence is basically the crux of this book, though of course I have a lot more to say.

I am always in search mode. I always look for deeper meaning. It is exasperating, my need to dig. I rarely allow things to be what they seem to be on the surface. Instead, I am always looking for the significance. What does it *mean*? What are the *implications*? Of course I have heard the old saw that sometimes a spade is just a spade, but then I remember that, according to surrealist painter Rene Magritte, the pipe is not a pipe. It is a picture of a pipe. And so begins the peeling of the layers of the onion—if an onion is indeed what it is.

This book recounts a phase of my life when I took a quantum leap along my journey, using the gospel according to Brazilian Jiu-Jitsu to help me on a search I had started years earlier for purpose and fulfillment—those things that sound banal when you try to describe why you care about them, but that are fundamentally important for human beings, if the fact that countless minds far stronger than mine have spent centuries contemplating them is any indication.

This has been a bruising, blind faith quantum leap that continues to influence my every subsequent decision. In this book, I try to describe the initiation of the jump, the sensation of being mid-air for months on end, and the realization that I have yet to fully land.

1

"Oh, no, I'm fine—I just dropped my pencil," I heard myself say, though I had actually just put my head between my legs to stave off the panic attack that had started in my feet and quickly spread to my everything else. I had not been holding a pencil.

My freak-out was self-imposed, caused by the sentence I had just spoken to my realtor, Melissa, who was sitting with me at the kitchen table in my Chicago condo. She had helped me find my home three years earlier, and now, in the spring of 2006, I had just said, "Please put this place on the market." I did not have another home lined up. Frankly, I did not have much of a plan of any kind. I was almost 36 years old and had no idea what I was doing: with the condo sale, with my life, with anything.

I only knew two things for sure. The first thing I knew was that I was miserable, and that something had to give. I was worried that if I kept to the path I was on, that that "something" would be my soul. This is why I had also, much to my terror, begun the process of quitting my job, going from a fairly high-level position to a part-time role at my company about three months earlier. In the coming months, I would see through to completion the process of dismantling my professional life as I knew it.

The other thing I knew for sure was that the only happiness

I derived at that time was participating in—also known as "training"—a martial art called Brazilian Jiu-Jitsu (BJJ) or submission grappling. BJJ had been my hobby since 1998, though over time it had become more a way of life than just a hobby. In fact, it was my love of BJJ and the sheer joy it brought me that awoke me to the stark absence of joy elsewhere in my day-to-day life. While I believed I had been sleepwalking through an ill-fitting existence for several years, BJJ shoved malodorous dissatisfaction under the nose of my conscious awareness.

The more I devoted myself to training, the more it drove a wedge between me and the life I had created for myself, making it more and more difficult for me to deny the contrast between the exhilaration I felt while training and the emptiness I felt at every other waking moment. On more occasions than I want to relive, I would head to training after a soul-sucking day at work, on or past the point of tears. Then I would spend a few blissful hours immersed in a training session, only to get buffeted by giant waves of despair as reality re-set in after class was over.

A series of events over a number of years cascaded over me like a waterfall, with the speed and intensity of these events having increased in the previous half year. Finally, they culminated in my uttering the aforementioned sentence and precipitating the aforementioned panic attack.

"Well, now is a good time to sell," Melissa said. "What prompted the decision?"

"The big one is money," I said. "I'm not sure what I want to do professionally, but I'm definitely looking to downsize. So I won't be able to afford this place anymore."

"Oh, wow. That's a big decision. Do you want to talk about it?"

"Nah, it's no big deal," I said, and then promptly launched into a minutes-long monologue about how I had been feeling unfulfilled in my job and that it was depressing me. Melissa nodded sympathetically and asked guiding questions. I got the feeling she had done this before. She was a good listener, and apparently I had needed a safe place to unload. If I had not already known her because of our interactions around my purchase of the condo several years earlier, that exchange would have confirmed for me that I could trust she would look out for my best interests.

I spared her these details, but a significant contributor to my upheaval was the sudden passing of my BJJ teacher, Carlson Gracie Sr., which had occurred a few months earlier. February 1, 2006, to be exact. Those in the grappling community, a small but growing one that reveres excellence, will recognize Carlson Sr.'s name as a legendary one. I had the good fortune and honor to learn from the man behind the legend for the final four years of his life, after he moved to Chicago to live near his son, Carlson Jr., my other teacher during that time and a successful and beloved instructor himself. I always feel a bit reluctant to "claim" Carlson Sr. because I learned from him for a fairly short time compared to many of his more famous students, a veritable who's-who of grapplers of their era who knew him in childhood as a father figure and coach. Following Carlson Sr.'s death, the Brazilian population of Chicago increased as friends and loved ones descended on the city to pay their respects.

I found out Carlson Sr. had passed early on the morning it happened. It was about 7:30am, and I had just exited the El on my way to work in Chicago's Loop when my phone rang.

"Val?" It was Natasha, a good friend of mine from jiu-jitsu. I noticed I had missed a few recent calls from her because I had been in a tunnel. She was a personal trainer at the gym where the Carlson Gracie academy was housed, so she spent most of her workdays in close proximity to the training space.

"Tash? What's wrong? I can barely understand you." My stomach clenched in dread. Natasha was sobbing.

"It's Senior," she managed. "He died this morning."

I stopped in my tracks for a few seconds, but then it registered that I was hindering foot traffic. I moved to the side of the closed-in Merchandise Mart walkway to get myself out of the stream of commuters and to lean against something solid. "What? But he was fine last night. The doctors said he was recovering."

"He took a turn for the worse in the middle of the night." She dissolved into more sobs.

I kept my head against the wall. "But...but he was fine."

"I know," she choked, "but now he's gone."

"Where's Junior?"

"He's at the hospital."

"Where are you?"

"I'm at the gym."

"What can we do?"

"Nothing right now. Just go to work, but stay close to your phone, okay? I'll call you in a little while."

"Okay." I paused. "Are you absolutely sure? Maybe it was a mistake."

She had already hung up.

I stayed bent over with my forehead against that comforting wall for several minutes. I felt like I never wanted to leave it. I cried for the first of many times.

Later that day, the students at the academy got confirmation that there had been no mistake: Carlson Gracie Sr. was gone. In the days that followed, Internet jiu-jitsu forums blew up with the news, friends reached out with condolences, and those of us who were in the area pitched in to provide what support we could. We got together at the academy more to try to find comfort in each other's presence than actually to train, though we tried to do that too, imagining Carlson Sr. would have chided us for getting sidetracked.

I got very little done at work or otherwise as reality set in and as I did what I could to stay connected to Carlson Jr. and my fellow students. I also found myself fielding numerous phone calls and texts from friends and acquaintances from other academies who wanted to convey their sympathies.

Later in February, there were three commemorating events to say good bye to Carlson Sr.: two memorial services in church settings in Chicago and the internment of half of his ashes at a cemetery in Evanston, IL. The other half were returned to his birthplace in Brazil.

At one of the church events, held on a somber, snowy,

and frigid day, Carlson Sr. was lying in repose, in an open casket at the front of a softly lit room. Fittingly, he had been dressed in a gi. A gi (pronounced "ghee," with a hard G) is like the familiar karate uniform of drawstring pants and collared jacket, though made of heavier woven cotton, and it is the traditional uniform jiu-jitsu practitioners wear for some forms of training and competition. Historically, gis have come in white, royal blue, and sometimes black, though more recently gi companies have gotten flashier, including red, yellow, and even tie-dye and camouflage patterns in their inventories. On this occasion, Carlson Sr. had been dressed in white.

The gi jacket is held closed with the practitioner's belt, also made of heavy woven cotton, and corresponding to the rank the practitioner has attained under a qualified instructor: white, blue, purple, brown, or black. White belts are at the inexperienced end of the spectrum, and some black belts have held their rank for decades. A scant few practitioners attain the rank of red belt, an honor reserved only for those who have attained the highest levels of skill, experience, and wisdom over the course of a lifetime.

Although he was more than qualified to wear a red belt, Carlson Sr. refused to do so during the time I knew him, claiming that it was for "old people." So his gi was always tied with a threadbare, faded black belt. Now, the black belt it was tied with was new and dark, and someone had coiled a red belt and placed it on his abdomen.

All of the stereotypes about the recently deceased applied to him: He seemed so peaceful; he looked as if he might soon open his eyes as if he were just waking from sleep; he could not really be gone. Throughout a long, emotionally enervating day, mourners came in to pay their respects, sometimes standing with downcast eyes and folded hands, sometimes kneeling on a bench that had been placed in front of the casket to facilitate contemplation and maybe even final communication with the departed. People clustered in small groups around the room or sat quietly in pairs or alone, holding hands, putting arms around each other, dabbing at their eyes. Some people kept vigil for the entire day, while others paid their respects to Carlson Jr. and his mother and then discreetly took their leave.

One teammate, named Carlos, had just been promoted to black belt by Carlson Sr. just the previous month. Carlos was fluent in Portuguese and had been in the middle of his medical training when Carlson, Sr., became ill. He had taken on an ad hoc and much-appreciated role as liaison among the students, Carlson Sr. (whose English was limited), and the doctors treating Carlson Sr., translating among English, Portuguese, and medical-speak for the several days he was hospitalized before his condition deteriorated and he ultimately passed away.

When he had an opportunity, Carlos approached the casket, accompanied by a small boy. After the two spent some time kneeling on the bench, they stood up. Then both, prompted by Carlos, solemnly placed their hands at their sides and, in a gesture even non-martial artists would recognize, bowed to their professor one last time.

I was just a random jiu-jitsu fan who had come to know Carlson Sr. long after he had made the name that many strangers and would-be intimates have gone on to drop. I worry that I will be accused of the same thing. The simple fact, though is that I loved him, I am grateful to him for what he taught me about BJJ and about life, and my world is better for having had him in it. People who have been around grappling long enough to have observed Carlson Sr.'s excellence in action, either through his own competition accomplishments or through those of the stable of high-level practitioners he coached, speak respectfully about the legacy he left behind. Unlikely though it may seem, I am a very, very small part of that legacy.

Others have documented Carlson Sr.'s legendary contributions to the world of vale tudo ("anything goes") fighting and Brazilian Jiu-Jitsu far more eloquently than I could, and with much more firsthand knowledge of them. For instance, in his book *The Gracie Way: An Illustrated History of the World's Greatest Martial Arts Family*, author Kid Peligro devotes a chapter to Carlson Gracie Sr. and his influence on the grappling world. In it, Peligro details the role Carlson Sr. personally played in upholding his family's reputation as a martial arts powerhouse by defeating multiple larger, more experienced opponents in no-holds-barred match-ups, starting when he was a very young man.

He also describes how Carlson Sr., through his coaching, "created some of the best Brazilian jiu-jitsu (sic) fighters in the world,"[1] dozens of high-level practitioners who went on to leave their imprimatur on the grappling world through their own competition records and through coaching their own students. Whether we are steeped in this history because we started training while he was active, or whether we developed an interest in Brazilian Jiu-Jitsu since his passing and view him as more of a historical influence, those of us who invest in the grappling lifestyle and strive for excellence in that world have him to thank for the major role he played in shaping and bringing honor to the sport we love so much. Carlson Gracie Sr. is one of the grappling giants upon whose shoulders today's practitioners now have the opportunity to stand.

I knew this before I met him because I trained at Carlson Jr.'s academy for two years before he arrived—and people talked, of course. Then after I met him, I got to observe the impact of his stature firsthand. Whenever he walked into our academy, he immediately became the focal point of the room, a tractor beam wrapped in a gi. Well before the time of his passing, he had probably forgotten far more about BJJ than most grapplers would ever learn in multiple lifetimes. I was routinely astounded by his teaching and his knowledge over the four years I got to know him, and as a blue belt, I was ill-equipped even to do that properly. In a proud moment for me, Carlson Sr. and Carlson Jr. eventually promoted me to purple belt, with Carlson Sr. himself tying the belt around my waist.

It is probably not surprising that in the weeks and months after Carlson Sr.'s death, those of us left behind were thrown into a tailspin, both as a team, and, if I was any indication,

[1] Peligro, K. (2003). *The Gracie way: An illustrated history of the world's greatest martial arts family.* Montpelier, VT: Invisible Cities Press.

as individuals. To me, it felt like one of the support beams on which I had built my day-to-day existence had been knocked out from under me, and that, coupled with how much I had been struggling at work, reminded me of the stages of losing baby teeth. Before Carlson Sr. died, I felt like my life was a little wobbly but not poised yet for any major action. After his passing, though, I felt like I had crunched on a hard piece of food at an angle that removed all connection between my tooth and my jaw but the tiniest bit of sinew, leaving the tooth hanging by a thread. His death added to an amalgam of confusion, recklessness, and general existential itchiness that had already begun to collect in my mind partly as a result of my BJJ training, leading me more and more regularly to take actions and think thoughts that before BJJ would have shocked me or seemed beyond the pale.

In that springtime meeting with my realtor, fueled in part by the subversive effect BJJ had on me in general and by the aftermath of Carlson Sr.'s death in particular, I continued this behavior, with one half of my psyche standing by, helplessly disembodied, silently screaming "What the $&%#!! are you doing??" as the other half took over my person, particularly my voice, prompting me to vomit the aforementioned sentence.

Melissa was very patient, telling me that in her field she had seen many people before me experience a similar level of difficulty in taking the plunge and actually putting their homes on the market. Apparently it is usually an emotional experience, sometimes because people have grown to love their homes and cherish the memories to which those homes have borne witness, sometimes because the act of selling is fraught with questions about the future, and sometimes both.

For me, while I had had some good years in the condo, the focus was definitely on the future, particularly since I did not have any idea what it was going to look like, nor any inspiration about how to figure it out. I did not have a place to move to, and I did not feel compelled to look. Here, Melissa was at a loss. Apparently her clients usually did not just gloss over what they planned to do once they were literally out on the street.

"You're not looking for another place in Chicago?"

"No."

"Are you looking for a place in a different city?"

"No."

"Where are you going to live?"

"I don't know."

"Well, what are you going to do?"

"I don't know."

"Are you going to move back in with your parents?"

"No."

"..."

"I might just drive around."

"Oh. Do you have a car?"

"No."

"I guess you'd need to get one."

"I guess. At least I'll have money after the condo sells, right?"

"Yes," Melissa said, forcing a laugh. I forced one as well.

And just like that, an idea materialized. A completely wrong-headed idea. An idea that would ultimately inspire me to quit my job and use the proceeds of my condo sale to buy a car and drive it back and forth across the continent, training Brazilian Jiu-Jitsu at many of the academies scattered throughout the United States and Canada.

A plan for a jiu-jitsu walkabout, kind of an *On the Road* meets *Kung Fu* meets *Eat, Pray, Love*; a plan that also seemed to be a fitting homage to my recently departed teacher. As I have learned during the process of making many decisions since I made this most momentous one, it was the act of speaking the idea, even in my irreverent way, that brought it into the realm of possibility.

As with many of those subsequent decisions, this one had no real details attached to it. While I was in the process of hatching what would become a plan, I only ever got a vague sense of what my immediate next step needed to be. There is some movie—or maybe I dreamed it—where the protagonist pursues the antagonist through a space-age landscape. He comes to a chasm that is too wide to jump across. The bottom is invisible in the blackness.

A disembodied voice tells him to trust and to walk, which he does after some hesitation, and a lighted square zips into place under his foot just as he takes his first step, remaining in place long enough to support him and flying away as a new square speeds in to support his next step. In this way, he stays aloft across the chasm. All that exists is the square supporting him, the square meeting his next step, and the square disappearing behind him.

As he moves farther from solid ground, he must rely more on faith that the squares will fly into place at the moment he needs them. Eventually, as he gets closer to the ground in front of him, he becomes more confident that he will make it safely across.

This tableau feels like what I was experiencing: as fearful as I was, I just had to keep moving forward and trust that the squares would appear when I needed them.

I did not tell Melissa this part either.

- - - - - - - - - -

If I had to assign a time frame to it, I would say my dissatisfaction with my life came to a head in December 2005, some two and a half years before I went on to become a BJJ purple belt world champion. To put it another way, that is when I finally and officially went bat-shit crazy. I had been employed at an education corporation for a few years by then, working with professors in various locations around the country, doing my best to encourage them to converge on shared ideas of an ideal curriculum for their respective programs that would become the common core for every student in every campus location.

I say "doing my best" because in my role I did not have direct authority over anyone. This means if I wanted any support for them, I had to convince my colleagues that the goals I had been tasked with were great ideas.

The job had been fine. I was not leaping out of bed in the

morning to rush to my office, and I did my share of clockwatching, but I had managed to create a reasonably agreeable life, complete with enough disposable income to keep myself in jiu-jitsu gear, academy tuition, and some grappling-related trips—even a visit to Rio to watch the 2003 version of the world tournament I alluded to earlier.

And beyond the benefits this lifestyle conferred on my budding BJJ preoccupation, its trappings were also consistent with the kind I had grown up expecting I would have: a white collar job, a nice home in a desirable neighborhood, friends who had similar sensibilities and priorities, and, perhaps, eventually a family. I was following to a "T" the blueprint I had always believed would help me put together a fulfilling life. So I was happy.

Right?

As it turns out, not so right. Back then, I was among the one in ten Americans who pursued better living through chemistry[2][3] (and these numbers are not decreasing). I took Prozac to treat my depression, characterized in my case by crying jags; periodic feelings of despair, particularly when I contemplated a future of more of what I had in the present; and a tendency to sleep too much or too little, depending on how long I had been doing the one or the other. I had been taking Prozac for several years, starting in graduate school. In 1995 I had moved to Michigan to pursue a doctorate in educational psychology, which is basically the study of learning—processes, motivations, and influences. I did and still do find the subject matter fascinating and unexpectedly relevant in almost all aspects of my life.

If I had to describe my day-to-day life in my first year as a graduate student in one word, it would be "insecure," in the literal sense of feeling "without security." I was lonely, I was

[2] Wehrwein, P. (2011, October 20). *Astounding increase in antidepressant use by Americans*. Retrieved from http://www.health.harvard.edu/blog/astounding-increase-in-antidepressant-use-by-americans-201110203624

[3] Pratt, L. A., Brody, D. J., & Gu, C. (2011, October). *Antidepressant use in persons aged 12 and over: United States, 2005-2008*. Retrieved from http://www.cdc.gov/nchs/data/databriefs/db76.htm

not sure I could do the required work, and I was surrounded by people who seemed to know what they were doing. Little did I know that apparently most everyone suffers from "impostor syndrome." While it might have helped to know I was not alone, it would not have stopped me from feeling stupid and berating myself for it on a regular basis. I subjected my parents to countless phone calls during which I cried and they tried to comfort me. One time in particular, after months during which they had been endlessly patient and supportive, I finally brought us all to our breaking point.

"Hello, Mom and Dad? It's me," I snuffled.

"Hey there. How's it going?" my father said.

"Not good."

"What's going on?" from my mom.

"I don't know. I just...I'm just unhappy but I don't know why. I don't know if I can hack it here."

"So, quit," said my dad.

"What? I can't do that," I whined. Even at the time, though I was genuinely upset, I knew I was acting like a child.

"Well, honey, what other options do you have? I mean, we've gone around and around about this for months now. You're not happy, and it's not worth it for you to stick with it if it's going to make you miserable," my father replied.

Inwardly, I panicked. Not get a doctorate? Both my parents had them, and my sister was working on hers. I could not be the only one in the family who did not have a Ph.D. Right or wrong, my entire body rebelled against that thought—it could not happen.

Plus, if I was being honest with myself, I liked what I was studying. I just was not confident I was smart enough to study it, and I did not like where I was living. Among other things, with all due respect to Michigan and Michiganders, the locals joke with good reason that there are only two seasons: winter and construction. At that point, I had experienced the full spectrum of construction and was more acquainted with winter than probably anyone would like. I had also found that my east coast sensibilities did not play well in the kinder, gentler Midwest, with more than a few people finding my sense of humor to be mean, or at least not at all humorous. I eventually grew to appreciate Michigan, but at the time, I felt like a fish out of water.

Yet: "No, I want to stay."

"Well, then you have to be able to make it work, honey," my mother said. "You can't spend all your time crying. It makes us sad that we can't do anything to help you." Ugh. I was a terrible daughter.

"Well, Joyce had a suggestion." Joyce was the psychologist I had seen off and on throughout my post-college young adulthood. I had been consulting with her more regularly since I had been in school.

"We're all ears," my father said.

"She mentioned Prozac."

Truthfully, this was part of why I was so upset this time. My conversations with Joyce were very similar to the ones I was having with my parents, in that there was a lot of crying but very little progress toward figuring out how to stop the crying. I was miserable, but in my mind, not getting a doctorate was not an option. I was not even trying to be difficult. It is just that a world that did not involve me pursuing a doctorate did not compute in my brain. Just like division by zero, it was a mathematical impossibility.

I was not able to articulate this at the time. I just said, "No, no, no, I'm staying." This is when Joyce had gently raised the suggestion of an anti-depressant.

"What? Drugs?" I cleared my throat and took a deep breath, like an opera singer preparing to belt out an aria, only I was fixing to pitch a major fit.

"Hear me out," Joyce had said. She anticipated and countered my main concerns, namely that drugs meant I had *really* gone around the bend and that using them would make me somehow not me. "If you don't like the way they make you feel, you can always taper off them again. But it's a viable option that could really help you, Valerie. Many people report that an anti-depressant enables them to feel *more* like themselves, not less. Many people just like you go on them. They aren't crazy. They are just affected by rogue neurochemistry."

I digested this and still felt nauseated. The problem, I felt, was not that drugs could help me. The problem was that I apparently needed the kind of help that drugs could provide. This seemed momentous, and yet, I still made no connection between my mood and my choices.

I do not have any qualifications other than my own experiences to support this claim, but I believe many people do suffer from the rogue neurochemistry Joyce referred to, myself included. I further believe that for those people, and for countless other people, anti-depressants are a viable remedy. That being said, I also believe that at that time in my life, some different situational decisions on my part could have served a purpose similar to the one Prozac did.

In the words of Martha Beck, who is an author, a life coach, and a columnist for *The Oprah Magazine*, I was moving away from my north star—my right life—and in my case, the fact that my situation had given rise to a need for medication was a huge clue about this. I just did not yet know how to read the signals my own body was giving me.

After much keening and wailing, I eventually conceded that I had nothing to lose by trying Prozac, and I had to admit that it helped me. A few weeks after I had taken the plunge, during which time the medication built up in my system, I distinctly remember waking up one morning feeling like Josh Baskin, the Tom Hanks character in the movie *Big*, after he had, well, you know... For a time, I felt "fixed." I had to check in with Joyce and the medical doctor who served as my Prozac connection once in a while to make sure things were continuing to go well, to make sure there were no adverse effects, and to renew my prescription. I had no complaints, however, no need for talk therapy. In fact, those check-ins eventually became kind of awkward because there were lots of silences punctuated by my comments about how fine I felt.

This proved to be temporary, however. Slowly over the next several years, as I completed my degree and moved to Chicago, the dissatisfaction crept back in, gradually transforming back into despair, prompting me to up my dosage. By the time I arrived in the Windy City, I had also developed severe allergies. I consulted a specialist, who was unable to pinpoint their cause. I followed the advice to avoid food allergens and dander, and although I did not seem to have a problem with anything environmental, I nonetheless experienced bouts of sneezing, itching, and tear-filled eyes—the works—at least once or twice a month, every season of the year. This sent me hurrying for the relief of antihistamines, a cure that was frequently worse than the disease.

The fact that these allergy attacks disappeared completely once I left behind my job and the accoutrements of the life I had spent so much time carefully constructing, combined with the fact that I was Prozac-free for over a decade at the time of this writing, has convinced me that I had in fact been allergic to that job and that life. I never say never when it comes to Prozac or other medications, but I make sure I have explored my other options before I choose it. Now that I have an expanded sense of what those options are, I believe that my neurochemistry is such that I am often—though obviously not always—able to manage my moods on my own.

When people ask me now what was so wrong with my life back then, I find it difficult to give a convincing answer. I did not have one back then either. Every now and then I became overwhelmed with feelings of despair about my life, that I was doing it wrong, and that everyone else had it all figured out. I felt like something was missing, but I did not know what it was or how to get it.

Then I felt ungrateful, because by any measure I had had every advantage, and here I was pissing it away by crying and eating ice cream out of the carton while watching syndicated television alone in my apartment when there were countless people who would have killed to have the opportunities I had.

A friend of mine is the seventh of ten siblings who were raised in poverty in inner-city Connecticut, among other places, by an alcoholic, abusive father and a mother who had all she could do to keep it together for her children. My friend's childhood concerns included protecting herself and her siblings from her father and never being sure where her next meal was coming from. She told me her mother observed that in that kind of situation, depression is a luxury.

When you are worried about issues like personal safety and getting enough to eat, you do not have the space to experience ennui, or to consider whether you are living your right life. Or maybe you do think about those things, but you are rarely able to indulge them. Instead, you have different, more immediate battles to fight every day, and you likely have no opportunity to do much else. This is not to say that my friend's mother believed, or that I believe, the depression many people suffer is unjustified or an overreaction. Rather, depending on the context, it may not be the front burner issue it is for some, including, historically, me. It was not for my friend's mother because it could not be.

It is a tricky tightrope to walk. I remember when *Eat, Pray, Love* thundered onto the cultural landscape. Readers— mostly women—loved it so much we wanted to marry it, and not just because we suddenly had a built-in excuse, even a compelling moral imperative, to gorge ourselves on pizza. The book seemed to tap into some kind of zeitgeist of dissatisfaction. But author Elizabeth Gilbert endured pot shots from some commentators who, among other things, described her as a whiny rich girl who did not appreciate her advantages and oversimplified what it takes to reach spiritual enlightenment.[4] To say I do not have as much wealth as Elizabeth Gilbert reportedly has is to split hairs. I know I am a person of privilege.

I puzzle over how to square this with the fact that sometimes I genuinely feel bad. I do my best to strike a balance between honoring my own experience while always counting my many blessings. Back then, the way I handled it was to berate myself for not being happier and more grateful. And I might have continued to do so indefinitely had I not made what looked to be a great career move but ended up being the final straw for life as I knew it.

---

[4] Meier, P. (2010, August 12). *Life isn't fair and Eat, Pray, Love*. Retrieved from http://www.morepaul.com/2010/08/life-isnt-fair-and-eat-pray-love.html

Before I was able to free myself from the wrong life I had spent five years building for myself in Chicago, I waded one step deeper into it: I got promoted. Doing anything other than accepting did not occur to me. I was offered a significant salary bump and more visibility and authority. After I signed on for the role, I received many congratulations and good wishes from colleagues, family, and friends. It was consistent with the blueprint, the next step toward securing my everlasting happiness.

Yet the low-grade depression that had gradually returned during my time in Chicago kicked into high gear directly after I took the new position. I was looking to the promotion to snap me out of my funk, but for the first month after I accepted it, which was actually about as long as I lasted, I went into my office every day when I got to work, closed the door, sat down and put my head on my desk, and cried for anywhere from a few minutes to an hour before I pulled myself together and got on with my day.

In my more lucid moments, when I thought to try to identify what was really upsetting me, I entered familiar territory: Just like when I decided to go on Prozac in graduate school, I could not pinpoint anything specific, like a breakup or a loss or a disappointment, that was causing my upset. Just general dread, an almost unbearable feeling that I wanted to be anywhere but faced with the work I had signed on to do.

It was when I caught myself thinking, "Not this again," that it finally started to click. I realized I had to take a different course of action.

- - - - - - - - - -

"So...just so I'm clear, you want to step down from the promotion?"

"Yes, that's correct," I intoned to my boss. "I've realized it's not a good fit."

"Well, you've only been at it for a month," he responded. "Can you give it a little more time? It could just be growing pains."

"I can see how you might think so, but it isn't," I said, recalling the countless tears I had cried and the waves of despair that had bowled me over in the single month that had elapsed since I had accepted that expletive-deleted promotion. "I've had the opportunity to think about it a lot, from a lot of angles. It was a tough decision, but I feel it's the right one. Like I said, it just isn't the right fit." In other words, if I don't get out, I will come completely unglued. "So, I would like to go part time and work on the other project I have been assigned to." I was careful to maintain an impassive expression.

"And there's nothing we can do to change your mind?" He did not say he was annoyed, but I picked up the meaning in his clipped tone and repeated sighs. The meaning was that I had bungled a huge opportunity: I had been invited to sit at the adults' table with all the sophisticated conversation and the fancy cutlery, but instead of capitalizing on the invitation, I had breathed on my spoon and hung it on the end of my nose.

Now my boss was going to have to come up with a way to explain my rapid departure. He had, after all, sent many laudatory emails and announcements to colleagues around the organization about my appointment to this coveted position. He had shepherded me around the office, showing me off like a prize-winning spaghetti squash—and letting me know through his body language that he expected the same amount of participation from me in these interactions that he would from an actual root vegetable.

I did not tell him I wanted to spend more time training BJJ, and he did not ask. In the past, when he had been showing muckety-mucks around and happened to bump into me in the hall, the fact that I train BJJ was always included as part of my introduction, along with my actual professional qualifications. I am willing to bet I was the only person thus described, though for me it was an awkward interaction every time, partly because everyone involved in the interaction except me insisted on busting out with what we grapplers call "karate chop hands." In BJJ, there are no chops or kicks of any kind; these are characteristic of more traditional martial arts like karate and kung fu.

This distinction, important to the jiu-jitsu practitioner, is lost on the blithe layperson, which means that people who "air chop" or crane kick are revealing themselves as outsiders, on the non-righteous side of the shibboleth. When it was handy to use my quirky hobby for some benefit, my boss did not hesitate. Now, though, whether he realized it or not, it was that siren song that was partly responsible for my recent life decisions. He was annoyed because this time it was personal. I did not blame him, but I also did not intend to do the thing that would have made his life easier: stay.

"Well, you've always been a good employee, and I know you would have done a great job in this position," he said, as if he were reading off a cue card behind his eyelids. "But if we can't change your mind, we'll set the wheels in motion to adjust your pay and find someone to replace you."

"Thanks a lot. I really appreciate it, and even if it doesn't seem like it now, I know it will be for the best."

"Yeah, sure," my boss sighed.

I scurried away while the scurrying was good.

Things had gotten serious. For the years I worked there, everyone at my job indulged my cute stories of sore muscles and scrapes on the tops of my feet from repeated rubbing on the jiu-jitsu mat, and even the black eyes I tended to get on a regular basis, when it came to me pursuing my endearing, off-the-wall diversion, as long as I pursued it outside of the confines of my work. As long as I did not challenge anyone's sense of propriety or of what constitutes normal—which is to say, a 9-to-5 job with all the trimmings—I could probably have come to work in full head-to-toe gi regalia with two black eyes, and everyone would have confirmed with me that I had met my deadlines before even inquiring about it. ("Val, did you get that email sent out? You did? Great. By the way, is it Halloween or something?")

By quitting my job without having a bigger, better job lined up, and instead retreating into part-time obscurity and offering only a vague idea of what I was going to be doing with the rest of the hours in my workday, I broke the fourth wall. With my actions, I declared that some set of unknown variables was preferable to what was in front of me, though everyone around me had opted for what I was now turning my back on. That was not likely to be considered quite as adorable as my scrapes and scratches, and as I found out, people did not become *more* understanding.

Take, for example, my colleague Joe[5], who was the first to reach out when he heard the news that I was quitting my promotion.

"Val, do you have a minute?" he asked, knocking on my open office door.

"Sure, Joe, come on in," I chirped, though I groaned silently when I saw who it was.

Joe did not have direct authority over me, but his actions did affect my day-to-day life. My experience of him was that whenever he appeared, progress slowed or tasks landed on my desk that were outside of the scope of my job. He struck me as a "company man" who invested himself in knowing the right people to the exclusion of doing any measureable work. Today he was wearing a bolo tie. This was not going to be good.

"What's up?"

"Did I hear you quit your promotion?" Joe demanded, visibly agitated.

"Apparently so," I snipped. One saving grace I had learned about Joe was that sarcasm was lost on him. Of course to me this was akin to an invitation to lay it on with a trowel. I figured it was preferable to relieve some of the build-up of annoyance in this way rather than allowing the disdain to accumulate over time until I lost control and shouted in his face.

His eyes widened. "I mean, I heard it, but I couldn't believe it. So it's true?"

"Yep. I'm stepping down from the position and going part time. I'll be working on another project." I ended up lasting in the part-time position for roughly three months. Then I and my teammates lived through Carlson Sr.'s death, and then I went full-on crazy and decided to leave Chicago. Right now, though, I was beginning to see a side of Joe I had

---

[5] Not his real name

never before observed and did not like.

"But why? Why on earth would you do that?" His voice trailed off, and he looked like he was about to cry.

"Well, um...Joe, are you all right?"

"I just don't get it. I mean, you got a promotion, you got a nicer office, you'd have a bigger leadership role. And I assume you got a raise?"

I said nothing. It was none of his business.

"What more do you want? Is that not good enough for you?"

"Wait, what? No, no, no, Joe, that's not it. I didn't want more. I realized I want less."

"You wanted less work? You think you should be allowed to work less than the rest of us?"

"Excuse me? Joe. Please calm down. I realized the job wasn't making me happy. I want to be happy. I believe I'll be happier if I step down from this position."

"You think you're special. Why do you get to be any happier than the rest of us?" Joe closed the distance between us, and while I did not for a second believe he would get physical with me, I also did not like where this was headed. I began to try to angle myself closer to the door and to keep my chair between us.

"I don't, Joe. I—I'm not entirely sure why you're so upset. This is my decision and it doesn't affect you," I offered carefully, keeping me hands out in front of me, palms facing him, moving my arms up and down like I was a conductor of a very distraught soloist. "I mean, it won't make additional work for you or anything. The position I just stepped down from isn't even in your department."

"You just shouldn't quit. What if you never get another job? What if you regret this decision? How can you not want this? I mean, you're not even going to something better. You're taking a step backward professionally."

"I guess I'll worry about it when the time comes. I just don't want this right now. I've thought about it a lot and weighed all the pros and cons, and I feel really sure that it's the right decision for me."

"You can't do this. It's not right," he said, almost under his breath. "The rest of us are sticking it out. We're doing what people are supposed to do."

Joe looked at the floor for a minute, lost in thought. I kept the chair between us and racked my brain for a way to end this interaction. He looked up and said, "I mean, I know I should probably say something nice to you, but I think you're making a big mistake."

He turned and left, unconvinced and unassuaged, and I closed the door with shaking hands, my heart slamming practically through my rib cage. I sat down heavily, assuming the same pencil-dropping position I soon found myself in during my conversation with Melissa. Why would Joe react so vehemently about decisions I had made—had the right to make—about my future, or even my present, for that matter? When you do something that makes you happy, people are supposed to be happy for you, right?

At the time, sitting in a heap on the floor of my office, Joe almost had me convinced that I was making a huge mistake. Maybe I could go crawling back and convince my boss to let me change my mind—again, I thought, my mind racing. I mean, after all, a promotion is a positive thing. It is something most of us would agree is normal to strive for and then to celebrate, but mine had very quickly come to feel like rocks in my coat pockets. Was there something to his implication that there was something wrong with me?

I am not alone in my confusion, given the preponderance of anecdotal and scientific evidence that most of us do not like our jobs. Witness, for example, "Working for the Weekend," "Take This Job and Shove It," the concept of TGIF, and author Po Bronson's 2005 best-seller *What Should I Do with My Life?*,[6] which spent close to a year on the *New York Times* bestseller list. Bronson's book features case studies of individuals who left their careers, explaining why and how they did it. As an aside, it may come as no surprise that reading anecdotes about the inspirational and fulfilling things people discovered they could do with their lives also provided me with much-needed hope during those times

---

[6] Bronson, P. (2002). *What should I do with my life? The true story of people who answered the ultimate question*. New York: Random House.

when I was not sure what I was doing with mine.

Further, a 2013 Gallup poll on the state of the American workplace found that only 30 percent of full-time workers in the U.S. report being actively engaged in their jobs.[7] According to this, then, it turns out that we as a population appear to seek advancement in careers we regret having chosen in the first place. When you look at it that way, it sounds kind of barmy. Why on earth would we do this? Why on earth would I do this?

In her book *How to Be Happy, Dammit: A Cynic's Guide to Spiritual Happiness*, author Karen Salmansohn describes a parable about a criminal who is brought to justice in a kingdom. When given a choice between being hanged or whatever is behind Door Number One as his punishment, the criminal immediately chooses hanging, whereupon the king comments that nearly everyone does the same. The criminal then asks what lies behind the door, pointing out that he is now in no position to reveal the secret, and the king responds, "Freedom, but it seems most people are so afraid of the unknown that they immediately take the rope."[8]

And yet, for all the aversion we as a species seem to have to drastic life changes, we still make tons of them. Relocation. Marriage. Parenthood. Job changes. Joining and leaving religions. Divorce. In my case, detonating a perfectly good, steady existence to pursue a more volatile, doubt-riddled one.

In her book *Finding Your Own North Star: Claiming the Life You Were Meant to Live*, Martha Beck acknowledges the difficulty most of us have in making drastic life changes but observes that, throughout our lives, there are times when the compulsion may become irresistible. She also counsels that the experiences most of us have as we undergo a life

---

[7]Gallup (2013). *State of the American workplace: Employee engagement insights for U.S. business leaders*. Retrieved from http://www.gallup.com/strategicconsulting/163007/state-american-workplace.aspx

[8] Salmansohn, K. (2001). *How to be happy, dammit: A cynic's guide to spiritual happiness*. New York: Celestial Arts.

transformation, are, while scary-seeming, actually quite predictable and consistent. She describes three categories of impetus that compel people to transform their lives, to veer off the predicted trajectory and end up in an unexpected field of clover—or perhaps something a bit more pungent, depending on where you are in the process and what you bring to it. These three categories are shocks, opportunities, and transitions. Shocks can be anything from a layoff to a severe car accident to a death in the family. The common denominator among shocks is that they are externally imposed. The main characteristic of an opportunity, on the other hand, is that it offers what appears to be a chance for positive change: a dream job offer or requited love, for instance.

And then there are transitions. Beck says that transitions are initiated from within, and as such, they are much harder to justify, especially if nothing appears to be wrong, exactly, in the transitioner's life. She suggests that "transitions begin, deep down, the minute you set out to live a life that doesn't jibe with your essential self. Over time, the dissonance, the sense of never being who you really are, starts to bother you. A lot. In fact, it finally becomes intolerable...Either you end up having a nervous breakdown...or you simply decide that you have to acknowledge your real thoughts, preferences, desires, and identity."[9]

I am a poster child for Beck's model. My life in the early 2000s was starting to become intolerable, though I felt guilty for thinking so, because I could not identify anything that was truly wrong with it. If anything, I was fortunate, given all the academic, professional, and familial options and support I had always enjoyed. In the midst of this, I got the promotion. Then, about a month or two after I began to extricate myself from it, Carlson Sr. passed away. The transition (my vague but profound dissatisfaction with my day-to-day routine), the opportunity that turned out to be anything but (my promotion), and the shock (the loss of my teacher) that clustered together in my life during that time

---

[9] Beck, M. (2001). *Finding your own north star: Choosing the life you were meant to live*. New York: Three Rivers Press.

frame created the perfect storm of conditions to shove me out of the known quantity of my life and into an unknown new one.

All of this is nice to know now. But back then, I had no idea what was happening. Like the iconic if dated scene in the 1981 movie *An American Werewolf in London*, I was transforming before my own eyes into something I was not yet able to recognize or control—and it was painful as hell.

- - - - - - - - - -

"Okay," Melissa said, after we got back on track. "Let me take some pictures of the place, and we'll get you listed...Val?"

"Nope...Fine...Good...Dropped the pencil again."

2

In the last week of June 2006, the boy from Hopewell Valley Central High School in Pennington, New Jersey, who had been voted Most Likely to Succeed by his fellow seniors in the class of 1988 probably expertly attended to the medical needs of multiple patients in his capacity as a licensed physician, spent quality time with his wife (also a doctor) and children, and otherwise enjoyed the benefits and status of an adult who had lived up to the potential of his 18-year-old self.

The girl from that class who had been named his female counterpart spent that same week running around the Lakeview neighborhood of Chicago; trashing some belongings (including dismantling a woodgrain bookshelf with a hammer and some anxious aggression); donating others; and putting the rest in storage in preparation for moving out of her condo. She also spent quite a bit of time crying, looking at road maps and AAA triptychs, starting a travel blog, not sleeping, and training Brazilian Jiu-Jitsu. Yes, during that week, the girl who had demonstrated such promise that her classmates immortalized it through the democratic process was reluctantly staging her teenage rebellion, almost 20 years late.

Allyson and Kyler had been voted Most Athletic. Jen and Adam got Most Musical. Michele and Josh scored Class

Clowns. Kim and Tim were Most Artistic. Corky and Pete got Best Looking. And then there were P.T. and me. To this day, P.T. is one of the smartest people I have ever met. He aced every course he took in high school with no apparent effort. He got into every college he applied to. After graduating from Stanford, he entered medical school, where he probably crushed the curve before becoming a physician in California. There were lots of smart boys with bright futures in our class, but P.T. was the obvious choice for Most Likely to Succeed.

On the other hand, I am not sure why I got the nod for the girls in the class. There were so many talented and ambitious girls who maintained schedules in those formative years that were exhausting just to hear about, but somehow I got the nod. Just like all the other pairs of class superlatives, P.T. and I got our picture taken together for the yearbook. When it was our turn, we wore sunglasses and stood shoulder to shoulder, trying to look smug, powerful, and wealthy. I held up an issue of *Money* magazine, and he held a sports paper.

When my classmates voted for me, I doubt they imagined I would get to a place in my life where, at the risk of sounding cliché, I was not sure who I was. Yet here we were. I could no longer point to my job title for assistance in identifying me because I had given up the job. I was no longer a member of the club of people who lived in a certain neighborhood in a certain city because I was selling my condo and, for all intents and purposes, moving into my car. I was still someone in relation to other people— daughter, sister, aunt, friend—but, rewarding though that always will be to me, it will never be enough. There is more to me than who I am to other people. At that time in my life, I just did not happen to know anymore what that was.

The fact that I had to do something with my belongings exacerbated that feeling. I could only take so much with me, and I had to decide what to do with the rest, which for the most part translated into divesting myself of it. By the time I left Chicago, I had given away dozens of boxes of books and clothes, furniture, knickknacks, and the like. I gave my bed, the only really nice piece of furniture I owned, to a friend to babysit.

Eventually, once I decided to stay in California for a while, I sold it to her. I did keep some things: bound photo albums and other personal mementoes; CDs; books, including textbooks and edited scholarly volumes from graduate school; best-sellers and highbrow literature; some clothing; and some housewares. I found a storage facility on Broadway, north of my place but still in Lakeview, and when I described what I needed to store, the guy behind the counter at the facility suggested a 5'x10' unit. I said, "Okay, fine," until I saw it, and then I was brought up short.

The space was smaller than some walk-in closets I had seen. It was probably the size of the bathroom in my condo. Five hundred cubic feet to accommodate all of the worldly possessions that survived my weeding frenzy.

When I had moved everything I owned into the unit, I was disconcerted to see all that was left of me crammed into what basically amounted to The Wardrobe, only dingier and in a more industrial neighborhood. I remember wondering if Hiro Protagonist and Vitaly Chernobyl lived next door, in their own windowless, dusty and concrete-floored storage unit, and whether they, too, kept it secure with a self-purchased padlock. I was very satisfied with this joke and looked around in vain for someone to share it with. Then I felt lonely, small and ill-defined, and once again wondering what I had gotten myself into.

The real countdown had begun. In that last week of June, I was waiting for two things to happen. First, my parents were due to arrive in Chicago with my new home: the car I had bought in Florida, near where they lived. Once they had come to terms with the fact that I was essentially going to become a vagabond, my father had taken me to a dealer he trusted there, and he and my mother had floated me a loan to buy the car outright that I would repay as soon as the money from the condo sale came through.

This was the second thing I was waiting on: the condo sale. It was scheduled to happen on June 30, 2006, that Friday, at which point the net profit I had made after fees, taxes, and the like would sustain me until it no longer did. I figured I could make the money last for about six months if I was frugal, but since I did not know how or where this chapter of my life was going to end, I had no idea whether that was long enough.

The profit from the sale, minus what I owed my parents for the car, was my travel money, so I had to stay in Chicago until the funds had actually been transferred to my bank account. That meant that during that final, liminal week, I was left with lots of time to twiddle my thumbs, play "What If" until I lost my marbles, and repeat.

One morning during that week, I woke up feeling an almost unbearable desire to jump out of my skin. I had hated my job, and yet, lying in my condo, which had become increasingly echo-y as I put more and more things in storage, I felt myself wishing I was on my way back to it. I craved some semblance of normalcy. I wished I had chosen the rope.

I got myself to the morning training session that day, became completely absorbed in it, and then returned to feeling squirrelly when I came out of the BJJ reverie and started home. That told me that at least the guiding principle of the trip, jiu-jitsu, was a good one. With the benefit of hindsight I can say that should not have been surprising, but when I was anticipating the start of my journey I was going on faith, knowing I had to trust that the next lighted square was on its way, but not entirely believing it. I had no idea whether I was making sound choices or whether I was in the process of ruining my life, and it was all I could do not to stop in the middle of the busy Chicago streets, sit down on the curb with my arms wrapped around my stomach, rock myself back and forth, and repeat ad nauseam, "Oh my god oh my god oh my freaking god oh shit oh shit what the hell am I doing?" I waited until I was alone to do that—usually.

Finally, the day arrived when my parents drove into town in my new car. I had already fallen in love with it, a 2002 Toyota Camry Solara that we had registered in Florida, as my address of record was going to be my parents' place for the foreseeable future. It was gold. It was gorgeous. It was the closest thing I had to a home, one I got to take with me, like a fuel-injected turtle shell. When my father drove up in it that morning and parked it under a tree, my mother waving from the passenger's seat, I finally felt some excitement. Of course it helped that my mommy and daddy were there.

Thirty-six years old and feeling no shame that I wanted them as viscerally as if I were four years old and had just skinned my knee. When I pressed "unlock" on the key fob and the car responded with a "beep beep" as the mechanism shifted, I was reminded of the affectionate nickering sound a horse makes in the movies when its owner comes near. When I got inside, I immediately felt safe. My car had already become a giant mechanical security blanket and my partner in crime.

Then Friday, June 30, 2006, arrived. The day of the condo sale. Melissa had told me I didn't even need to show up for the closing, so I didn't. Attending would have made me even more nervous. I did, however, check my bank account incessantly. The closing was scheduled for mid-morning, and Melissa promised me the funds would be transferred later in the day. That did not stop me from checking as soon as I got up and every five or ten minutes thereafter until the account had hit pay dirt. My other security blanket was now snug around me. It was time for me to fly.

On the morning I left Chicago, I loaded my car with my grandfather's duffel bag, army green and stamped with the letters BHS, for Belleville (New Jersey) High School. I added the new laptop I had bought for blogging and taking notes on moves I would be working on during training, a few milk crates containing paperwork and manila folders, the CDs I had not put into storage, and snacks. Then, with no other excuses to keep me there, I held the wheel and drove, as Incubus might say.

My mother had predicted that I would feel much better once I got on the road, and she turned out to be right. Not that there had ever been any doubt. She is a mother, after all, so she knows things. For minutes at a time, I was able to forget that I was not just en route to visit some dear old friends for the weekend. That was all it had to be for the moment, just a holiday visit with good people, I kept repeating to myself, every time I remembered that it wasn't.

The dear old friends I was on my way to see were Darin and Linh. Darin had been one of my favorite teachers and training partners at the academy in Chicago, but he and Linh had moved back home to Somerset, Kentucky. While my general trajectory was westward and Somerset was east of Chicago, I reconnected with him when I realized they were relatively nearby. I thought it would be nice to start my trip surrounded by friendly faces.

As with all of the friends I reached out to in anticipation of driving through, they enthusiastically invited me to stay, train, hang out, whatever I wanted to do. This became one of the most gratifying aspects of the trip: the uniformly positive reaction of old friends from all walks of my life to the prospect of seeing me again when I passed through. Even friends of friends were gracious and welcoming. Time after time, to my scared and uncertain self, those reactions were like cool water on a sunburn.

I pulled into their driveway at dusk, and Darin came outside to meet me, their dog Bandit serving as advance team. The first thing Darin said upon seeing me was, "Valerie Worthington, you fuckin' blueblood!"

Darin was the latest in a long line of people, starting with my college friends, who gave me a hard time about my name because they thought it sounded snooty. Before they met me, my freshman year college roommates, upon seeing my full name, "Valerie Lynn Worthington," in an official college document announcing our roommate status, became convinced I was "sixteenth in line to the throne or something" and were worried they might have to deal with my bodyguards and other security measures. Other friends started calling me "Valerie Worthington of the Pennington Worthingtons" and affecting a sort of British accent while speaking the words.

I guess it did not help that my hometown in New Jersey, the aforementioned Pennington, apparently sounds snooty too. Another friend said that "Worthington" should be the name of a great hall where people have tea and crumpets, pinkies extended, of course, while peering at each other through monocles and saying things like, "What, what, old chap." I pictured a room full of Mister Peanuts upon hearing that one. Then there was Darin. Apparently it was lost on him that, as he proudly showed me, he had just that week gotten the outline of his own family crest tattooed on his arm, yet I was the blueblood. The fuckin' one.

My trunk was one giant suitcase: gis and other training gear on the left, t-shirts and shorts in the middle, jeans and hoodies on the right, and unmentionables shoved into a corner. I had not thought to pack what I needed to take into the house, so while Darin chatted in welcome, I discreetly grabbed t-shirts, underwear, and toilet articles that I would need for the night, cramming them into a cloth grocery bag.

"I told all my students you were coming, so you've got a real Welcome Wagon for your stay. There are lots of things going on for July 4th." One of the reasons Darin and Linh had moved back home, in addition to wanting to be closer to family, was for Darin to be able to open a jiu-jitsu academy of his own, a Carlson Gracie affiliate. "We've been invited for a barbecue, and I can show you around a little bit. And of course we'll train."

We went inside, where Linh greeted me with a huge hug that I returned in kind. We stood for a few seconds and then I started to pull away, but she hung on. I squeezed again too, feeling a tear or two well up in my eyes and an itch in my nose.

"We're so happy you're here!" she cried. "What an exciting adventure for you. We're glad you made us part of it."

"Yeah, I'm still a bit shell-shocked," I said.

"Well, you are welcome to stay as long as you want. There are lots of people excited to meet you."

"Don't tempt me. It's going to be scary heading into the great unknown."

"Oh, you did the hard part already."

As Linh and Darin got dinner ready, Darin told me a little about his academy, The Submit Pit. I loved the place as soon as I heard the name.

"It's a small student base so far, but it's growing, and we have a lot of families, which is nice, because they encourage each other to come to class. It's something they can share. There's class tomorrow at 11, so you can see for yourself."

"Sounds great, Darin. I can't wait to train with you again!" This was true. I usually always enjoy training jiu-jitsu, but there are certain people who elevate a simple roll, which is a sparring session between two practitioners, from fun to profound. Darin has always been one of those people for me.

Imagine a game like chess or Risk, where you must anticipate an opponent's moves and have counters ready, as well as your own attacks. As with these games, the goal in BJJ is to win, to dominate the other's position and impose your will, and the key to winning is to out-strategize your opponent. Now imagine that those moves, counters, and attacks happen instantaneously, rather than stretching out over hours or even days.

Imagine further that the pieces in this game are your and your opponents' bodies and that for this game you must train yourself to perform complex psychomotor tasks, in a prone position, in a way most people probably have not since they were babies learning to walk. It is doubtful that any of us has any recollection of that process: the concerted effort, the trial and error, the successive approximations of this crazy process of moving effectively through space while balanced on two very small-seeming feet.

As we learned to walk, we pulled ourselves up, maybe using a table or a chair, or even a parent, and then we fell over. We pulled ourselves up again, and then maybe we stood on our own for a split second until we hit the deck, and so on and so forth until, after countless attempts and countless setbacks, we walked. Staggering around like an overserved bar patron at first, and then with more ease and skill as we got more practice.

Learning BJJ is like this. Unlike learning to walk, though,

when we learn BJJ, most of us are aware of what is happening, where we are succeeding, and, especially in the beginning, where we are failing. Especially in the beginning, our minds are willing but our bodies are simply unable, and this makes our egos revolt. We mix up left and right, fling ourselves into moves, and create anxious tension in our bodies so great we are in danger of snapping like violin strings. We long to move like the great practitioners: effortlessly and almost as if we can see a few seconds into the future, but instead our bodies seem to be encased in quick-drying cement.

In BJJ, the ultimate intention is for practitioners to position their bodies relative to their opponent's so they can execute a submission. To achieve such a position, practitioners must first execute combinations of movements including sweeps, guard passes, establishing side control, taking the mount (straddling the opponent), and taking the back (controlling the opponent by getting behind him or her). Working for these positions is known as training or rolling.

There are many submissions, and they generally fall into two categories: chokes and joint locks. These are physical manipulations of one or more body parts that apply painful and potentially damaging pressure to some major body part. Chokes have colorful names like guillotine, rear naked, baseball, loop, cross collar, and head-and-arm or triangle. Joint locks have names like arm bar, shoulder lock, foot lock, knee bar, wrist lock, and heel hook. If caught by a partner in one of these submissions, the trapped person must tap his or her fingers to signify defeat, either on the mat or on the partner. To refuse to tap when truly trapped is to risk bodily harm or unconsciousness.

Probably the closest analogue to Brazilian Jiu-Jitsu or submission grappling for the non-practitioner is wrestling, particularly since in both activities participants compete for superior physical position relative to their opponents. As with any analogy, the one to wrestling is imperfect, but the two are part of the same family—grappling—so they do overlap.

In BJJ, for every move you make with your body, there are countless responses—defenses and reversals. Just like the

37

letters of an alphabet, these moves are building blocks that create a complex physical language of movement patterns and sequences, feats of body awareness, and demonstrations of kinesthetic intelligence. Despite the fact that control, domination, and even pain are the immediate and ultimate goals, this language, when spoken by skilled practitioners like Darin, can be as graceful as dancing. It is in this aspect of BJJ, the casual beauty and seeming effortlessness experts reflect in their movements, that its moniker makes sense. "Jiu-jitsu" translates from the Japanese as "the gentle art."

From the get-go, I have never in any other context felt by turns as exhilarated, as stupid, or as in the moment as I do when I am training BJJ. In my first few months of training, I came to the painful realization of how disconnected I had become from my body, living at that time an almost complete life of the mind as a graduate student. BJJ required that I fully and consciously re-occupy my body and find a way to get it and my brain to work in tandem so I could perform physical acts that seemed completely foreign. I had to learn to "speak" jiu-jitsu with both my brain and my body, and fluency has been slow in coming. I am not a native speaker like many high-level practitioners who started earlier in life and work harder at it, but I do know enough now to be able to recognize the beauty in the cadences.

- - - - - - - - - -

"Here we are," said Darin, as we pulled up to a storefront adorned with the words "The Submit Pit" and a stenciled logo of a jagged-edged dog. The latter was a variation on the iconic Carlson Gracie logo depicting a bulldog with a bloody muzzle growling at its mirror image. It was about 10:30 on the morning following my first night in Somerset, time to get ready for the 11am class. I had slept the sleep of the dead and was looking forward to living in the moment, during the next several of which I would get my training fix.

Darin unlocked the doors and turned on the lights in his academy. It featured an entryway/reception area and a perimeter of regular flooring around the main attraction: the mat, those spongy puzzle pieces, 3x2 foot rectangles, or huge, single roll-outs where all the jiu-jitsu magic happens. Where pairs of grapplers get so engrossed in their physical chess games that they run into each other. Where unwitting visitors get roundly criticized if they try to walk without taking their shoes off—wearing shoes on the mat is strictly forbidden because we put our faces there, among other body parts. Where people stand at the edge and bow, either to signal that they are ready to focus on training if they are stepping on or to signal that they are putting an end to their training for now if they are stepping off. Where I would soon be feeling Darin's top pressure.

- - - - - - - - - -

"This is very much like nursery school," I thought.

I do not remember much about nursery school, but I have watched and been involved in many interactions where a toddler of nursery school age wants to do something that an adult will not let her do. The toddler reaches for the electrical outlet. The adult gently pulls her away and tries to distract her. The toddler turns back and makes a beeline for the outlet again. The adult again prevents the toddler from doing her thing. Perhaps this time the distraction works, but the toddler becomes interested in another thing that the adult wants to keep her from, say a flight of stairs. Again, the adult gently redirects the toddler in her endeavors. The toddler starts to screech in frustration at not being able to do what she wants. Maybe she throws a full-on tantrum, and the adult is patient and kind.

When I thought my thought, I was lying on my back, in Darin's side control, contemplating life and what it would be like to spend the rest of mine here, on this mat, in this position, in the event Darin decided not to let me move. He is not a particularly large man. At 5'8" or so, he is about an inch taller than I am, and depending on how often I have

39

had dessert in the previous week, maybe a few pounds heavier. Regardless, I was utterly contained.

I was lying on my back while Darin lay facing down, perpendicularly across my chest, controlling my movements by applying pressure downward. In this imperfect analogy, he was most definitely not the toddler. I screeched inwardly, not as much in frustration as in awe. Darin had invited me to pair up during the first round of the live training, which followed a warm-up and explicit instruction in jiu-jitsu technique.

"It's like being back in Chicago!" he said.

From almost the moment we gripped up with each other, I was reminded, at least at the awareness level of a purple belt, that Darin was one of Them.

By the time I departed on my trip, I had been training BJJ long enough to begin to appreciate how little I actually knew about BJJ, but one thing my years of training had given me was the murky stirrings of an ability to detect where on the spectrum of uncoordinated to undulating my training partners resided. Were they tense, herky-jerky, and desperate like I was, or were they smooth, effortless, and serpentine, like Darin was? After rolling with Darin for several minutes, during which time he repeatedly cut off my intended movement as if he had read my mind, I almost stopped midstream to ask, "Can you please tell me what I'm planning to do next?" because he clearly knew better than I did. Unlike many other people I had rolled with, he was not struggling or straining.

Of course, this was due in large measure to how much better he was at BJJ than I was, but there was more. I had trained with other people who were significantly more skilled at BJJ than I, but not all of them were in constant, effective motion, thwarting their partners through a perpetual series of instantaneous physical actions and reactions. Some of Them were. Darin was. Not all of them could refrain from tensing up while training and using brute force to finish the sweep or lock in the submission. Some of Them could. Darin could.

As a man he has more muscle mass than I, but even though he could have contained me with strength, as some practitioners try to do, he did not. Rather, he anticipated and deflected my strategies. He redirected my energy instead of fighting it head on, so that my movements were not hindered as much as they were co-opted for his intentions, which were the direct opposite of mine.

Martial arts legend Bruce Lee was famously quoted as saying, "Be like water." When I found words, a long time later, to describe what it is like to train with people like Darin, I was reminded of this imagery: Rolling with Them is like sitting in a bathtub and trying to push the water away. I can move all I want. I can push and push in any direction. If anything, that just makes things wetter.

The buzzer sounded. I sat up, turned to face Darin, extended my hand, and bowed over it. "Thank you," I said, smiling—and meaning the smile. I did *not* tell Darin he had rolled well or say, "Good job," even under my breath. Different practitioners have disagreed with me on this point, but I believe it is not my place to praise the technique or movement of someone who outranks me.

I remember one time in my academic career a visiting dignitary from a different university participated in a Q&A with me and some other young scholars. We got together to have lunch and hear from him in a relaxed atmosphere about his experience of conducting research as well as his life as a university professor, because this was the career path most of us were likely to follow.

One student who knew the professor's work made a comment that had the same effect on me as fingernails on a chalkboard, and that comment went something like, "I'm so proud of how you've grown as a scholar." As someone who had been studying for just a few years, it sounded presumptuous for this person to give him what amounted to a verbal pat on the head about his career, which had probably spanned about thirty years by then.

The group recovered and went on to have a lovely discussion, but I always think of that interaction whenever I hear a white belt say something like, "Nice work," or "You have really good base. Normally, I can sweep most everyone with that sequence" to a purple, brown, or even black belt, or anyone who is outranked by anyone else, for that matter. Maybe it is one thing when you are a blue belt and your longtime purple belt training partner/teammate hits a move he or she has been working on after several weeks of near misses, and you say, "Hey, you got it! Nice job!" but it is another thing altogether to say to a complete stranger or someone who is light years ahead of you, "Your technique is really impressive." Two responses come to mind: One, no kidding. Two, if you think my technique is really impressive, maybe I need to work on my technique. No offense meant to lower belts—or to young scholars. Grapplers spend a huge proportion of our careers in the lower belt category, and we are working as hard as anyone else to get out of it. That being said, I always say, only half-jokingly, that if someone who is better at BJJ than I am wants my opinion about technique, I will wait for him or her to give it to me.

One liberty I *may* have taken after my roll with Darin is to ask him for any feedback he might have had about my rolling. During the 30 to 60 seconds that is usually allotted between rolls to allow for the collection and retying of belts and the selection of a new training partner, lower belts will frequently ask the upper belt they were just training with questions like, "Did you notice anything while we were rolling that I should be working on?" or "Do you have any advice?" especially if they have never trained with that person before. For the first years of my training, I was guilty as charged, asking anyone who outranked me at any opportunity for any tidbit that would help me crack the BJJ code.

I stopped doing it to higher belts I did not know when lower belts I did not know started doing it to me and I realized that though I know it was not anyone's intention, being asked those kinds of questions put me on the spot. For one thing, I was usually just trying to get my own work done, which means I was probably not paying attention to what my partner had been doing except insofar as it affected my own movement, so I had probably not been observing that other person's movement in any sort of evaluative way. For another thing, once the roll was over, I was immediately going to be looking for a new training partner while also retying my belt and re-corralling my hair. Finally, as I rose through the ranks, I realized two other things.

First, assuming I had been paying attention to my partner's movements, any complete answer to that question had the potential to engender an entire conversation that would take far longer than the 30 to 60 seconds we had to do a switcheroo and would be better handled in a private lesson, which upper belts everywhere offer their students, guests, and visitors for an extra fee. Second, the fact that I was more and more able over time to answer those kinds of questions (again, assuming I had even been paying more than cursory evaluative attention to my partner) reflected the fact that I had worked hard for a long time and accumulated knowledge that was apparently valuable (See above about private lessons).

When chatting about his job as a college professor with my grandmother (his mother), my father once commented, "I get paid for what I know."

In response, my grandmother quipped, "You must not get very many raises."

She was busting his chops, of course, because that is how my family shows love for each other, but there is a germ of truth in their exchange that relates to the grappling world: Everyone who trains BJJ wants to be good at BJJ, but not everyone who wants to be good at BJJ recognizes what I have come to believe, which is that there should be some kind of exchange for the knowledge that can help us improve. If I want you to share something that you have (in this case, knowledge about jiu-jitsu technique) because I perceive that it has value, then by definition I should be willing to compensate you for that valuable something. My expectation that you share without being willing to give you anything in return creates an imbalance.

It was perhaps slightly different with Darin since we were friends, and since we were animatedly discussing differences and additions in each other's games since the last time we had trained together. If he did feel put on the spot in this way, he did not show it. Perhaps with people he knows less well, he responds with the answer I have learned to give: "Let's discuss it after class." I do this because, as often as not, the person does not remember to check back with me, and if he or she does, then there is time for that lengthier discussion during which the shrewd upper belt will share some feedback and raise the topic of private lessons.

One of the most beautiful and awful things about Brazilian Jiu-Jitsu is that just when you think you might have a handle on some aspects of it, someone comes along and thoroughly cleans your clock, making you feel like you do not know anything about anything. Darin was one such person. It had been some time since he and I had trained together, and in the intervening time, he had transformed his game. Rolling with him was a stark reminder of how little I knew and could do compared to how much it was possible to know and be able to do, and I was catapulted back to the memories of my very first day of training.

In that first class, sometime in 1998, I was paired up with a man about my size.

The instructor, Julian, had said, "Andy[10], please work with Valerie. It's her first day, so be nice!"

My experience with Andy was the first of many that led me to conclude that, as a rule, blue belts like him have little patience for white belts. Since they are a level above rank beginner, blue belts have advanced somewhat in their training, but they are still relatively low on the totem pole.

They are likely to try to ensure that the only group of people they outrank never forgets it. It is the law of the jiu-jitsu jungle. I learned this lesson thoroughly both because many blue belts throughout my tenure as a white belt engaged in interpersonal gerrymandering to avoid pairing up with me, and also because when I got promoted I did the same thing.

Andy heaved an audible, dejected sigh when it became clear he was not going to be able to escape working with me.

"Okay, let's get on with it," he said.

---

[10] Not his real name.

I smiled a weak smile and pulled at my droopy gi. The sleeves looked more like those you might find on a traditional silk Japanese kimono, which is to say wide and baggy. The crotch of the drawstring pants had fixed itself at thigh-level, about where a pair of Daisy Dukes might end, and the cuffs of the pants spilled well lower than regulation ankle height, pooling on the floor like the sprawling hooves of a Clydesdale. I had not had the gumption to ask anyone how to tie my snow-white belt, so it was double-knotted on top of my belly button, and the two ends were so long I was in danger of tripping on them. Eventually I acquired better fitting gear, but at that moment, I looked the part of the three-year-old playing dress-up in her parents' somewhat strangely appointed closet.

Julian arranged us in two rows on the mat, each person facing a partner.

"Okay, guys. We're going to jump guard and work from there."

Julian demonstrated what he meant on one of the other students. While the student stood stock still, Julian leaped toward him and landed with his legs wrapped around the student's waist and arms around his neck, facing him, as if he were a little boy who had fallen asleep in the student's arms after a long day at an amusement park. An outsized little boy with a five o'clock shadow. The student responded to the force of Julian's weight by bending his legs slightly and giving just a bit but staying solidly on two feet.

Julian said, "Notice how he's leaning back to counterbalance my weight," as he leaned back himself—all the way back, in fact, so that he was upside down and extending his hands over his head in order to touch the ground behind him. His legs were still clamped tightly around the student's midsection, and then he pulled himself back to the sleepy child position.

I learned later that that was what was known as a "jiu-jitsu sit-up," though at the time, I looked around to see if anyone else noticed how completely insane this was. Nobody did.

"Any questions, guys?" Julian asked. "Okay, you're going to jump guard, do a sit up, dismount, and then repeat. Ten each and then switch. Let's get started."

Andy balefully eyed me again, and said, "Okay, I'll go first. Try not to drop me."

He put his hands on my shoulders and flung himself toward me. Just in time, I managed to remember to lean back and bend my legs a little bit so my thighs would create a platform for him to rest on. I struggled to keep myself upright—more to his point, I struggled to keep myself from pitching forward and dropping him on his shoulders and neck. Suffice it to say that my discomfort and lack of coordination probably renewed his dislike of white belts, though I am pretty sure I only dropped him once. My story, which I am sticking to, is that it was an accident.

Then it was my turn, to jump, to wrap, to lean all the way back, to reach, to clamp, and to pull. I was gratified to observe that my cantankerous partner had a bit of trouble keeping me aloft himself. I would even have endured a drop on the head to stick it to that guy. It was not that far, after all. I had not yet gotten to the point in my training where I was able to see behavior like this for what it was, even and especially when it came from me: so much hot air from an insecure dirigible.

At that moment, it felt like a stab to the heart. I did not even think the girly thought of how this guy struggling to hold me up must have meant I was fat. I also did not point out to my partner that he did not seem all that great himself. I was breathing too heavily and concentrating too hard. I did notice with satisfaction that 180-degree sit-ups were actually in my wheelhouse. Who knew? When I was watching Julian do them, I had been more than a little skeptical that I would be able to follow suit. I think the exact thought that had popped into my head had been, "Oh, hell no."

After two or three sets each, depending on how fast different pairs were able to execute the movements, Julian yelled, "Time!"

He walked us through several more drills that taxed my brain, my body, and my partner's patience, and then we moved to the technique section of the class. In typical BJJ classes, a warm-up like the one Julian put us through is followed by technique, where the instructor leads the class through a series of positions and sequences.

"Today we're going to do a sequence starting from closed guard. We'll stand up, open the guard, and then pass to side control," Julian announced.

I knew the words he was speaking were English ones, but as with many things he said that day, I did not understand their meaning. Either I had not heard them strung together in this specific sequence, or I was suffering from some kind of aphasia. Regardless, the effect was the same: I was completely lost.

Julian beckoned with his finger to the same student he had worked with when he had demonstrated how to jump guard. This time, he knelt on the ground and the student lay down facing the ceiling and wrapped his legs around him. For the uninitiated, the picture would have looked more than a little sexual, but as anyone with any experience in sport BJJ can tell you, it is not. Julian took hold of the student's gi collar with one hand and his sleeve with the other. He put one foot on the mat and leaned all of his weight on it so he could bring his other foot under him, and then he stood up.

The student kept his legs closed around Julian, which meant his lower half accompanied Julian up and off the mat. Only his shoulders and head stayed down. The rest of him hung in mid-air by his legs, which were still closed around Julian's waist. He was in a position similar to the one we had been in at the bottom of the jiu-jitsu sit-up, only this time more of his shoulders and upper back were on the mat. Julian stood up straight, continuing to hold the student's collar and sleeve. He dropped to one knee and then the other, returning to his original position where both his knees were on the ground and his butt was on his heels, the student's legs still shelved on Julian's thighs and his feet still hooked together around Julian's waist.

"Okay, guys, this is called standing up in guard."

Sure, whatever. I would eventually make the connection that having someone "in the guard" is to have someone between your legs as a means of control, either completely wrapping them around that person as the student had done with Julian, or otherwise using them to keep your partner from moving toward your side. Standing up in guard is exhausting on a good day, and on a first day, it was batty. When it was my turn, I again struggled not to pitch face-first into my partner's chest while getting my legs and hips under me, like a slimy newborn foal testing its balance for the first time. When I posted a foot, I had to really lean into it to get my other foot in a reasonable position to support both my weight and my partner's. My partner stared into space, his shoulders on the mat and his arms splayed out, creating a dismissive plus sign with his body. When it was his turn, my hopes that it would be easier to be the person who was picked up were dashed, as I kept sliding around and losing my grip with my legs.

"Can't you hang on better?" he asked.

I was concentrating so hard I had no mental capacity left for formulating sentences. It was just as well. He would not have liked the one I came up with.

From standing up in guard, Julian taught a sequence for opening and passing the guard. I realized this meant there were strategies for getting a person to open their feet. No wonder my partner was annoyed that mine kept opening of their own accord. I was supposed to refuse to let that happen so he could practice making me, and then apparently once a person had opened the guard, it was beneficial to pass it. This involved a series of leg and hip movements to get past the legs and, to oversimplify, end up basically perpendicular to your partner, lying chest to chest, one person facing down and the other facing up. This position was called "cross-side," "cross-body," or "side control," the position Darin had placed me in that had prompted my trip down memory lane in the first place. My partner had obviously done this sequence before, and he obviously had expectations about what I was supposed to do to help him.

"Okay, try not to be so floppy. Don't just lie there, but don't defend too much." I had not yet regained the power to speak, but that was just as well. I did not speak this particular English.

Just as I started to panic, anticipating my turn but knowing full well that there was no way I would be able to remember how to do all these new guard opening and passing things, let alone make my body do them, Julian came by, pointed at me, and said, "Okay, you're just going to continue practicing the stand-up."

Thank you, thank you, thank you. I continued gamely to stand up in guard while my partner hated the player.

"Time!" Julian shouted, after what seemed an eternity. Were we done? I felt like maybe the sun had started to poke through the clouds. But no. My humiliation and enervation were not yet complete.

"Grab a drink of water and find a partner. Time to roll."

Most BJJ classes end with "live rolling." This, enthusiasts, claim, is one of the things that distinguishes BJJ from other martial arts, and this is what practitioners live for: the opportunity to try to use technique on a resisting opponent.

Julian pointed at me, smiled, and said, "Let's go." I assumed my partner had gotten a better offer. Pairing with Julian was both better and worse than rolling with Andy.

I said to Julian, "I don't really know what I'm doing."

He said, "That's okay. We'll just move around a little bit. I'll start in your guard." Okay, that sentence I almost understood! Baby steps.

Very quickly, Julian used the sequence he had showed in class to pass my guard and get to side control. I did not know this then, of course. I just spent the whole round doing my best impression of a fish that had jumped out of water and onto an electrified floor. At some point, Julian's gi top fell across my face, and since I have a bit of claustrophobia, I clawed at it, panicked when I could not get my nose and mouth free, and tapped. Slapped Julian's back frantically, if I am being perfectly accurate. He stopped and asked me why I had tapped because he knew he had not been applying a submission.

I stupidly told him the truth: "I couldn't breathe because your gi top was on my face, and I started to freak out."

He laughed, said, "Well, then, honey, you're in the wrong

sport!" told me to keep going, and then proceeded to cover my face with his gi at every opportunity. He did check in regularly, saying, "How are you doing under there?" and I realized that this was the first of many times in my BJJ career that I would be forced to face my own limits.

I managed to keep myself reasonably together and to refrain from convulsing in terror, but only barely. Julian kept getting that cross-side position, and usually he had my arms pretty well tied up so I could not get the gi out of my face. I almost tapped again, but the reality of my mostly immobilized arms required me to refocus on staying calm, breathing deeply, and doing my best to move. I have been trying to do pretty much the same thing for close to two decades since.

At some point years later, I heard a buzzer sound.

"Switch partners!" Julian yelled. To me he said, "Stick with me."

I did, gladly. This time, Julian let me start in his guard, and after I awkwardly stood up in it, he walked me through the process of opening and passing it, moving my chest and arms to their proper positions in side control—a process I promptly forgot and would need to see and practice many more times before it started to stick.

After several more buzzers, Julian called, "Time! Okay, guys fix your gis and line it up."

I looked down at my gi and realized my belt was missing. It had come undone during the rolling, as it did again and again, thousands of times, over the years. I located it, secured it insecurely around my waist, and watched the other students mill toward the side of the mat to form a tidy line facing Julian, desperately trying to suss out where I should stand. I quickly figured out that white belts were on one side of the line, and I walked to the end of that side. Good guess, apparently, because nobody pointed or laughed or rolled their eyes. Not even my blue belt friend.

Julian said, "Thanks for a great class, folks," put his hands at his sides, and bowed to the line.

We bowed back. Julian approached the student at the head of the colored belt side of the line and went down it, shaking hands. The students followed behind him, slowly forming a human bobby pin as we all shook hands first with Julian and then with each other. Class was over.

"Thanks for coming," Julian said to me, as the group broke off into smaller clusters and some students made for their gear bags and the changing rooms. "See you tomorrow?"

Oh yeah, I had to do this again. And again. "Yes," I said, with zero hesitation, surprising myself. Hey, I could talk!

Thus did I enter the world of Brazilian Jiu-Jitsu, clumsy and exhausted in mind and body, feeling like one of the ballerinas in *Harrison Bergeron*.

It may sound like an inauspicious beginning, but I am here to tell you that Brazilian Jiu-Jitsu blew my mind in a way few things before or since have been able to do. I was sold from the first crazy guard sit-up, from the first time I mentally soiled myself because my instructor's gi was on my face. I had never done anything even close to BJJ before, and I wondered where it had been all my life.

Even when I felt the full force of my physical exertions two days later, I laughed. That morning I tried—and immediately thought better of—sitting up in bed. Instead, I was forced to lie back down, roll to the edge of the mattress so my stomach was facing the floor, heave myself out, and land on all fours. From there I pulled myself to a standing position, bypassing the use of the abdominal muscles I had burned out in the class. I was glad my partner was not there to see that, but I did not mind the actual pain. Sometimes love hurts.

Perhaps this should have foreshadowed to me how demanding a mistress BJJ would prove to be at times, how completely and utterly she would come in and dismantle my entire adult life before helping me put it back together in a far more solid fashion than it had ever been. In those months before she revealed her true nature, I was overwhelmed by a buoyant feeling like the one you get when you find out that your secret crush likes you back. You know the one: where you are inspired to find any lame excuse to cross paths with that person, but then you act like a total moron if you happen to make eye contact, and then you giggle as you run away, already plotting your next encounter.

- - - - - - - - - -

By the time I had landed on Darin and Linh's doorstep, I had had thousands of such encounters with BJJ, which ran the gamut from exhilarating to devastating. The ones I had at The Submit Pit were definitely toward the happy end of things, and I had learned to recognize the phenomenon in others as well. I recognized it in Chad, one of Darin's students. He was a white belt, and at maybe 20 or 22 years old, he was still what I at my advanced age considered a kid.

He had been waiting outside the academy when Darin and I pulled up, the first one to arrive for class, and as we exited the academy, he was lingering there again, the last one to leave.

"There he is, the man of the hour! Val, I think you rolled with Chad during class. He is one of my best students. And Chad, Val is my dear old friend. We go way back to when we were both training under Carlson Sr. and Carlson Jr. in Chicago. She has been around BJJ for a long time, like me. So when she talks, pay attention."

"Haha. He's just being nice. I'm learning like everyone else. Thanks for the roll earlier. How long have you been training?" I said

"Oh, not long. I just started earlier this year, but Coach thinks I'm improving, and he said maybe I could help build up a kids' class in the next couple months. I want to compete too. I need to work on my stand-up, but I really like playing from my back, so I'm trying to focus on triangles and arm bars as my go-to finishes. I wanted to thank you for training with me. I don't get to train with many upper belts besides Darin, and it was really fun, and I learned a lot."

"Uh-oh, Darin. He's a goner."

"Well, I hope so! We have a lot of work to do, right Chad?"

Chad beamed.

"I'm sure you do, but remember, guys. There's more to life than jiu-jitsu."

Chad and Darin looked at me inquisitively. "There is?"

"I mean, there's eating and sleeping and making enough money so you don't end up living in a refrigerator box. Don't let this guy forget about those things, Darin."

"Should we really be taking home ownership advice from a goddamn gypsy, Val?"

"Okay, good point, but I'm still really good at eating, and speaking of that, I'm starving."

"Then it's a good thing it's almost time to barbecue! We gonna see you over at the party, bud?" Darin asked Chad.

"I'll be there," he said.

"That kid's a goner," I said again, as Chad walked away.

Darin put his hand on my shoulder. "Friend, it sure as shit takes one to know one."

From the academy, Darin took me back to the house, where we collected Linh and got ready to head over to the house of a family whose members—a mom, a dad, and a son—all trained at The Submit Pit. They had invited us over to celebrate the July 4th holiday, and they regaled me with stories of how much they loved Darin and Linh, and how much they loved jiu-jitsu.

"Oh, we walk around the house with our shoulders hunched, because you never know who's going to launch an attack on your neck from behind!" said Carey, the mom, as we sat around the kitchen table drinking beer and husking corn.

"Sounds like you don't let your guard down in this house if you know what's good for you," I said. "Maybe I should sit with my back to the wall."

"That's not such a bad idea," said Alan, the dad. "But everyone in this family should know better than to attack you. We might not like what we get in return. Hear that, Justin?" he yelled to his son.

"Nah, such as they are, I use my powers for good," I joked.

"Maybe you can get Darin to do the same," Carey

joked back. "When I roll with him, it feels like resistance is futile."

"It pretty much is," I said, flashing Darin a smile as he passed the table with a plate full of burger patties.

"Hey, you're making me sound like a monster," Darin mock-complained over his shoulder as he headed outside to the grill.

Linh pointed after him and nodded solemnly.

"I don't understand quite why getting smashed is so much fun, but it is," Alan observed. "And I've lost weight, and I swear Justin behaves better, along with the other kids who train over there."

"Plus, you get to meet amazing people. It's been way too long since I got to see that guy," I said, pointing to where Darin had exited the room. "He's always been a really welcoming person, even when I first started at Carlson's and was terrified."

"That's how we feel about him too," Carey replied. "I never thought I would have liked to do something like this, and I think a big part of it is how easy Darin makes it. And Linh, you're at the academy all the time too! I know you are a big help in keeping things running."

"Well, Darin's going to train whether I'm there or not, so I might as well try to catch a glimpse of him every now and then," Linh joked. "But seriously, he's really invested in the school and in the people." She turned to me. "I think he's just thrilled to be able to show you what he's done."

"I'm thrilled to be able to see it."

"We're so glad you came!"

It is almost too precious that I embarked on my jiu-jitsu adventure over the Independence Day holiday, though that is just something my mom would have described as "serendipitous." Yet as my visit in Somerset progressed, the awareness grew in my mind that resolving to choose the unknown instead of the rope might end up being pretty cool at times.

- - - - - - - - - -

After living in a state of abject panic in the months and weeks before I left on my journey, and after many people I told about my journey looked at me like I had sprouted an extra head—while many others asked if I had room for them in my suitcase—I decided to capture a play-by-play of the absurdity as it happened. I decided to maintain a blog of my travels.

I suppose I could be described as a somewhat early adopter of jiu-jitsu blogging, just as I suppose I could be described as a somewhat early adopter of the traveling grappler lifestyle. Nowadays, if you Google "jiu-jitsu blogs," you get dozens of results. None of them point to mine, and this is fine with me. Many jiu-jitsu websites these days tend to be polished, professional, and consistent. In my case, only the last adjective accurately described my five years of blogging. In addition, these days it is quite common in the jiu-jitsu world for people to couch surf; log hundreds if not thousands of plane, train, and automobile miles; and otherwise live an itinerant lifestyle devoted to training BJJ, especially if participating in competition is part of the equation.

In recent years, when I have read or heard about these travelers and bloggers, I have felt a little bit smug, allowing myself to channel the late, great George Harrison's appearance in an episode of *The Simpsons*. Toward the end of it, as part of the story arc, Harrison drives by a building and observes the Be-Sharps, Homer's a capella group, performing on the roof. He rolls down the window of his limo, takes in the scene, and sniffs, "It's been done" before riding away. This is a reference to the fact that the Beatles did something similar years earlier, in non-cartoon form, performing on the roof of the Apple building in London one day in January 1969 until they were asked to shut down.

While I am not nearly as good at blogging as the Beatles were at music, I allow myself this bit of high-and-mighty attitude because in 2006, when I left on my journey, blogging in jiu-jitsu seemed relatively new. Further, as evidenced by the general reaction to my trip among my small but growing circle of BJJ acquaintances before I left, so did the concept of the BJJ walkabout. In fact, when I started to tell my jiu-jitsu friends about my plans prior to carrying them out, their reactions fell along the spectrum from good wishes to good-natured envy. I am sure some people also expressed some misgivings, but I did not clue into the fact that I might need to be worried about anything at first. Of course, I did not invent the BJJ walkabout, but still, at the time I did mine, I did not have any blueprint to follow, whereas in recent years more than a handful of would-be travelers have approached me to request advice on how to travel and train. Countless others have done it with no assistance from me. If I am approached, I am always happy to pay it forward to help others avoid my mistakes and assuage for them some of the fear I felt about the unknown.

So my plans were remotely exotic and trail-blazing. They were exasperating as well, apparently: During the countdown, one friend posted a response to an advice-seeking thread I had started on an online jiu-jitsu forum that went something like, "Who does Val think she is? She's going to prance around the country training jiu-jitsu while the rest of us have to live normal lives? She sucks." And lo was a title born: from that moment on, my blog was known as Prancing and Sucking.

3

A few days after I had left Darin and Linh's, I woke up in a motel somewhere in western Tennessee and began to plan my day. It took me a minute or two to figure out where I was and what I was doing there, but as would also become part of the routine, once it registered I smiled and jumped out of bed—and began humming. Could not help it. This, for me, is a sure sign of contentment. I do not sing to myself unless I am in a really fabulous mood. It may sound somewhat sketchy—the anonymous motel room, the disorientation on my part, and even the smiling. It was all pure, though: the joy, the intentions and actions that had so far taken place in that room, and, for the most part, the personal private thoughts of the room's occupant. I had not awakened in an ice-filled bathtub missing a kidney, nobody was pursuing me that I knew of, and I was going to be able to pay the bill when it was time to check out.

I was chipper even though I had gone to bed probably only 5 hours earlier, because when I arrived at what would be my home for the night, I spent a few hours blogging about my stay in Somerset. Not only had it been a fantastic visit, but I had had the opportunity to relive it by writing about it and sharing it with my friends and family. Today I was going to drive from where I was in Tennessee to St. Louis,

Missouri, arriving in time to train at an academy run by a venerated black belt named Rodrigo Vaghi.

On this particular July day, I found a hotel that offered the best of meals—breakfast—for the best of prices—complimentary. I went to the lobby area to check out the offerings, arms full of my AAA maps and triptychs. I planned to spread out the maps of Tennessee and Missouri on the table and look at the close-up inset of St. Louis on the other side of the Missouri map. Those inset maps only showed the main streets, but I also had separate maps of some of the major U.S. cities along the route I had originally specified to AAA. Pretty soon I papered my breakfast table with numerous possible trajectories.

I wore what became my unofficial uniform for the driving days of my trip: cutoffs, Havaiana (a Brazilian brand) flip flops, and a grappling t-shirt, at this stage of my BJJ career usually one that was adorned with the Carlson Gracie mascot. I typically twisted my hair into a bun that I held in place with a cloth-covered elastic band, both to keep it out of my face and so that when it was time to train, I already had a hair tie at the ready. As the day progressed, strands would fall out of the bun, creating a messy effect, with the overall image calling to mind someone who had just helped a friend move or clean a house.

This morning I had grabbed my windbreaker, the one that had seen me through training for two marathons in inclement Michigan weather and that was probably two sizes too big for me. I was tying it in place when I first entered the area of the lobby where breakfast was laid out, my maps and triptychs squeezed between my elbow and my ribcage, and one or two tucked precariously under my chin.

The young woman behind the registration desk smiled and said, "Wow, looks like you have your hands full. You got everything okay?" in a Tennesseean drawl.

I smiled back and said, "Oh, probably not. But that's the story of my life," in my own New Jersey accent—not quite Tony Soprano, but closer to that than to Dolly Parton. "I should be fine once I get some breakfast and maybe an extra arm."

"Well, the arm I can't help you with," she said, laughing, "but breakfast is that way. Good luck!"

I smiled at her over my shoulder as I kept walking and balancing all that was in my hands. I entered the dining area as my head turned back around to face forward, just in time to get a load of the business-suited professionals, truck drivers, and vacationing families who were already enjoying their morning coffee and reading the paper getting a load of me. Kids who had been playing with the cereal dispenser and business people who had been tapping on their laptops stopped what they were doing and snuck glances or openly stared my way.

I was not the only person traveling alone. I was not the only person from elsewhere. I was not even the only person dressed like a vagabond, but something about the way I combined these features with my armful of maps made me the obvious correct answer in that old game from *Sesame Street* called One of These Things Is Not Like the Other, which the entire group of us seemed to have spontaneously started to play.

I felt my scalp tingle and my step falter. I stopped dead in my tracks and opened and closed my mouth like a snail attached to the inside of a fish tank. Then I did the only thing I could think of to do: I smiled. Broadly. At everyone and no one. It was actually pretty easy to make it look natural, because I just thought about how surreal my life had become and accepted that the surreal was obviously at least somewhat visible. All I could do was throw up my hands and appreciate the spectacle. I smiled, as if to say, "Believe me, I know."

All of this nonverbal communication occurred between me and the entire room in a single second, and that is all it took to break the spell. Some people smiled back at me, and some people simply resumed what they had been doing. I could feel my breathing deepen as the energy in the room shifted back to neutral and the ambient noise went back to a low hum. Later on, one elderly couple even stopped at my table to ask politely why I was fumbling with all the maps.

"Wow, looks like you have a ways to go," the man said.

"Well, I'm trying to figure out the best way to get to St. Louis," I responded, trying to refold Memphis.

"Oh, it's not too bad a drive from here. You have relatives there?"

"No, actually, I'm going to a martial arts academy," I replied.

"A what now?"

"A martial arts academy. I participate in a martial art called Brazilian Jiu-Jitsu, and there's a school there that has classes later today."

"Oh, how fun! Our grandson has a black belt in tae kwon do. Got it just before his tenth birthday."

I heard this kind of comment frequently when I mentioned that I train BJJ. It was always from well-meaning people, but it was also a bit trying. Grapplers as a species tend to look askance at promotion practices in some of the more traditional martial arts, where it is not unheard of for a young child to be awarded a black belt. On the other hand, the International Brazilian Jiu-Jitsu Federation (IBJJF) stipulates that a jiu-jitsu practitioner must be at least 19 years old[11] before he or she can be awarded a BJJ black belt. Further, it is common for practitioners to spend a good decade or so training before they are considered eligible. Even though increased access to more and more highly skilled practitioners may have reduced that average in recent years, earning a black belt in BJJ is still a huge accomplishment and is, grapplers will argue, on a different plane than black belts in more traditional martial arts because of the different levels of perceived rigor.

However, I took this couple's comments in the spirit in which I believed they were intended: as a means of connecting with me.

"That's fantastic. Martial arts can be great for kids," I said.

"Oh yes. He is learning discipline, and respect, and all those forms and things. He has fun with it. Now, I'm going to

---

[11] International Brazilian Jiu Jitsu Federation (2012). *General system of graduation*. Retrieved from http://ibjjf.org/wp-content/uploads/2014/02/IBJJF-Graduation-System-v1-ENG.pdf.

mind my Ps and Qs around you. I don't want you beating me up or anything!" Cue karate chop hands.

"Oh, no, I would never do that. I can't run very fast, so I'd definitely get caught afterward," I responded, smiling. They seemed like a really sweet couple. I forgave them, for they knew not what they did.

The man hooted with laughter at my comment and the woman chuckled, "Well, you enjoy yourself, sweetie. Kick 'em first, before they can kick you!"

"Thank you so much, and safe travels to you as well!" THEREISNOKICKINGINJIUJITSU. But there are people in the world who are kind and decent even if they do not understand this, and just like that, I had connected with two more of them.

Between all the maps, I managed to calculate that I would need about five or six hours to get to Team Vaghi, depending on traffic. In the process, I also managed to spill jam on Cape Girardeau, Missouri, and salsa on Humbolt, Tennessee. It seems so quaint now, when I think back on how I relied on paper maps and wrote turn-by-turn instructions down in a spiral-bound steno book so I could refer to them while driving. How I had to find a coffee shop or other place that had wireless—and usually pay for it—and fire up my computer if I wanted to recheck some information I had found online. It was necessary, though, as phones were not nearly as smart in 2006 as they have become a decade later.

According to my math, if I left soon, I would have plenty of time to stop for lunch and maybe even schedule in opportunities to be spontaneous. I was in America's heartland in the summertime, and in my travels I had already seen numerous Airstreams and other recreational vehicles filled with families on their way west, probably headed to major tourist destinations like Yellowstone National Park or the Grand Canyon. The people in the communities along the highway appeared to be banking on this. Signs advertised delicious home cooking, playgrounds, and strange and fascinating museums. The world was my oyster—maybe even a two-headed one, or one that could jump farther than any other east of the Mississippi River. I just had to go out into it and keep an open mind.

- - - - - - - - - -

It was almost go time. I had arrived at Rodrigo Vaghi's academy, which was situated in an industrial-type complex. I arrived early, so I had already cased the joint like an inexperienced bank robber, driving by at a snail's pace and trying to peek inside while at the same time appear nonchalant and detached. Over time this became part of my routine: I always allowed way too much time to get to any destination, but doing so enabled me to familiarize myself with the surrounding area and sometimes sneak a glance at the mat space, on which I would soon be rolling with strangers. Doing that recon gave me some comfort and some illusion of control. It also gave me lots of time to lose my nerve, regain it, and then will myself to stop thinking at all. This feeling, of wanting to go inside and simultaneously wanting to do anything but, was familiar, and as I sat in the car, watching the minutes pass and growing more and more nervous, I started to think about what it had been like when I first started training, how daunting a prospect it seemed simply to walk inside the academy.

By the time I left Chicago, I had gotten to a point where I felt completely comfortable at the Carlson Gracie academy. It had become my home, but that peace of mind had been hard won over the span of years. A Brazilian Jiu-Jitsu academy is an intimidating place, especially if you are new. This is true for anyone, but as one of the few women I knew of at that time who was training regularly, I felt particularly conspicuous and out of my element. Many academies are in areas that are a little bit off the beaten path, such that there would not be many alternative reasons for you to find yourself there.

Or they are in store fronts, where the people inside can see you approaching. At any academy, regardless of location, there are intense-looking, sweaty, mostly male people contorting their bodies in weird positions, and some of them look downright bad-ass while doing it. The stink of "excellence" is often almost visible, to the point where it stings your eyes. For someone like me, who for the most part lived the kind of life represented in white, middle-class family-based sitcoms, the proportion of shaved heads, tattoos, cauliflower ear, and piercings—again, on mostly male bodies—is high if compared to what you would find in other parts of my life. There are rituals and expectations at a BJJ academy that the novice might not track effectively, and more seasoned participants endure transgressions of these with varying degrees of patience. In other words, there is always a good chance that the newcomer will step in it, and step in it again, with both feet.

As I developed more perspective, I realized that it had actually been kind of narcissistic for novice me to think that anyone gave more than a passing crap about my presence, even if they had had to work with me during a class. If upper belt me was any indication, I might have noticed that a lower belt was making mistakes, but as long as that person did not act like a chump, I tended to have a very short memory about them. My blue belt partner that first day at Julian's academy seemed plenty annoyed with me, but he probably spent very little time moaning about it once class ended. After I gained some experience, I entered a different phase of narcissism: total focus on my own training and how I was going to get it done.

When you are new and inexperienced, though, you do not realize this. You do not yet understand what constitutes normal behavior in this social environment, so you feel like you are surrounded by land mines, where one false move could be the game-ender. You feel like you are the student in dance class who only had an hour to memorize the routine before the big recital. Since you do not know what else to do and you cannot just stand there, you do the steps as well as you can, aware that everyone around you is doing them better. Of course, another thing I have learned as I have put in more time is that *everyone* feels like the person with two left feet at different times, and that feeling does not go away nearly as quickly as you would think.

You do not know that as a beginner or as a visitor. I did not know that when I was sitting outside of Vaghi's. As I discovered during my travels, it was harder for me, a woman with a purple belt to blend in than it would be for a male white belt, especially at an academy where no one had ever seen me before. Male white belts were de rigeur. Female purple belts stood out like the target in a game of Whack-a-Mole. All in all, taking into account all of my perspectives as novice practitioner, seasoned practitioner, novice visitor and seasoned visitor, I have come to the conclusion that anyone who even crosses the threshold of a grappling academy as a newcomer, both those who are new to BJJ or new to a given school, possesses serious cojones, whether these happen to be internally or externally attached.

For that reason, it may come as little surprise that when I had first fallen in love with training, I was constantly of two minds: the one that could not wait to train and the one that could barely summon the courage to walk into my academy. Every time I went in, I was sure I would feel stupid and out of place, and I was unsure of just about everything else, though every time I left, it was atop a wave of exhilaration and amazing brain fry that I had never experienced with any regularity in any other environment. The fact that this was the feeling I was left with even though I surely messed up, embarrassed myself, and in some overt or subtle way reminded my teammates of both my newness and my femaleness every time I trained should convey a sense of the strength of that high. Every time I pulled up to the academy, I wished I were already done with training so I could just skip to the transcendent feeling. I would often sit in my car beforehand, arguing with myself about whether to go in, vacillating between trying to gird myself for battle and capitulating to my overwhelming desire to go home and curl up on the couch with some *Law and Order* reruns.

One time the choice was inadvertently made for me. I was sitting in my car in the parking lot of my first BJJ academy, the one where Julian had covered my face with his gi and my partner in the first class I ever took had been impatient. It was about 15 minutes before class was due to start, and I had that familiar anxious feeling: by this time I knew what lay beyond the front doors of the gym, but I still felt equal parts drawn to and repelled by it. I had gotten out of my car and was rummaging around in the trunk for my gear bag when a huge wave of the screw-its washed over me. I had decided to get back in my car and drive home, convincing myself that I did not feel like shoring up my confidence and going inside. Basic cable had won the day. I was already debating what kind of ice cream I would pick up from the Quality Dairy on the way home when...

"Val?"

I heard a voice behind me, and I stopped, half in and half out of the driver's seat.

"Oh, hey," I said, falteringly. It was Vicki, one of the employees at the gym, a feisty girl in her late teens. She attended BJJ class sometimes, but she preferred Muay Thai and was on reception duty in the evening, so she was not someone I could glom onto as a regular partner. "How's it going?"

"You leaving? Class is starting soon!" she said. She seemed young. I felt old.

"Oh, yeah, I was just going to go run an errand. I thought I'd have enough time beforehand." Please don't ask what errand. Please don't ask what errand.

"Well, you'd better hurry. You don't want to miss the warm-up!"

"Speak for yourself," I returned, lamely. "Hang on a second while I grab my bag. I'll do the errand later." Ice cream would have to wait. The chance to walk in with someone rather than all by my lonesome like always was too good to pass up.

It took a year or more before I was able to go inside my own school without having to endure that anxious feeling. Then, just as I started to feel comfortable at this academy, I made the tactical error of graduating and moving to a different part of the state, where I trained at a different academy for a year. After my subsequent move to

Chicago, I had to start over at Carlson's. At each new place, the same anxieties caused me to play the same bargaining game. As my skill level and my familiarity with my teammates increased—oh so slowly—I started to feel more and more like my academy was my home, a place where I was welcome and where the others would wonder where

I was if I failed to show up for a while. This became particularly true in Chicago, where I stayed for six years. Of course, I still got creamed all the time, but the people kicking my butt had at least started to learn my name and to give me suggestions here and there on how to suck a little less. Students and instructors alike had started to see that I was there to stay. I became more comfortable with the discomfort BJJ inspired in me, discomfort I felt because I was terrible at it and because of the battle I waged against my own doubts and the ones I imagined the other students held about whether I belonged there. I started to realize that the discomfort I felt was the price of admission to the happy place I had quickly become unable to do without.

Now I had decided to leave behind the familiarity I had finally established—again—at my home academy and embark on a trip where I would have to endure that same constellation of feelings of insecurity, anxiety, awkwardness, and stupidity every time I decided to train. At most, I would train maybe twice or three times at any given school before getting back in my car and moving on to the next one. The fact that I was not place-bound was good in that if I did something dumb at one academy, I could quickly leave the scene of the crime. It was bad in that if I did not do something dumb at a given academy, there was always next time, with new rules and expectations to get up to speed on.

All this ran through my mind as I sat in my car in a large parking lot in St. Louis, trying to act natural. This whole road trip endeavor was feeling pretty stupid right about now. No one—not Darin, not Carlson, not Jack McCoy—was going to come to the rescue this time.

According to the schedule I found online, there were going to be two classes on the day I visited: a no-gi session followed by a gi session. I planned to go to both. I parked far away from the door to the academy, several rows away. This looked conspicuous because the lot was empty except for the growing number of cars clustering right around the academy, but I figured it would have been even more noticeable if I had sat right outside for close to an hour, trying to look busy.

I spent way too much time deciding when I should go inside, and I decided to make my move at 15 minutes before the start of class. My repeated calculations suggested that would be enough time for me to introduce myself and still be able to get to the bathroom and change without being late—something I dreaded. Far better to be in from the get go than to risk all action screeching to a halt and all attention turning to my meek and apologetic self as I stepped on the mat after class had formally started. I took a deep breath and opened the car door. I popped the trunk and grabbed my gear bag, which I had packed before I arrived, to make sure I did not draw attention to myself by futzing around.

"Hi, how you doing?" I said as I went inside and made eye contact with the first person I saw, trying to smile while at the same time looking like a badass. A friendly badass. "I'm in town for the day and wondered if I could join the class. You've got a no-gi session coming up, right?" I would learn the drill: no matter the academy, there was always a waiver to sign, there was usually a mat fee of maybe $25, and there was the quick tour of where to change, where to go to the bathroom, where to put your gear. So, I signed, paid, and took note of the surroundings.

There were already a few guys—always guys—warming up on the mat: stretching, engaging in a fundamental BJJ movement called hip escaping, taking practice wrestling shots. They were also kibitzing with each other, but they were not so busy that they neglected to get a load of me, a stranger, and a chick stranger, no less, trudging into their space and apparently planning to invade their class. I did not sense any hostility, but nor did I sense any active welcome. If anything, the energy I imagined I felt directed toward me was equal parts bemusement, detachment, and curiosity. This became a common theme of my entrance into most any academy during my journey: everyone would wait and see. I did not blame them, though as an attempt to create some comfort for myself, I started to make a game out of trying to make at least someone in every new crop of people laugh. Laughter is disarming, and people like the way they feel when they are doing it, and eliciting a chuckle or two was a way for me to try to ingratiate myself into the group. On the other hand, I tried not to assume too much closeness. I just wanted to be able to interact comfortably and register on people's radar as "friend" rather than "foe."

I went toward the bathroom the guy who took my waiver and mat fee had directed me to. While I was inside dressing for the no-gi class, I debated hiding in there until everyone left or finding a window or other escape route back to the haven of my car.

Some jiu-jitsu practitioners do not like to train no-gi. For one thing, you are that much more up close and personal with your partner or opponent because you are not protected by the heavy cotton gi. The no-gi uniform has traditionally consisted of a rash guard, like the ones surfers wear, and board shorts, also a staple of surfer fashion. Increasingly, both male and female practitioners are opting for spats (tights) instead of board shorts, or spats underneath board shorts. Also, no-gi grappling tends to be more fast-paced and intense, for multiple reasons.

Since there is less clothing, participants more quickly become sweaty and stay that way, so it is easier to slip out of submissions or positions of control. This frequently translates into an increased need for explosiveness and timing, which are important in gi grappling but even more so in no-gi. There are also positions and submissions that are allowed in no-gi training that are generally not allowed in gi training, and some people find those positions and submissions more dangerous than those allowed in gi training.

I emerged from that bathroom, dressed for no-gi but prepared for disaster. It had not escaped my notice when I entered the academy that, not only were there no other women on the mat, but also that the men occupying it looked to be nothing short of enormous. Brobdingnagian. The number of people in the room had increased, and it appeared the average size had as well, which contrasted starkly with my own 5'7", 145-pound frame. I felt like I was about to walk through a forest of redwoods, and I kept waiting for someone to tap me on the shoulder and say, "Nice try, Pee Wee, but you must be this swole to ride this ride." Nobody did, but I did look around to see if the whole situation was a joke.

"Okay, guys, let's get started!" The instructor for the class was an advanced student, or so I assumed.

One of the challenging things about no-gi, particularly when you are trying to get your bearings, is that since you are not wearing a gi, there is no need to wear a belt to keep it closed. This means it can be difficult if not impossible to tell who is of what belt rank. There are no-gi ranking systems, and nowadays, gear companies also make board shorts and rash guards that indicate a practitioner's belt rank—overlays of correspondingly colored belts on the shorts and different colored shoulder panels on the rash guards—but back in those days, those clothing items were not the norm, so it was not clear across the board who was what rank.

All the guys probably knew where they fell relative to each other because they trained together on a regular basis, both in and out of the gi, but I had no idea about them, and they had no idea about me. This made it challenging for me to place myself in the group, though it also had the potential to work in my favor: Since I was a woman and women were still relatively scarce in the BJJ world, I predicted that everyone would assume I knew nothing. This was not an insult to me. It was a reflection of the times. Anything I did know would be unexpected and maybe impressive, and perhaps that would get me a check in the "plus" column.

"Okay, we're going to start with the Peruvian necktie," the instructor said, as the students sat down on the mat around him in a semicircle.

The Peruvian necktie. A neck crank/choke combo, one of

the sequences that was more common in no-gi than gi training. I could not wait to show everyone back in Munchkinland. The instructor selected a student to demonstrate the sequence on, which from this setup culminated in him using his arms to encircle the head and one arm of the student, who was on his elbows and knees, and then throwing his legs over the neck and back of the partner.

"Guys, with this setup, I can use my arms to isolate my partner's neck and throat, and then when I throw my legs over his back and neck, my body weight causes a lot of pressure." The instructor demonstrated a few more times, and his partner tapped early and often, as we might say in Chicago.

I thought wryly that I should have eaten a bigger breakfast.

The instructor said, "Any questions? No? Okay, let's give it a try." With that, he signaled to the class that it was time to find a partner and start drilling the sequence.

In my case, it was time to try to find someone—anyone—to make the mistake of making eye contact with me. I got used to this part of every class at every academy, learning that lots of people were good at the eye glaze—they might accidentally meet my eyes for a split second, but then they looked away before I had a chance to say anything. I also learned to become more aggressive. In a friendly manner, of course, but in a way that ensured I had a partner, even if I had to encroach on a pair and make it a group of three.

This time, the game of partner musical chairs proceeded until the only two left standing were me and a twenty-something kid, who at about six feet and 180 pounds was kind of puny compared to the rest of the guys in the room. To his credit, when he saw that we were the only two left unpaired, he motioned me over, introduced himself, shook my hand, and asked, "Do you want to go first?"

From my perspective, he and I actually went on to have a pretty awesome drilling session. He was a wrestler and an aspiring practitioner of mixed martial arts (MMA), which is a combination of grappling and striking arts that has become exceedingly popular in recent years. Nonetheless, he patiently endured our size difference and my lack of familiarity with the sequence, saying things like, "Bring your elbows close to your body. It's tighter that way," and, "Don't be afraid to really sit through." I did, and I was, but I tried not to be. I could not help thinking that to anyone watching me try to execute a Peruvian necktie on this guy who barely even had a neck, I must have looked like a baby koala clinging to its father.

"Okay guys, bring it in." The instructor, who had walked around among the pairs of grapplers correcting movements and answering individual questions as we were drilling, brought us back to the large group and said, "Now we're going to move on to the anaconda. As you'll see, the Peruvian necktie and the anaconda are related, and we can get to them from the same setup."

Yes. True. Only in the case of the anaconda, another choke that involves the practitioner controlling the head and one arm of the opponent with both of his or her arms, we were required to roll ourselves underneath our partner to secure the proper position. Theoretically, if I rolled properly, I would be able to move my partner off his elbows and knees and onto his side, which would make it easier for me to finish the choke. Also theoretically, there are planets in the universe besides Earth that could be hospitable to human life.

"Guys, a common mistake for this choke is keeping your arms too loose. You have to maintain tight control if you're going to get your partner to roll," the instructor said. "You also need to kind of throw yourself underneath your partner—don't just roll them on top of you, because that's a good way to get squashed. If you are the person being choked, don't just give it to your partner. You're not being a good partner if you make them think they have it when they don't. Make sure they're actually *making* you roll."

As we worked on the sequence, my partner did as the instructor said, making sure to roll only when I was executing the technique properly.

This meant he rolled exactly zero times.

I really appreciated and really hated him for that. I mean, I did not want to go away thinking I had this move down when I did not. I really, really did not have it down, and that sucked. Especially since when it was his turn I discovered it was not a question of whether I would cooperate. Time after time I ended up on my side, tapping like The Little Drummer Boy, and it was not just because of the size difference. He was certainly not rough in his movements. Rather, he was effective.

This is how it goes with me and learning new sequences sometimes. I try and try, I get nowhere, and I throw a tantrum inside my mind. Then, when I go back the next day, I have more success. It is like my brain and body need time to combine and cook together any new sequence, and if I give myself that time, I can eventually execute some approximation of what we had been working on. At that point, though, my attempts to anaconda my partner must have looked to my hypothetical observer like a lollipop stick trying to roll under a table leg.

"Okay, guys, let's get some water and then it's time to train," said the instructor. Time for more tragicomedy, in other words. "Stick with the partner you have and then we'll switch."

I downed some water, and re-found my partner, who had staked out a section of the mat, which was dotted with pairs of grapplers. I gamely faced him, both of us on our knees. When the instructor said "go" and the timer dinged, we slapped hands and bumped fists, in what in grapplespeak is the international symbol for "Here's to a good training session. Let's go hard and learn something but not be jerks to each other."

That is what it should symbolize, at least. Some permutation of the hand slap/fist bump/handshake/one-armed hug has preceded and ended almost every roll I have ever participated in, whether at my own academy, at any academy I have ever visited, on my trip or since, or in competition. I am pretty sure that is true for most every grappler. Given the storied history of martial arts in general, particularly the fact that martial arts are traditionally about self-defense and personal honor, it is a fitting way to make sure both partners remember what they are doing and why, just like bowing to the mat to step on and off helps practitioners remember their purpose in entering the training space. It is important to decide to think about it, every time, and not allow the action to become rote.

While rolling with my partner, I felt like the squirmy puppy, sometimes jumping around but more usually being pinned under the older, more world-weary dog. At any time, he could probably have batted me with his mature-dog paw like a bear swatting at a fish, but he did not. There is debate in the grappling world about whether it is even worth it for two people to train together if there is a huge size and strength discrepancy. The fact that we can have that debate nowadays is a luxury I did not enjoy when I started grappling. Back then, it did not even occur to me to be frustrated that I could not find people to roll with who were my size and skill level. There just were not that many. There were not as many people, period. If I wanted to train, I trained with whoever was available who was also willing to work with me. That session was an extreme version of what I experienced pretty much every day: size and strength discrepancies galore. I think this is why I was not that much more freaked out by what I encountered in academy after academy, though in retrospect, I probably should have been a little more on guard. It was not until I had the opportunity to reflect on my trip after it was over that it dawned on me how much I had relied on the kindness of strangers, both in terms of safe, productive training opportunities and in terms of helping me feel like I belonged to a larger community.

Vaghi's academy was a case in point. After I rolled with my drilling partner and everything seemed to go semi-normally, I felt the energy toward me become a little warmer and more interested. Another student came up to me and asked, "Hey, do you want to roll?"

"Sure," I said. Slowly, I started holding my own in partner musical chairs. With each new partner, I got the same few questions before the buzzer sounded to end the rest period and signal the start of the new round. "Where are you from?" "What brings you here?" and, increasingly, "How long are you staying?"

By the time the no-gi class ended and it was time to get ready for the gi class, I had managed to capture the ongoing interest of a handful of the guys.

"You're coming from Carlson's? Chicago, right? My condolences. Huge loss to the whole community. Some tough dudes in Chicago."

"Wait. You're just traveling around, training jiu-jitsu? That is the *shit*. Can I come?"

"Where are you going next? You should really check out this place I know in Texas/Wisconsin/Arizona. Really nice guys and super tough. They'll take good care of you."

"Not a lot of women who train. Props to you, man."

"Yeah, can you talk to my girlfriend? She won't even try it!"

One guy in particular went out of his way to be friendly. His name was Tracy, and he and I are still acquaintances to this day. After training was over, he said, "What are you up to tonight? There's a UFC, and some of us are going to meet at a bar in town to watch. You should come."

The UFC, or Ultimate Fighting Championship, is an MMA circuit that in recent decades has contributed to the rise in popularity of MMA and has itself become a popular cultural phenomenon. The UFC is only one of multiple circuits of its kind, and yet, like Jell-O for gelatin and Kleenex for tissues, it has become almost synonymous with MMA. Live events regularly sell out, bringing in astronomical pay-per-view and arena dollars, and popular television shows like *Law and Order: SVU*, *CSI: Miami*, and *Hawaii 5-0* have reflected the influence of the sport on popular culture by airing MMA-themed episodes in recent years. Even *Friends* demonstrated a certain clairvoyance back in 1997 by featuring a story arc in which a boyfriend of the character named Monica wanted to fight. This was before MMA took on the monstrous proportions it has now, but that episode foreshadowed the sweaty pop culture juggernaut that was looming on the horizon.

"Oh, I don't know. I have to do some laundry—I'm out of clean gis."

"Screw your laundry. You can do that any time. Come hang out."

To this day, I have not asked Tracy why he was so nice to me. He was not being weird—I could tell that at the time. Like the older couple that chatted with me about karate chopping, Tracy simply decided to make a connection with me that day.

It took a phone call, some cajoling, and the actual completion of at least one load of laundry before I finally agreed to meet up with Tracy and his friends, some of whom were guys from the class that day. The show that night was UFC 61: Bitter Rivals, featuring two main events: Tim Sylvia vs. Andrei Arlovski and Tito Ortiz vs. Ken Shamrock. I do not remember much about the fights, the venue or the conversation, and I turned into a pumpkin shortly after they were over, but Tracy taught me an important lesson about actually acting on my claim that I wanted to be open to new experiences on my trip.

When faced with an opportunity to get to know some new people who loved BJJ as much as I did, my knee-jerk reaction was to say no. Regimentation at its finest. I had planned to do laundry, and by God, I was going to do laundry. Tracy did me the huge favor of telling me I was full of shit and that I should come out and enjoy the evening. He gave me a chance to exercise the spontaneity muscle.

Partly as a result of Tracy's cajoling that one night, I recommitted myself to saying yes to opportunities for adventure, though I cannot say for sure that I am any less full of shit.

4

After I said goodbye to Tracy and the rest of the Vaghi crew, my journey continued westward. It was mid-July, and the next big stop on the itinerary was Littleton, Colorado, where my former colleague Lacey lived. If I do say so myself, Lacey and I had done good work together at the company where we met, where I took a job after I spent a year at a post-doc.

Through our collaborations, we had realized we had a lot in common both personally and professionally, and we had become friends, staying in touch after she moved west and I moved onto the next job(s) I would eventually quit. Littleton, in addition to being forever associated with the tragic Columbine High School massacre in 1999, is also within spitting distance of Denver and Boulder, both places where BJJ had established a solid foothold by the time I came through in the summer of 2006. My plan was to spend a few days reconnecting with Lacey, taking advantage of summertime activities in John Denver's heaven on earth, and training at several academies in the area. To break up the journey from Missouri, I added an intermediate stop in Kansas, where some Internet research had turned up a small academy that was en route.

After having spent some time in Kansas, I now feel protective of it, just like I feel about my home state of New

Jersey. Smug Manhattanites, Los Angelenos, San Franciscans, and District of Columbians abound, and they are smug because they believe that Kansas and New Jersey are two of the ugly ducklings of the USA, if they even think about them at all. Yes, the Jersey Turnpike is far from picturesque. Yes, you have to take an exit off of the Turnpike to get elsewhere in the state, though I am pretty sure that is true of most highways everywhere in the country. How else do you get off a highway? So the question "What exit?" that some snide non-New Jersey-ites ask when they find out where the person they are talking to is from is not really that funny, which, in my opinion, is actually a bigger transgression than the attitude itself. If you try, you can find areas of beauty, tranquility, historical significance, even lush greenery in New Jersey. We are known as the Garden State for a reason. I sound defensive. I am.

Kansas appears to have a similar PR problem. It is flat, and it is home to a lot of cornfields. It is squarely in what I and countless others have referred to as "flyover country." Though that may seem boring to some people, I encourage you to stop at one of the scenic outlooks along Route 70 near Lawrence, Kansas, and really take a look. The University of Kansas is located there, and they have installed plaques with explanations and diagrams that can help the uninitiated fully appreciate both the beauty and the utility of the crops. I admit that when I first entered Kansas on my journey I considered it mostly something I needed to get through as quickly as possible on my way to Colorado. Once I slowed down a little and realized how good Kansas is at being Kansas, I started to become a fan.

Once I had identified an academy to visit, I initiated my typical sequence for locking a grappling academy in my sights: I found it on the map, calculated roughly how long it would take for me to get there, and worked backwards from my current geographic location to figure out when I would need to leave in order to arrive an hour or so before class started so I could do my vaguely creepy recon. As I did this, I blithely drove on, not realizing that my visit here would be my first encounter on this trip with some of the warts of the BJJ world.

"Hi, I'm just driving through the area and I wondered if I could jump into a class. I train in Chicago," I said to the guy I encountered when I walked into the academy, which was housed in a squat building off a major-ish thoroughfare.

"Oh, sure, welcome," he said. "I'm Jeff[12]. I'll be teaching."

"Nice to meet you," I said. "So I'm in time for class?" I managed casual glances at the pictures on the walls, which included several shots of gi-clad grapplers as well as a logo painted directly on the underlying paint that matched the patch on the gi Jeff was wearing. I noticed he was also wearing a blue belt, which meant I outranked him. I had not foreseen this. I had assumed the instructors at all the academies I visited would be run by men—they were virtually all men in those days, though this is now changing—who outranked me. I doubted he would be expecting it either. Then again, I also doubted he was used to having many visitors come through, let alone ones who might know as much as he did about BJJ. This would probably be uncharted territory for both of us.

"Sure, everyone is just starting to trickle in. We are affiliated under a black belt who lives in another state. He comes to town a few times a year, and I keep things running around here in between."

At the time of this writing, close to ten years after I visited this academy, the affiliate model is still quite common. According to this model, a lower-ranked practitioner essentially runs an academy under the auspices of a black belt who lives elsewhere. The black belt instructor typically visits the academy on a regular basis, and the affiliate instructor regularly makes the trek to train with the main instructor and vice versa, thereby ensuring some consistency and mentoring. A major difference between the way the model worked in 2006 and the way it is likely to work today,

---

[12] Not his real name.

however, is that affiliate instructors now can typically be expected to have higher rank. In other words, it would be far less likely nowadays that a blue belt like Jeff would be left to run an entire academy on his own because now there are more people with more experience. Identifying a purple, brown, or even black belt to run an affiliate academy would be easier now. Jeff himself would have many years more experience by now, enough under most affiliations to have earned his black belt.

This is not to say blue belts never run academies under the auspices of a remote instructor, but it happens less often. To my mind, this is a good thing, because even the most well-meaning and eager blue belt is likely to lack the experience and accumulated wisdom of a more seasoned practitioner, which means that blue belt will be less equipped to deal with challenges and set an appropriate example.

Jeff gave me the typical orientation. I signed a waiver and paid a mat fee, and then he showed me the bathroom, where I could change, and the mat space, where we would be training. Out of the corner of my eye, I could see guys walking in and doing a double take when they saw me talking to Jeff. I never got used to that part, but it became one of the things I learned to expect. As a woman, I turned heads, and as a purple belt, I turned heads completely around. At this place, other than their black belt instructor, it appeared *anyone* who had earned a rank higher than blue was like a yeti—there may have been stories chronicling their existence, but actual sightings seemed to be few and far between. They had not yet seen me wearing my purple belt, but the time was nigh.

Upon emerging from the changing room in my gi, I steeled myself twice as much as usual. Outwardly, I was all smiles, especially to Jeff, as I quickly surveyed the room and took in the reactions of the assembling students—all white belts with a couple blues—to my appearance on the mat and the color of my belt. Jeff and I were now in an officially awkward situation: This was his academy, but I outranked him. On one hand, I would have felt rude walking in and throwing my weight around, but, on the other hand, judging from the way he froze, staring at my belt, mouth half open, it appeared he was frantically trying to figure out how to keep from being rude himself. How could he acknowledge my rank but still maintain authority over his students? I was some random itinerant grappler. He was their day-to-day leader. Or was he, when I was around? It appeared nobody knew. The students stood quietly, waiting to see what was going to happen next.

Making a game-day decision, I walked up to Jeff, bowed, and shook his hand, saying something like, "Thank you for having me in your class. I'm looking forward to it." Jeff returned my handshake and immediately snapped into leadership mode. "We're really happy to have you here. Thank you for coming." Thank you for the other thing too, his facial expression said.

"Okay guys, start running!" Jeff said.

Many jiu-jitsu instructors, of every rank, start off their classes having the students run in a circle to begin the process of warming up. Jeff took us through the various types of running that are frequently employed at the beginning of jiu-jitsu classes everywhere—knees high, heels high, shuffling side to side, a movement called grapevining or karaoke (think Riverdance), skipping—and then transitioned us into some line drills that more closely approximated BJJ moves—forward rolls, hip escapes, backward rolls, and the like.

I do not remember what he taught by way of technique, but I do remember what happened after that.

"Okay, guys, let's get some water, and then it's time to help Ed and Timmy[13] get ready for the competition," Jeff said. To me, he explained, "These two guys are going to do a local tournament next week—their first one, so we're going to do King of the Hill to help them get ready. Only they'll stay in the whole time. We'll get them some prep first, and then while they're resting after, the rest of us can get in our own rounds too."

"Oh, cool," I said. "Sure."

King of the Hill, also known as "pass, protect, sweep,

---

[13] Not their real names.

submit," is a drilling game frequently used in jiu-jitsu classes. Some number of grapplers, five, say, position themselves on the mat while the rest of the class lines up against the wall. Each of the first five students in line pairs up with one of the students already on the mat to make five pairs of students who will train with each other. The rest of the students in line wait and watch. The student already on the mat is "down," seated or on his or her back, and the other person is on top, in that person's guard.

Then, when the instructor gives the signal, the person on top starts to try to pass the guard of the person on the bottom and get to a side control position, the way Julian showed in the very first class I took. On the other hand, the person on the bottom starts to try either to sweep the person on top, where "sweeping" someone involves reversing position with that person—putting him or her on the bottom and coming on top—or submitting that person.

In competition jiu-jitsu, there are different rule sets depending on the tournament, but generally there are several ways to win a match. A competitor can earn points by successfully executing certain movements for which points are awarded. These movements include, but are not limited to, passing the guard and sweeping—the movements the top and bottom person will most often try to execute in King of the Hill—taking the mount, and taking the back.

In the absence of a submission, the competitor who earns more points—executes more sweeps, guard passes, and other movements that earn points—in the designated time frame will win the match. If a competitor is able to submit his or her opponent, that competitor wins as soon as the referee sees the opponent tapping and stops the match, even if the opponent had earned more points by then, and even if there is still time left on the clock. If no submissions occur and the number of points is the same, matches may go into overtime or be subject to a referee's decision.

In King of the Hill during a typical jiu-jitsu class, pairs follow these competition rules, but unlike in a competition, they go only until the first points are scored. If someone executes a submission, the round ends as it would in a competition. The person who was submitted or scored upon leaves the mat and returns to the end of the line while the person who did the submitting or scoring stays in place, squaring off against the next person at the front of the line. The winner usually assumes the "down" position—trying to sweep or submit— even if they had won the round by passing the guard, so the next person in line comes in "on top."

Usually if a student "wins" some number of exchanges— perhaps three or four—that student will come out and get back in line to give other students an opportunity and to give that person a bit of a rest. This is particularly useful if there is a big discrepancy in skill level—in other words, if there is one black belt in a group of white and blue belts, it is likely that the black belt will be able to out-maneuver the rest of the group for the most part, so putting a cap on the number of exchanges ensures that the black belt will not be "down" the whole time.

This is how King of the Hill usually goes, unless the instructor changes the rules, like Jeff did for this particular game. This time, Jeff had Ed and Timmy stay "down" the whole time. This meant that even if someone passed Timmy's guard or swept Ed, for instance, he would stay "down" and take on the next person in line, continuing to try to sweep or submit them until Jeff called time. The goal was to help them work on their cardio and retain their composure as they got more and more fatigued. The energy and intensity requirements in a competition are usually much higher than those in a class situation, particularly for new competitors who may not yet have learned how to manage their nerves and the accompanying adrenaline dump, so drills like these are good for simulating that. The other pairs on the mat would follow the "four and you're out" protocol, but Timmy and Ed would soldier on.

With the cap in place, King of the Hill could take place for as long as the instructor liked, anywhere from 15 to 30 or even 45 minutes, though much more than that and people were likely to get bored or exhausted. The guys who were waiting in line kept up a steady patter of cheers and coaching for Ed and Timmy as they started to sweat and breathe more heavily.

"Get it, Tim! Pass, pass, pass!"

"Come on, Ed! Pick it up, pick it up!"

"Sweep!"

"Good hustle, guys! Go hard here so you can go easier in the competition!"

"Push it! Let's go!"

We had been going for about 10 minutes, with Ed and Timmy staying in the fray while the rest of us cycled out. I had just reached the end of the line when I heard Jeff say sharply, "What's up, Ed? Why are you stopping?"

Ed had sat up and had held out his hand, palm facing away from him, toward the student approaching him from the front of the line. His face was creased in what looked like concentration or consternation, or a little of both. The other student stopped uncertainly and looked toward Jeff.

"I'm starting to have trouble breathing, Coach," Ed wheezed. "Can I get my inhaler?"

I nudged the person next to me, a young, eager-looking white belt. "What's up?" I asked.

"Oh, Ed has exercise-induced asthma," the kid said. "Makes it hard for him to breathe sometimes. He's working on controlling it."

"You won't be able to get your inhaler in the middle of your competition matches, Ed!" Jeff yelled. "Suck it up and get back to it."

"Yes, sir," Ed responded, breathing heavily. He lay back, and when his partner approached, he put him in his closed guard.

I kept my eyes on Ed as the pairs on the mat engaged and disengaged and the people tacking themselves onto the back of the line put me closer to the front.

So did Jeff. "Ed, stop being a pussy!" he yelled, as Ed appeared to start moving less and gasping more. His partner dutifully put pressure on him, working to open and pass his guard and staying tight with his hips and shoulders, compressing Ed's chest in the process. Ed's breathing became more and more audible, rattly, and moist.

"Coach," Ed rasped, "this is feeling pretty bad."

Unless I am actually playing poker, I have a terrible poker face. I flinch at any violence or gore in movies, watching through my fingers and half-closed eyes. I must have shown what I was feeling when I watched the exchange between Ed and Jeff: extreme discomfort and concern. I am guessing this because Jeff started to respond to Ed with, "Ed, for God's sake, shut up and fight," but stopped short as his eyes fell on me, so his response sounded more like: "Ed, for God's sake, shut up and f..."

I stared at Jeff, unable to contain my surprise, and then looked at Ed and back to Jeff again. I had never seen anything like this before. Sure, on one hand, I had seen people get hurt or have to stop physical activity because of sudden incapacitation, and on the other hand, I had seen my coaches encourage my teammates to fight harder and refuse to give up. Even in my case, there had been times when they had encouraged me to dig deeper. When I did, I had been heartened to find a reservoir of badassery within me that I had not known existed, and that I know I would not have found without their collective shoe up my butt. As the recipient of good coaching, I had reduced my knee-jerk tendency to assume I could not do something just because I had not yet tried.

I had never seen the two together, though: an athlete in obvious physical distress and a coach insisting that that athlete disregard that physical distress and keep at it. Apparently, up until that point in my various sports endeavors, my coaches—both jiu-jitsu and otherwise—had known when it was time to require their players to rest or sit out, even going so far as to protect the overzealous ones from themselves ("I'm fine, Coach! You can barely see the bone protruding through the skin, and the blood is slowing to a trickle. Tape me up and put me back in!"). Thus far in my athletic life, what I had observed of my coaches was that they knew how to walk the line between pushing an athlete outside of his or her comfort zone and pushing that same athlete into the danger zone. In my experience, their coaching decisions did not reflect an abusive streak, a desire to live vicariously through another person, or a need to process unfinished emotional business. I had never encountered any of those motivations, which might come to mind when contemplating the over-the-top reputations of coaches such as Olympic gymnastics coach Bela Karolyi or Indiana University basketball's Bobby Knight.

In Jeff's case, I believe his actions reflected a fourth possibility: naïveté. I got the sense that his intentions were good, and that he was honestly trying to help Ed with his mental toughness. As a blue belt, and as young man, Jeff was relatively inexperienced, both in jiu-jitsu and in life. He was unlikely to be as skilled at evaluating and controlling a potentially dangerous situation as a more experienced coach, and he was also unlikely to be particularly skilled at evaluating and controlling the role his ego was playing in his coaching.

Perhaps the combination of the two led him to come down extra hard on Ed to make sure neither of them looked inexperienced or weak in the presence of a visiting upper belt. The fact that he had gone about it all wrong if he wanted to impress me was beside the point. All that provided cold comfort as I watched Ed struggling to breathe. I was particularly sympathetic because of my own claustrophobia, but based on what I saw, and what I felt in my gut, Ed was not dogging it. He was in distress.

As I watched Ed struggle for breath, I was reminded of how I had felt while rolling with Julian on my first day. I had been hamstrung by fear, and only Julian's encouragement had enabled me to cling to a shred of sanity while I faced that fear. I started to clue into how fortunate I had been that my trust in Julian was well-founded, given how little I had known him before letting him into my physical space, and given how much stronger and more skilled at jiu-jitsu he was than I.

Legendary boxer Mike Tyson once said, "Everybody has a plan till they get punched in the mouth."[14] While there is no

---

[14] Berardino, M. (2012). *Mike Tyson explains one of his most famous quotes*. Retrieved from http://articles.sun-sentinel.com/2012-11-09/sports/sfl-mike-

punching in jiu-jitsu, being rolled up like a carpet while a more skilled jiu-jitsu adversary calmly anticipates and neutralizes my every panicked flail and flop is just as big a head game as I would imagine a good punch to the money-maker in a boxing match is, though of course a punch also rings the bell. In very few other situations are people like me required to face physical intimidation of any kind, and then, to add insult to injury, evaluate how well or poorly we handled the threat, knowing that we have to face our shortcomings if we are to fix them. In jiu-jitsu, we do this over and over, some of us almost daily, and some of us even more often than that.

In order to do it safely and effectively, we must be able to trust one another, quite literally, with our lives. Unfortunately, sometimes this trust is unwarranted. Inexperienced practitioners are particularly vulnerable, both because they do not have much skill to defend themselves if necessary and also because they may feel like they have limited recourse if they find themselves in situations where their wants or needs are at odds with the instructions of the teacher.

"Okay, time!" Jeff called, keeping his eye on me. "Everyone, grab a drink, and Ed, go do your thing."

Ed made a beeline for his gym bag and Jeff made a beeline for me. "Ed's kind of soft," Jeff confided, his comments meant only for my ears. "We've talked before about mind over matter and whatnot. When we first started preparing him for this competition, he asked to stop like every 30 seconds, so he's improving."

"Uh huh," I said. I didn't know what else to say, or what to believe. I guess I did not have a reason to doubt Jeff, other than that the entire situation *felt* absolutely wrong, and that what I had seen Ed experiencing did not seem to be about mind over matter. Out of the corner of my eye, I saw Ed shake his inhaler, put it to his mouth, and take a deep, raggedy breath. I was overwhelmed by the desire to just turn

tyson-explains-one-of-his-most-famous-quotes-20121109_1_mike-tyson-undisputed-truth-famous-quotes on my heel and leave immediately.

"Seriously," Jeff said, trying to catch my eye and probably sensing that I was unconvinced. "We're toughening him up a little bit, and it will be good for him when he competes. He can rest now while the rest of us train."

"Sure," I intoned absently, though upon hearing Jeff speak, my mind started racing. Dammit. I had forgotten that we were not done with the class. Ain't no way I am training live here, I thought. Putting myself in a situation where these guys might very well be able to physically overpower me. Yes, I was the highest-ranked belt, but I was also a woman, very likely weaker than these men if they chose to "muscle" me—use brute strength instead of jiu-jitsu technique. What if they tried to take it to me harder because they were reacting to the purple target on my back? I was used to that, but then I asked myself a question that had never ever crossed my mind before: What if they got me in a compromising position and did not respect the tap?

In every academy in every country around the world, grapplers share a tacit understanding that if I tap to the submission you have put on me—the choke that could put me unconscious or the joint manipulation that could lead to a fracture or a dislocation—you let go of that submission. It is the single most important, most fundamental expectation grapplers have of each other, so much so that it frequently goes without saying, though since it is so important, it should be discussed frequently.

Far more often the issue is that someone who is legitimately caught in a submission refuses to tap. Sometimes this is because the trapped person does not recognize that he or she is in danger, but more often people refuse to tap because their egos forbid it. In those latter cases, the person who has applied the submission is placed into the untenable position of having to protect the other person from him or herself by opting to let up on the pressure rather than put the partner to sleep or inflict serious injury on the trapped joint.

In this case, it dawned on me that if it was acceptable to do what I perceived as playing fast and loose with people's safety in one way, where did the line get drawn? Was it beyond where I was used to finding it? I honestly did not sense any malice among these guys, but an injury was an injury, accidental or not.

"Oh, about that," I followed up, aloud. "I realized while we were doing King of the Hill that I actually have to get going. I have to go make a phone call."

My lie sounded pathetic. I stuck to it, though, even when Jeff asked, "Are you sure?"

"Yes, sorry. I forgot until just now."

Every impulse in my body was propelling me toward the door. I was not going to ignore it. I did not seem to be able to. Whereas a few minutes before I had felt surrounded by "my people," eager, excited disciples of the sport I loved, within the last few seconds the academy had become a foreboding and dangerous place. Everyone was still smiling and friendly, but I did not want any of them near me anymore. I no longer trusted them to know how to put my well-being—and their own, for that matter—first and foremost. It was because of the absence of that confidence here that it started to dawn on me, with just a glimmer of realization sinking in at that particular moment, how much I had relied on it so far on my trip.

In his best-selling book *The Gift of Fear and Other Survival Signals That Protect us from Violence*, Gavin de Becker argues that human beings are equipped with a built-in system for protecting ourselves from harmful forces: our intuition. In its purest form, our instinct for survival comes into play just when we need it for protection from harm. To have such instincts is just step one, however. It is only when we *act* on these instincts that we can benefit from their protective power.

Over time, we as a species have developed a tendency to act in opposition to those survival instincts that kept humans alive in prehistoric eras if those instincts challenge our more modern senses of propriety and etiquette. Women in particular have a tendency to worry about being rude to others, especially men, when faced with the threat of real physical danger and the additional tendency to allow that worry to override their instinctive, self-preserving inner voice. "A woman who is clear and precise is viewed as cold, or a bitch, or both. A woman is expected, first and foremost, to respond to every communication from a man. And the response is expected to be one of willingness and attentiveness."[15] In this context, it becomes more apparent how women might feel cognitive dissonance in the face of an encounter that feels uncomfortable.

In the book, de Becker, a threat assessment specialist, relates stories from actual clients—survivors of violent and devastating crimes such as rape, assault, and harassment—in which he explains how he and each client worked together after the fact to pinpoint moments in the interaction with the perpetrator before the violence occurred when she might have been able to identify the threat and, then, perhaps, neutralize or at least reduce it. In most cases, the survivor said something along the lines of, "I could just tell there was something off about this guy," or "Something didn't feel quite right." In the absence of hard evidence, and not wanting to rock the boat, she went along with what was more socially acceptable: "He said he wanted to help me with my grocery bags, which is the *polite* thing to do, right?" "I hoped he'd leave me alone if I was just nice to him at first." "He said he loved me." "I didn't want to seem like a bitch."

This phenomenon is not a justification for blaming the victim. Every one of us is socialized from early on in life about what is appropriate behavior and what is not, and too often, individuals conflate behaving "appropriately" toward another person with granting that person permission to violate our physical, emotional, or psychological boundaries. We assume others are acting according to those same rules and interpreting them in the same ways. As de Becker describes in his book, in the case of the survivors—and those who did not survive—all too often there are people who will act in a predatory manner, manipulating what is considered acceptable for malevolent purposes.

---

[15] de Becker, G. (1997). *The gift of fear and other survival signals that protect us from violence*. New York: Dell Publishing.

Anyone can manipulate the tacitly accepted rules of social interaction to their own advantage if they are so inclined, and sometimes the intention is less predatory than it is passive-aggressive. Consider one of my favorite/least favorite examples: the pedestrian with poor timing. While driving your car, have you ever been stopped for a red light at an intersection and then watched as a pedestrian started crossing the street in front of you while the red "DON'T WALK" light was blinking? Further watched as that pedestrian continued to saunter slowly past once "DON'T WALK" had stopped blinking and changed into a red hand, signaling "STOP," at the same time that your light had turned green, while that person was still squarely in the intersection and in harm's way, perhaps just in front of your bumper? Suspected in your heart of hearts that he or she was doing it on purpose? And, of course, done nothing until the pedestrian was safely across the street, even if it meant you sat at the intersection for another cycle because your green light turned amber and then red again as you sat and waited?

If you have ever experienced this scenario, you know that the pedestrian banked on you as the driver recognizing that the law against hitting an individual in an intersection with your car—even one who is asking for it—supersedes the law allowing you to proceed through that same intersection when your light turns green. Maybe you were infuriated because you knew the pedestrian was technically in the wrong, but you could not do anything about it.

Hitting someone with your car is still hitting someone with your car, even if the person who got hit was not acting intelligently. In a similar, more sinister way, predators bank on the idea that potential targets will allow their senses of propriety to override any messages they receive from their intuition that ignoring their intuition is a bad idea. Only, in these scenarios, potential targets are not infuriated but rather made uneasy. This is because, while on some level of consciousness they may know something is amiss, they may be unable to put their finger on exactly what the problem is.

In this situation, as I mentioned, I believe the issue was one of naïveté. I do not believe Jeff was trying to hurt Ed, nor did I believe he or his students would deliberately try to hurt me or anyone else. Still, the King of the Hill exchange set up a situation where the action my instinct was telling me to take—get the hell out of this unsafe-feeling place—was at odds with what I had been socialized to do—get ready to train because class was not yet over, and polite people did not disrupt class before it ended. I did not have any concrete explanation for why I felt uneasy. It was not *me* who was being put through the wringer, and I had heard a reasonable-sounding explanation for what he was doing.

Although I am an inveterate people pleaser, my intuition won the day. Over Jeff's protests of, "But don't you want to train?" I shook my head and said, "I really have to get going," excused myself to go change, and took a few deep breaths to steady myself when I was alone. When I re-emerged in the mat space in my street clothes, Timmy and Ed were sitting against the wall. Ed seemed to be breathing normally again, and the rest of the class was paired up and rolling. Jeff came up to me one last time and said, uncertainly, "Well, thanks a lot for coming by. Hope you had fun."

I shook his hand and said, "Thank *you*. Yeah, I have to get going. But enjoy the rest of the session." I waved to the students who noticed I was leaving, including Ed and Timmy. "Good luck in the tournament," I called to them. They smiled and gave me the thumbs up.

I walked out without looking behind me. I threw my gym bag into the passenger's seat, got in the car, and started it up, locking the doors as soon as they would engage. I drove a few blocks away until I found a supermarket parking lot, where I pulled into a spot far from the doors and sat. And cried.

In his book, de Becker argues that if we can do a better job of recognizing the dynamics that shape our day-to-day interactions with other people—how we negotiate power, and how we respect, enforce, and violate one another's interpersonal boundaries—we can better protect ourselves when some of those same people, from the passive-aggressive pedestrian to the predatory would-be attacker, attempt to manipulate these dynamics. Armed with that knowledge, we can then make wiser choices. We still might refrain from smacking the pedestrian, but on the other hand, we might feel more empowered to refuse to allow a stranger into our house even if the only reason we can point to is a sense of unease.

That day, I did not know any of this. My intuition still squelched any other impetus that might have tried to influence my behavior, but under other circumstances, my social conditioning has been far more powerful. After this and other experiences where my instinct and my conditioning have conflicted with each other, I have developed more empathy for someone who might decide to let the stranger into the house, neglect to check identification, or get into an elevator with a shady looking character. I am fortunate, though, not to have been the victim of any sort of attack as a result of my own tendency to do these things in the face of a foreboding feeling because I could not point to anything tangible.

I did not have the language to explain this to Jeff even if I had wanted to because I did not know that was what I was reacting to. I had had the presence of mind—or maybe it is more accurate to say the presence of my subconscious—to keep my exit conversation with him as short as possible so he did not have the opportunity to come back with counter-arguments about why I should stay.

I say this because after the fact I could not believe I had acted the way I did. It was very out of character for me, and it accounted for at least some of the tears—not just the idea that I might be in physical danger, but the idea that in my mind I had essentially accused someone of malevolence, in advance of it actually happening and with no way to prove it.

I had followed my instincts, though there was no way to confirm that doing so was the right call. Maybe I had avoided a potentially dangerous situation, but by definition, I will never know. I will also never know if there was no dangerous situation to begin with. That is where more of the tears came from: me second-guessing myself in the face of my social conditioning. Whether or not I was right, some primal part of me took over, the part that refused to allow me to ignore my inner voice and risk getting the worst kind of confirmation that I should have listened to it. As I struggled to process what I had just witnessed, I started to realize that the distance I had traveled since leaving Chicago was more than geographic.

In any relationship between two people, there is an end to the honeymoon period. Children eventually learn their parents are not perfect. A best friend disappoints us in some way. A spouse says something particularly vicious during an argument. The boss who usually has our back lightly scapegoats us "for the good of the project" and promises to make it right. Lousy though this may feel, if the foundation of a given relationship is solid, and if we expect it to progress in a healthy way, it is not only possible for each of us to recognize that everyone is imperfect, even the people we love the most. It is necessary.

It just is not fun. Or easy. Living in that perfect place is nice. We feel we are completely validated, connected, and heard, and it is a slap in the face to bump up against the fact that the Shangri-la is temporary. Sometimes we may hit that moment of realization and decide we cannot live with the other person's imperfections or with how the other person deals with them. If we decide the benefits of the relationship outweigh the negatives, we are then faced with a whole new mess of considerations.

When a given issue rears its ugly head, what do we speak up about and what do we let slide? Is that going to be the same strategy every time? Where do we draw the line, and what are we prepared to do if that line is crossed? One of the "relationship status" options Facebook allows users to choose from, in addition to "married," "single," and "in a relationship," is "It's complicated," and lots of people use it.

Perhaps it is evident where I am going with this. At the time of this writing, I have been training Brazilian Jiu-Jitsu for some 18 years. This is longer than many marriages last. In fact, I am sure I could name several celebrity couples who married after I started training and have since divorced. My relationship with jiu-jitsu is longer by far than any romantic relationship I have had (which is another story) and, I would argue, is as emotionally taxing and rewarding as a "real" relationship. As also happens in "real" relationships, my orientation to jiu-jitsu has changed through the years, such that while my ardor for it may have slowly transformed from a five-alarm fire to a quietly crackling Duraflame log, my commitment has deepened and strengthened over time. This is in spite of, or perhaps because of, my recognition over time that BJJ too comes with warts and all.

I remember as a white belt wanting to train all day every day and not noticing that I was being indulged when people who had been around for a lot longer would smile kindly at me when I said as much, exchange glances with each other, and reply, "Well, that's great. Hang onto that feeling for as long as you can." I was deep in the throes of the honeymoon phase, summed up in the song *Crush Story* by the band Too Much Joy: "Everything you've ever said is brilliant/Anything you want to do is fine with me." I had learned all there was to know about the depths and heights of BJJ's awesomeness. I mean, I had tons to learn where technique was concerned, of course, but BJJ as an entity was fantastic across the board. There was no downside, and there were no problems with the practice or the culture that had built up around it.

Then I encountered this situation. This was not the first time I had ever had a negative experience in BJJ. I had cried from frustration, gotten burned out from too much training, rolled with people who had had something to prove and were not concerned about their own safety let alone mine. Of course I had felt intimidated as hell pretty much all the time for the first few years of my training, and then again every time I entered a new academy on my walkabout, but I had taken those feelings on myself, assuming they all had to do with some shortcoming on my part, or that they were evidence that my deepest worry was correct: that I did not belong.

This was not the first time the pieces had fallen together in my mind in any way that could paint a picture of BJJ as anything less than the ideal I had created over time. It was the first time, however, that I had ever felt threatened. This experience drove home the fact that BJJ is performed by people, and that people are imperfect. By the transitive property, that meant that my experience of BJJ had the potential to be imperfect and even negative. The upshot was, I had to be on my guard even with my biggest crush. There were people who did things in the name of BJJ, or at least in the context of BJJ, that did not sit right with me, and this was just the tip of the iceberg. It seems obvious now, and I now know I was naïve, but back then I did not even know what I did not know.

Once I had collected myself, I started up the car and got back on the road. Lacey was expecting me in the next couple days, and I still had a long drive before I hit Littleton. It was a drive that would consist of more and more twists and turns and that increase in altitude through mountainous terrain after I crossed the Colorado border. Having someone waiting for me was nice, particularly someone who *didn't* do jiu-jitsu, given how I felt. I still planned to train when I hit the Mile-High area, though my excitement had been tempered somewhat. I pointed my car westward, putting the endless flat topography of Kansas behind me and hoping the anxiety would fade into the distance as the state did the same.

5

I was about 1200 circuitous miles from where I had started my trip. I felt both like I had traversed the globe and like I had used up a lot of gas going nowhere. After my experience at Jeff's school, the thought of being protected by my car for a while was comforting because nothing would be required of me beyond staying awake and steering. Since I could not be 5 years old again and encircled in my parents' arms, which is what I really wanted, it seemed like a viable alternative.

It was not quite enough, though. I called my parents as I drove, trying to combine the feeling of being safe in my car with the feeling of being safe at home.

"So, where are you now?" my father said when he picked up. This had become his favorite greeting since I departed, supplanting a simple "hello." He found it endlessly amusing to ask the question, and he also wanted the answer. As far as he knew, I was flirting with the edge of the earth, where sea monsters might dwell.

"I am in America's heartland," I said. I spoke loudly because of the noise from the car engine. "I am headed to the Denver area to stay with a friend there for a few days. She's excited to see me, and there are a few places in that area to train. So I'll probably hang out for a week or so."

"Colorado is so beautiful," my mother said, having picked up a different extension.

"Hi, Mom. Yeah, I'm looking forward to some different scenery, and it will be interesting to see how my car handles the mountains. So what's going on with you?"

"Oh, it's just another day in paradise," my mother said. She and my father had moved to central Florida after retiring. They had loved raising me and my sister in New Jersey, but they were happy to go someplace with warmer winters for their golden years, and they had landed in a golf community of like-minded partners in crime.

"What's the latest with the treatments?" I asked.

"Oh, it's the same as it always is. Dad is a real trooper, supporting me while I do my thing." Shortly before I departed on my trip, my mother had been diagnosed with breast cancer and had undergone surgery to remove the cancerous tissue. She was following up the surgery with a several-month course of radiation. As you might imagine, this had scared the living daylights out of me. At the time I heard her original diagnosis, I very much wanted to cancel my trip and be with her and my father, but my mother insisted I go, saying the best thing I could do for her was live my life. I did, with reluctance, but I made sure it was firmly tethered to hers and my father's through frequent phone calls and postcards.

"Dad is a trooper. Always has been. Right, Dad?"

"I'm definitely a keeper."

"Well, enough of that boring stuff. What's up with you? Did you train today?" my mom asked.

My mother was being evasive, but I decided not to press the issue, partly to respect her desire to talk about something else and partly because I was not in a frame of mind to be a good listener. I took a deep breath before I answered her question. I thought about where I had just been and willed my voice to keep from breaking. "I visited an academy, yeah. I didn't stay for training because I was a little bit tired, and I wanted to log some miles. I don't want to get to Lacey's too late tomorrow, so I'm doing a couple of hours in the car this afternoon."

"Anyone give you a hard time?" my father asked, ever protective.

"Nah, they were nice. A little bit green, and not just because they're all younger than I am, but welcoming. I outranked them all too."

"Oh yeah? You should have stayed and kicked their butts." He chuckled.

"Maybe on my way back. I just kind of wanted to get on the road and to hear your voices." My nose tingled, the first sign that I was about to cry.

"Well, we're always glad to hear from you. Not much changes around here, but we are only ever a phone call away," my mother said.

"I know. I count on it." More tingling. I swallowed.

"Well, go buy yourself a nice dinner or something, on us," my father said, "and remember, there are only three reasons to stop on the road."

"I remember, and thanks. You're seriously both okay?"

"We're fine. What about you?" said my mother.

"I'm fine too."

"Okay. Well, eyes on the road, and call again when you can. Love you, honey," my father said.

"Bye sweetie," my mother said.

"Bye. Love you too."

I got the words out and the phone disconnected before the sob came. Though they never said so, I knew my parents were always relieved when I called because they could hear for themselves that I was safe, at least for that day. I wanted them to be able to enjoy that, so I tried to keep my sadness to myself this time. I am thankful and relieved to be able to say that my mother has been cancer-free for many years now, but since I know the treatments took their toll on her and my father that summer, I suspected they had done the same for me.

- - - - - - - - - -

As my father implied, he followed an iron-clad rule of road trips: There are only three reasons to stop on the road, if you are not also stopping for the night. First, to get gas. Second, to go to the bathroom. Third, to eat. Ideally, every stop should involve doing all three, but at least two have to happen at once. To do otherwise is to waste time, and when there are many miles to cover, efficiency is the watchword. Given the size of both my bladder and my appetite, which seem to be inversely related, I sometimes had to stop before I needed to see to all three, but true to my upbringing, I never stopped for just one.

Not that day, and not at any point on my entire road trip. Given my commitment to experiencing as much as I could, I did add a fourth reason sometimes: to investigate something unique or crazy or interesting, like when I followed a sign advertising a store that sold "slightly irregular" candy at discount prices. I had to find out what that was. Turns out, it is when a piece breaks, or when two pieces stick together, things like that. Nothing to do with the ingredients or the edibility, for which I was glad, seeing as how I blew 20 bucks on what were supposed to be chocolate-covered toffees, though some of them missed the chocolate treatment altogether and others got it twice. But even at those times, I never technically broke the rule, again thanks to my appetite and a steady infusion of Diet Coke.

After I hung up with my parents and contemplated getting off the road to stretch my legs, I heard my father's voice in my head asking, "Do you really need to make this stop?" I mentally scanned the list of acceptable reasons. First, the gas gauge needle hovered somewhere between a quarter and a half a tank: good enough for topping off. Second, the thought of a bathroom break perked me right up: check. Third, I pictured the types of snacks that would be available at the next big convenience store and realized, yeah, I could eat.

I took the next exit, and in the distance along the local road I could see the tell-tale signs of a huge highway plaza, including a big neon sign and parking and gas pumps for both cars and trucks. I maneuvered to a vacant gas pump on the automobile side and filled the tank, shielding my eyes against the sun. "In New Jersey they pump your gas for you,"

I grumbled in my mind, while squeezing the handle and keeping the nozzle directed into the tank. I really had to use the bathroom, and the gurgling sound of the gas entering the tank was not helping, but it was more efficient to pump first, move the car to a parking space, and then go inside to do my business and get snacks than it was to park, run inside to use the restroom, run outside again to move the car and pump gas, and then move the car again so I could run back inside to get snacks. My father's influence was strong.

After moving the car to a spot near the entrance to the convenience store, I walked through the automatic doors out of the sunshine into the air-conditioned building, pushing my sunglasses up on my head. Upon reaching the restroom at the end of the beeline I made, I was glad I had chosen a big plaza to stop at, because, as I had predicted, the facilities were clean. The restrooms at some of the smaller places I had stopped at in a pinch earlier in my trip had fallen victim to the ravages of water stains, rust, and the calling cards of other, nastier customers, or were unisex, or were outside—or some combination of these. I was getting wise.

One section of the convenience store I was in had an ordering counter for fast food and tables where customers could eat. The rest was occupied by a row of aisles that featured the predictable convenience store offerings: candy, chips, energy bars, some overpriced household items like toilet paper and individual bowls of Dinty Moore beef stew, and beverages like water, soda, and milk in refrigerated cases along the walls. A man stood in the open doorway of one of the cases, blocking foot traffic and letting cold air escape, while he decided between Yoo-Hoo and Gatorade. I found a different way around him but not before noticing that he eventually picked up one of each.

People in pairs, groups, and families, and people by themselves stood in line to place orders at the fast food counter. Parents looked harried.

"I said I want a hot dog."

"Stop whining or you won't get anything."

I wandered the snack aisles, lingering over the beef jerky

and energy bar section, noticing that the items for sale looked more attractive than what I had brought with me, even though a few of the snacks I had in the car were actually the same things I was looking at right now because I had bought them during my last stop, at a convenience store just like the one I was in.

Closer to the register were rotating wire holders full of maps and postcards. I decided to get a postcard to send to my parents, and since the sign on that holder said "5 for $1," I took five of the same one, figuring I would send the others to other family and friends. I doubted they would be comparing notes to see whether their postcard from me featured the same Midwestern attraction.

Next to the wire holders was a pre-fab, waist-high box containing bargain basement cassette tapes. I leaned on the box and picked through them, finding Dan Fogelberg, *Guitar Rock*, and Joan Armatrading. My car had a cassette player, but nothing struck my fancy. I moved on to a set of shelves near the door that were stacked with beer cozies and baseball caps that said things like, "Wanted: Serious Overnight Relationship," or "I Used Up All My Sick Days, So I Called In Dead." Again, I passed, but I chuckled inwardly.

At the register, I smiled at the girl behind the counter and paid for my postcards.

She smiled back, putting the cards in a small paper bag.

As I left the store, I realized I was still smiling. My car was steps away, ready to welcome me back inside like a crate does a weary dog. In the store, there had been no expectations on me other than that I have the money to pay for what I wanted to buy. No one had eyed me appraisingly when I walked in, wondering what on earth I was doing there and trying to suss out my belt level. No one questioned why I was there, and it had not even occurred to me to worry that they might. I mindlessly navigated this interaction like I had countless others in my life. I had not had to think about it and anticipate the potential ramifications of using a dollar instead of four quarters, for instance.

As that registered, I realized that I was feeling relaxed and that this was in marked contrast to the previous few weeks, much of which I had spent feeling on guard. At a time when I knew very little else, including what might be waiting for me behind the door of the next academy, where I was going to be sleeping when night fell, or even whether I would be gainfully employable in a few years, I still knew how to navigate the business and interpersonal aspects of a simple financial transaction. In some small ways, I was still normal. As I continued west, I felt comforted.

- - - - - - - - - -

Lacey's home was in a development in Littleton that, like everything else in the Denver area, was flanked by beautiful, snow-capped mountains, even in the summer. When I arrived, I was welcomed by Lacey, her black standard poodle Tallulah, and a care package from my friend Chrissy.

In the early years of my training, I had not followed the competition scene or geeked out on instructional VHS tapes or DVDs like some grapplers did. (VHS was a viable delivery mechanism for sharing jiu-jitsu back in the day before Youtube and iTunes rose to prominence.)

It was through my participation in several online forums dedicated to jiu-jitsu that I slowly started to plug into the larger grapplesphere beyond my own academy. The ostensible purpose of these forums was to discuss jiu-jitsu, to get answers to technical questions from geographically diverse experts, to share and learn who had been promoted to the next belt—always a big deal and a cause for celebration—and to predict who would win the next big tournament, with competition news turning out to be something I took more and more of an interest in as time went on. These purposes were certainly served. There were grappling geeks aplenty who were always on top of the latest news and statistics and who were more than eager to share what they knew with those of us who were less informed.

However, those places, one in particular, served an even more important purpose for me personally: They connected me to a group of like-minded jiu-jitsu fans and practitioners who were scattered throughout the U.S. and the world. Between bouts of hating my job and my life while chained to my desk, I used company time, equipment, and broadband to point my browser toward a group of people who in this virtual rumpus room called themselves things like "Da Crippler," "Superstall," "The Vanilla Gorilla," and, in my case, "Valhalla." As many people did, I chose my screen moniker because it was vaguely related to combat and fighting, and I chose "Valhalla" rather than the even-more-similar-to-my-own-name "Valkyrie" because there was a gi company with the same name. Paradoxically, I also chose Wally, from the *Dilbert* comic strip, as my avatar. It seemed to fit. I have always had a nerdy, bookish side, but I guess I was starting to express my inner Viking too.

Over the course of several years, I became a pretty central part of what those in the know simply came to refer to as "the forum," or "the Monkey Forum," so nicknamed, I believe, because we acted in a less than distinguished manner in its confines. I, along with a few dozen other forum monkeys/mainstays, sometimes talked jiu-jitsu and more often talked smack. We shared random videos and pictures, had playful arguments, and reported back to each other when two or more of us had had the opportunity to meet in person: maybe "Joemoplata" (a play on a jiu-jitsu submission called the *omoplata*) had gone on a work trip from his home in Virginia to Florida, where "Letmbleed" lived and trained, or "Twerp" and "Wen" were taking a road trip to Vegas and wanted to connect with any forum members who lived and trained there.

As with any face-to-face group, each of us liked some people and disliked others, and there were some people everybody disliked but tolerated for their entertainment value. Each of us was more or less strident about our opinions, depending on our online personae, which, as I learned, did not always match up completely—or even remotely—with our face-to-face ones. On more than one occasion, as I met more forum members in person, I found myself surprised at encountering either a quiet, awkward actual person whom I knew on the forum as a contentious keyboard warrior, or the opposite: a circumspect virtual personality who turned out to be loud, crass, and in-your-face when in the same room as your actual face. Of course, there were those who were generally consistent across modalities—brash and funny online and brash and funny in person, or more of a lurker both on the forum and when actually sitting across from you at a table.

I became close, in a virtual sort of way, with a handful of people on the forum that I eventually went on to meet in real life, and this further strengthened my friendships with them. It may come as no surprise, then, that immediately after I had announced my half-baked jiu-jitsu odyssey plans to my realtor, Melissa, I then announced them to the forum at my next opportunity—as I had no computer at home at that point, I am guessing it was probably the only time during that dark period in my life that I was excited to get to work. As I knew I would, I got plenty of suggestions, even a few serious and useful ones in among the snark, about where to train and how to spend my time, as well as the suggestion by Anahi ("The Infamous Grip") about what to name my blog. I also got offers of places to stay and invitations to dinner if and when I passed through various parts of the country, such as where "Dr. Kimura" lived and trained, or "Loco Sano's" neighborhood, or a suggestion from "Pimpstein" that I look up his old instructor.

Chrissy ("Clinzy") was one of the people I came to know through the forum. We became virtual friends, chatting privately through the forum's email function as well as through the public discussion threads with everyone else, developing what felt like a real affinity for each other before we ever met in person. Our first face-to-face meeting was on the occasion of the grand opening of the academy of our mutual friend Andrew ("Goatfury") in Richmond, Virginia, in 2005, right when I was in the thick of my existential malaise.

She lived there with her husband Brian ("Brain") and their cat and three enormous, incredibly well-behaved dogs (a Weimaraner and two Rhodesian ridgebacks—no screen names), and I had come to town for the event. Chrissy and I seemed to be in the subsection of forum members whose online personae are relatively similar to our face-to-face personalities, so it did not take much for us to click in person as well as we had online. Our first real-life interaction involved BJJ, of course. We met at Andrew's academy for an afternoon training session a day or two prior to the academy's grand opening, and what was weird was how not-weird it was. We said hello, we got in each other's personal space, and then we went for Thai food. That was the beginning of a ritual that pretty much replicates itself to this day whenever Chrissy and I get together.

When I was on my trip, Chrissy was one of the people who kept tabs on me. She texted regularly to get a handle on where and how I was, and, of course, she kept in touch on the forum. She just generally let me know she was thinking of me and cheering me on. For that reason, I actually was not surprised to find a package from her. After an emotional reunion with Lacey and a snuffly once-over from Tallulah, I opened the package and read the note Chrissy had enclosed. It went something like,

"Dear Val,

As a fan of Douglas Adams, I'm sure you know the one thing you should always have when you're traveling. I saw this in a store and immediately thought of you, your trip, and the forum. So, think of it as a way to take us with you—well, those of us who aren't annoying, anyway. Drive safely and have tons of adventures.

See ya,

Chrissy"

I unfolded her gift: a white hand towel with gold fringe, sporting in embroidery the likeness of a smiling monkey that was enjoying the company of a blue bird fluttering overhead.

Douglas Adams is the author who wrote, among other novels, the cult classic *The Hitchhiker's Guide to the Galaxy*. In that novel, one sage piece of advice offered about travel is that you should never leave home without a towel. As a fellow fan of the entire series of *Hitchhiker* books, a proud and vociferous forum member (at several points, I believe, she had posted more individual forum messages than any other of the hundreds of members), and a good virtual and real-life friend, Chrissy had found me the perfect gift. The towel is still in my possession, having moved with me to and from numerous homesteads since I received it and serving as a reminder of all that has been and continues to be positive about my Brazilian jiu-jitsu journey, both the literal and the figurative one. It came along at the perfect time, reminding me that even though my trip was crazy, it was the good kind of crazy.

"So what do we have here?" Lacey asked, gesturing to the towel.

"Oh, it's a joke from a friend of mine." I told her about the Monkey Forum.

"Sounds like a crazy place," Lacey said. "So tell me what this is all about. I mean, I'm happy to see you, but you quit your job and sold your condo and are driving around the country? I didn't get the whole gist when you emailed that you'd be coming through."

"Well, all of those things, plus jiu-jitsu. Because of jiu-jitsu, really. I just hated my life, you know, and I felt like I had to do something drastic. I was ready for a change at work, and I was tired of Chicago, so I just kind of jumped into this trip."

We headed inside with my suitcase. Lacey showed me around her beautifully appointed home and gestured to the guest room that would be mine for the next week or so, complete with view of the mountains. There were many places to train in the Denver area, and I planned to visit the academies of Amal Easton and David Ruiz in Denver, and Mauricio Zingano in Broomfield. Lacey and I also planned to do some hiking—how could we not, given where we were? We were going to take a trip to Gunnison, where, as timing would have it, I would turn 36.

I had not mentioned this to Lacey, because I was not sure how or whether I wanted to acknowledge my birthday. At the moment, though, we were going to take Tallulah to Chatfield Park, a gorgeous, dog-friendly expanse that was consistent with the outdoorsy interests of the locals.

By this stage of my trip, I had gotten better about figuring out what I would need for different situations than I had been when I had arrived at Darin and Linh's. For instance, since I was preparing to go into Lacey's house, I did not need a gi, so those stayed folded in the trunk of my car. Instead, I had packed a smaller bag with sleepwear, a few changes of clothes, and shampoo and other toilet articles. If I needed something, I could obviously come back out and get it. I just wanted to minimize the need as much as possible. Everyone has to decide what to wear each day. I just seemed to require more costume changes.

I threw my bag on a chair, figuring I would unpack later. Right now, I wanted to hang out with Lacey and take advantage of the gorgeous summer weather and the mountainous landscape that was so different from Chicago's. I turned back toward the room to turn off the light and paused for a second to take in the scene—neatly made double bed, framed art on the walls, bathroom right outside—and this was just the guest room. I registered the contrast between Lacey's settled, adult life and my itinerant, grubby one, feeling wistful for just a moment as I wondered again for the umpteenth time why I could not be normal.

- - - - - - - - - -

"So, holy cow, Val. You have basically built your life around this martial art, at least for the time being. That's pretty intense." We stood in Chatfield Park, watching Tallulah frolic among a handful of other dogs.

"Tell me about it," I said. "I mean, I was training when you and I were working together, and I guess I did make a point of getting to work early so I could leave in time to get to class at night, but it didn't seem out of the ordinary, you know? By that time I had been training for a few years, so it had just become what I did every day, and I didn't seem to notice that I didn't have much time or energy to do anything else, really." I smiled, recalling the fatigue I felt in those days, when I tried to do enough to earn my salary though all I really wanted to do was train.

"You do it every day? Train, it's called? Wow. That's like a job. You must really love it."

"Yeah. Love," I said, widening my eyes as if contemplating an insurmountable obstacle. "I mean, I do love it. The physical aspects are unlike anything I had ever tried before, so at first I just felt clumsy. I've had enough years now, though, that I'm starting to feel like maybe I know how to move at least a little bit. It's also really mentally and psychologically demanding, though, both when I'm training and when I'm not. I mean, it's not easy to contort yourself into these crazy positions, but that just makes me want to try all the harder."

"Well, why? Why do you want to keep trying? What does doing jiu-jitsu give you?" Lacey was not judging me. She truly wanted to understand.

Tallulah was sniffing, rolling, play-growling, tugging, and chasing balls. She was completely focused on what she was doing, stopping only occasionally to check for Lacey, flashing her an adorable, joyful doggie smile, before diving right back in.

I pointed at the tangle of dogs, playing without a care in the world, no worries about needing to be elsewhere or with other dogs. "Flow," I said.

Lacey was familiar with psychologist Mihalyi Csikszentmihalyi's book *Flow: The Psychology of Optimal Experience* (1990). After I said the word, she just nodded and said, "Yeah."

In describing flow, Csikszentmihalyi references "[a]rtists, athletes, composers, dancers, scientists, and people from all walks of life [who], when they describe how it feels when they are doing something that is worth doing for its own sake, use terms that are interchangeable in their minutest details. This unanimity suggests that order in consciousness produces a very specific experiential state, so desirable that one wishes to replicate it as often as possible. To this state we have given the name of 'flow,' using a term that many respondents used in their interviews to explain what the optimal experience felt like."[16]

Flow, in other words, is a state of awareness that anyone can achieve who is engrossed in a task she finds worth doing and who feels equipped with the tools for the task. The flow state is not guaranteed, but it is achievable, and it is positive. While experiencing flow, individuals can become so focused that they do not notice the passage of time, or much else besides what they are doing, because in the moment they are performing the task for no other reason than that doing so fills the void in a satisfying way, without effort or resistance.

A person experiencing flow is intrinsic motivation personified. Flow is part heightened meditative meta-awareness and part don't-want-to-miss-a-thing. It is a lofty way to describe a simple state: one of all-encompassing contentment and focus, though in this case simple does not mean easy or banal. According to Csikszentmihalyi, everybody wants some. I want some too.

When I am training, I am in my own body, in my own mind, and I have no interest in being anywhere else—it does not even occur to me that there is anywhere else to be. I am simultaneously present and omnipresent, focused completely on the task at hand and meta-aware of that focus. It sounds high-fallutin', but it just means I am at peace, in a place where I do not see a distinction between myself and the rest of the physical world. When we are at our best together, BJJ takes me to the flow state, where I am present in my body and mind. During training there is no worry and no indulging in my favorite hobby: beating myself up for real or imagined shortcomings.

There is only encountering another person's energy, putting together a plan of attack and a logical defense, and adjusting and readjusting, split second after split second. Grappling is sometimes called a game of inches, and with good reason, because in countless training and competition scenarios, less than that—a hair's breadth,

---

[16] Csikszentmihalyi, M. & Csikszentmihalyi, I. S. (Eds.). (1988). *Optimal experience: Psychological studies of flow in consciousness*. Cambridge, United Kingdom: Cambridge University Press.

even—can mean the difference between things like base and instability, tolerable discomfort and physical injury, consciousness and sleep.

Unless I am burned out, sick, or feeling stressed, I experience some flow in pretty much every BJJ class. In other words, under normal circumstances, I always become engrossed, lose track of time, and spend the duration of the class with either a furrowed brow, signifying concentration, or a dumb, slightly slack-jawed smile on my face, signifying contentment—or both.

When the children of some friends of mine were toddlers, they would spend minutes on end totally immersed in important tasks such as carefully pulling all the toilet paper off the roll until they hit cardboard, with the paper itself ending up in an untidy, unusable pile on the bathroom floor. If anyone tried to divert their attention, they would either push that person out of the way or, if restrained, throw a big hairy tantrum until they were allowed to get back to it.

On the other hand, when Tiger, my childhood cat, was utterly content, she would lie belly-down with her paws underneath her, her head in a neutral position, her eyes half closed, her purring mechanism loud and, over time, her chin wet with drool. She could stay there for hours at a time, chirping slightly in affection if I petted her, and then settling back down as I scratched her ears. At different times in different jiu-jitsu classes, I have borne more than a passing resemblance to both a busy toddler and a happy cat, sometimes both in the same minute.

As I have improved at jiu-jitsu, I find the nature of the flow I experience during training sessions has changed over the years. In my very first class and for many beyond that, I was completely present because to be or do otherwise would be to fall behind. I had to ask my body to respond to commands that my brain barely understood, and I had to do this in an environment where I did not yet understand the rules of social engagement. Back then, I focused on each component of a technique or interpersonal interaction like a drowning woman locking her attention on the oar being extended to her by her rescuer. The twist was that I kind of liked the feeling. I skipped right over the fear to the exhilaration of knowing I was going to make it, and then I kept insisting on getting back in the water.

I continue to have this experience, but over time, more room has opened up in my mind to allow a complementary experience of the flow state. It is just as all-encompassing, but as I have become more able to operate my body and my brain as independent entities, I have found room for more of the meta-awareness. In these moments, what is striking is what is absent: fear, despondency, self-hatred. Imagine stripping your conscious awareness of all the negative thoughts and feelings you have in a day, and being left with just the good stuff: joy, love, connectedness, generosity. I know it sounds weird, because I am still trying to squish my partner, and my partner is still trying to squish me, but often the sum total of my BJJ experience after a class is over seems to contain only benevolence, good will, and gratitude. It is heady stuff.

"Okay, so help me out here," Lacey said, as we continued to watch the dogs play. "You go to the flow state when you do jiu-jitsu even though the entire goal is for you to hurt me or me to hurt you?"

"I know. It sounds completely asinine, but yeah, if I had to elevator pitch it, that's the gist. That's officially what we're trying to do, get superior physical position over each other so we can break each other's bones or put each other out," I said, hoping I was not losing her. "But there's...how do I put this? There's artistry and strategy and technique. There's beauty there. Not from me, but if you watch people who know what they are doing, you can see that jiu-jitsu can be beautiful."

We watched the dogs in silence. I wondered if I had just blown my cover as a semi-sane person, irretrievably revealing my true idiosyncratic nature. Lacey and I had been what I would consider good work friends back when we were colleagues, but I do not think she was privy to the extent of my immersion in the jiu-jitsu world. I had not allowed that world to collide quite so directly with my work world, and while Lacey and I were now "civilian" friends with no professional ties, that history persisted.

"Jeez, Val. I can't really picture you trying to do someone else bodily harm. The you I know is really gentle and kind."

"Thanks. I know, it seems really weird, and I can't quite explain it myself," I replied, "but for a while now, jiu-jitsu is the only thing that has made me happy. It kind of helped me deal with the fact that I was unhappy in the rest of my life. It's almost like I can become a different person when I train, because nobody who knows me through jiu-jitsu cares about what I do when I'm not in class. I mean, I feel awkward and clumsy and unsure of myself all the time, but there's this huge puzzle to work on, and the only thing that matters is getting better at the puzzle."

"So is it kind of an escape for you?"

"That's definitely what it became. It started out as just a workout, but then I realized I was using it to escape from the rest of my life. So I thought maybe I should try to create a life I didn't want to escape from. I don't know exactly what that means yet, but I think jiu-jitsu is a big part of it. And that's why I'm on this road trip."

"Well, I'm glad you're here, and I'm glad you're figuring it out."

"Oh, you're giving me too much credit. I have figured out what I'm doing today, and that's about it, but that's also enough for now, you know? I mean, look at Tallulah. She has some more dog butts to sniff, and then she'll probably take a nap, and then it's going to be time for dinner. She's pretty cool with that. I know my life is more complicated than hers, but that's at least partly because I make it more complicated. So today, I get to hang out with my good friend Lacey and my new friend Tallulah and stare at gorgeous mountains and feel the sun."

"That doesn't sound half bad," Lacey said, smiling.

"Yeah, and maybe there's a nap in my future too, and definitely dinner. I think I can be cool with that for now."

- - - - - - - - - -

"Great. Another one of Them," I thought, as I tried to keep moving but was thwarted at every turn. I felt like I was rolling inside a plastic bag, but I was actually rolling with Eliot Marshal, an instructor at Amal Easton's academy. Eliot had welcomed me to class, and after teaching a great lesson, he graciously invited me to train.

I thought of Darin and how he seemed to float on top of me when we rolled together, like a 150-pound cloud. Eliot was taller and heavier than Darin, but the effect was the same. I moved all I wanted, but no matter where or how, some part of Eliot was always blocking my hip or turning my face away from the direction I wanted to go, gently but definitively impeding my progress. I struggled hard to improve my position, always in vain, marveling at how my frustration was matched with an equal amount of exhilaration. Incapacitation can be fun!

When class was over and the students started to disperse, Eliot beckoned to me, sitting on the edge of the mat and gesturing for me to do the same. "Now, tell me again what brought you here? You're on some kind of jiu-jitsu road trip?"

"Yes," I said. I described, as briefly and non-emotionally as possible, the series of events that had brought me to their school.

By this time, Amal had approached us and sat down as well. While Eliot had been teaching, Amal had been otherwise occupied. Their flagship school was in Boulder, and they had recently opened a Denver location, in which we were sitting at that moment. They were open for business in Denver, but they were still settling in, which appeared to translate into unpacking, checking things off lists, and otherwise getting organized. I had met Amal when I walked in and then noticed his activity here and there out of the corner of my mind while trying to focus on Eliot's lesson and then on the specific ways Eliot hindered my movement when we trained together.

"So you're just dropping in at different jiu-jitsu schools?" Amal asked.

"Well, I try to call ahead, but sometimes I don't get an answer," I said. "So I either leave a message, or I just show up. But yes, I'm traveling around and training at different places. I've been to five or six so far."

Eliot asked, "Do you have a connection at the places you visit? Do you know anybody who trains there, I mean?"

"In some cases I do," I said. "Obviously, I didn't know anybody here. But I had a great time—thank you!" I smiled.

Eliot and Amal smiled back and then exchanged glances with each other. "Well, it sounds like quite an adventure," Amal responded. "But you should be careful."

"What do you mean?" I said.

"I mean..." Amal paused, looking for the right words. "Let's put it this way. Five years ago, you wouldn't have been able to take this trip safely."

Eliot nodded.

"Have you heard the term *creonte*?"

"Yes, cree-ontch," I said. "If I'm not mistaken, Carlson Sr. invented it. It means 'traitor.'"

- - - - - - - - - -

One of the many compelling aspects of joining a subculture is that when history occurs or the customs are modified in some way, you are likely to be only a few steps removed from the action. In other words, if something happens, good or bad, you might be able to hear the story from the horse's mouth or from someone who heard it from that mouth, or you might even have the opportunity to witness it firsthand. For instance, in the jiu-jitsu world, maybe you were front and center at the latest world tournament, so you saw that when the current black belt absolute champion was down on points in the gold medal match, he somehow summoned a wellspring of resolve and pulled out the submission in the last 30 seconds, snatching victory from the jaws of defeat as the audience went crazy.

Then maybe on the strength of that win, that practitioner conducted a seminar tour, including one at your academy, and you got the opportunity to learn directly from that person. Internet memes and adages abound pointing out that while it is pretty unlikely that the person who plays amateur basketball would ever have an opportunity even to talk to Michael Jordan, let alone play a pick-up game with him, it is very common in jiu-jitsu for hobbyists to have the opportunity to train and hang out with world champions—and then even become one of the people other practitioners hope to get the opportunity to train with.

Or maybe you were just drilling at your academy open mat at the exact time when a few creative teammates or instructors were off in a corner having a conversation that would eventually lead to the next popular gi company, jiu-jitsu publication, DVD series, or competition team. Maybe they called you over for a minute to ask you what you liked about the gi you were wearing, what BJJ topics you are interested in, what your favorite instructional videos were, or why you had chosen this specific academy as your jiu-jitsu home. You were present for the birth of this thing that would go on to have an impact on the rest of the community. Maybe you did not realize the significance at the time, but eventually, as it became clearer, you realized it more and more, and you also realized you had your own story to tell, because you were there.

Carlson Gracie Sr., was one of the people who had that kind of profound effect. I never saw him in action in Brazil, but I was around enough to hear stories about what it was like back then and also how things had changed and stayed the same as BJJ became more popular in the United States. Carlson Sr.'s influence extended beyond his own and his students' competition accolades. It has affected the actual language we use to describe who we are as a subculture and what we do in it. He coined the term *creonte*[17] that Amal had mentioned to me, a term I had heard before but had considered only in the abstract.

The story goes that Creonte was the name of a character on a Brazilian soap opera who was duplicitous and underhanded, changing alliances whenever it suited him. In the years before Carlson Sr. died, there was a split in his

_____

[17] Thomas, B. *Loyalty in Brazilian Jiu-Jitsu: What is a creonte, anyway?* Retrieved from http://www.bjjweekly.com/blog/post/loyalty-in-brazilian-jiu-jitsu-what-is-a-creonte-anyway

dynasty, such that a large number of students left his team, on contentious terms, and started their own organization. He called these students *creontes*, and since he was not an unassuming person, he called them that loudly and frequently. Over time, the term *creonte* was propagated throughout the BJJ world and became ensconced in the jargon, and by now it is synonymous with "traitor."

There are different opinions about what constitutes a traitor. Back in the day in Brazil, it was uncommon for people to leave their BJJ team for any reason. They progressed through the ranks from white to black belt under the same instructor, and they developed a sense of fierce loyalty to a team. They kept techniques and strategies secret, unveiling them only during competition so opposing teams would not have the opportunity to learn to counter them. They spent hours of every day together for many years, refining their jiu-jitsu and toughening up their mindsets.

They invested in each other and became a family. For some, then, just leaving one academy to join or start a different one is enough to warrant the epithet. For others, an academy-switcher is a *creonte* if he or she competes against his or her former team and shares secrets about how to beat those former teammates. For still others, it is the switcher who bad-mouths the old academy in addition to all the rest who is the traitor.

More recently, at least in the United States, it has become more common for students to switch teams for various reasons: geography, differences of opinion, or training goals that differ from the stated goals of the academy. Perhaps it is consistent with a more capitalistic mindset and with the often itinerant nature of the American professional experience. I pay you for a service, and if I do not like the service, I leave. Or, I like your service, but my job is taking me elsewhere, and I want to pursue that professional opportunity. This mindset does not account for the bonds that develop among teammates, and those bonds develop at academies in the States too, but U.S. students do seem to be more willing to vote with their feet than students in Brazil have historically been.

In my own case, I had already trained at three different academies during my jiu-jitsu career because I had moved around for jobs and school. Carlson Jr.'s was the third. Each time I made the decision to move away from an area, I had a conversation with the instructor to explain the circumstances, say thank you, and make my farewell. Each time, the instructor was understanding and wished me well, including and especially Carlson Jr. Some months before I started planning my walkabout in earnest, I approached him with the idea, and we had had an emotional conversation about how I felt the need to leave Chicago and what I planned to do.

He gave me his blessing, and we were both sad. He did tell me to be careful, but at the time I did not think of it as much more than a blanket statement that most people make when they find out someone they know is going to travel. It had never occurred to me that anyone would consider me a *creonte*.

"Things are still clannish in the States," Amal continued. "They are opening up, and they are maybe not quite as closed as they always have been in Brazil. Still, if you come from a different academy, especially one that has a lot of rivals, people at some of those rival places might think you had come to start trouble, and it's more than that. If you just show up on the doorstep of an academy, you might not be safe regardless."

"So they'd think I was trying to storm the dojo or something?" I asked. "But that would be stupid. I'm alone, and I'm a woman."

"And that's what makes it potentially even more dangerous for you," Amal said. "It's risky enough for a guy to do what you're doing."

"What's risky about it?"

"Well, like I said, five years ago if you had gone into a school that wasn't the place you regularly trained, let's just say you might not have been welcomed with open arms. Things aren't as closed in the States as they are in Brazil, but they're also not open."

"But I'm not trying to start trouble. I asked for Junior's

blessing before I left, and he was cool about it."

"It's not only your own instructor you need to be worried about. You may tell people at these places that you aren't there to start trouble, but there's a history of rivalry in this sport. It is a martial art," said Amal. "We're not just talking about techniques here. We're talking about loyalty and ritual and hierarchy. In the States we kind of play at that stuff, but in the places where these arts originated it is serious business."

I thought about what Amal was saying. We were not talking about naiveté, like with Jeff. We were talking about the use of intimidation to teach a lesson, which was...what? They were tough and I was weak? I deserved to be punished for being far from home but still wanting to get in some training?

"Well jeez," I said. Eloquent under fire.

"Yeah," Amal responded. "I mean, not everyone is like that, of course, but this is one of the aspects of jiu-jitsu that you need to keep in mind if you are going to go into unknown places."

"Well, I want to keep going on my trip. I've been to some places already where people have welcomed me with open arms. Like you guys. I know there are other places like that out there," I said, feeling defensive, though not at Amal. "I get what you're saying, and I really appreciate the heads up. I didn't even think about any of this before I started on my trip. Maybe jiu-jitsu academies are like people. Just because there are some bad ones out there, you can't become a hermit and never interact with anyone, right? I mean, if I hadn't gone on the trip, I wouldn't have gotten the opportunity to train with you and the other people who have been awesome to me."

Plus, I don't really have any other viable plans, I thought.

"I know I can't stop you, and you are also very nice, so that will help, but how will you be able to tell the difference between the okay places and the not-so-okay places?"

I thought back to Jeff's. "I'll be able to tell."

After a silence, Amal said, "We're really glad you visited, and we hope every place is just as glad. You know what they say about being forewarned, though."

"I do," I said with a sigh, extending my hand to Amal before getting up to stretch my legs and make my way toward the locker room. "I appreciate it. It's just a lot to take in."

"Well, thanks again for coming, Val," Amal said. "Do you need anything? Do you know where you're going? Here, take my number in case something comes up."

"Thank you so much. Really." I said, shaking his hand and then Eliot's. "I'll think about what you told me," I added, though I was experiencing a kind of existential whiplash. How could some strangers in the BJJ world be as nice as Amal and Eliot while others could apparently be far more dastardly? They had not told me exactly what they might have seen to prompt them to warn me, but they did not need to. I did not want to hear.

"I'm glad. I don't want to be an alarmist, but if I stop and imagine my girlfriend doing what you're doing, it makes me nervous," Amal said. "Just be careful."

Those words again.

"I will," I responded. "And I'll let people know that you and Eliot are two of the good guys."

He smiled. "We try."

I spent the rest of my time in Colorado, the better part of a week, going back and forth between giving into the exhilaration of the Rocky Mountain High—and I am sure some of that was dizziness from the altitude—and spending too much time inside my head.

The latter was nothing new, though, and the altitude probably did not help with that either. Resolving not to let fear rule the day, and still feeling compelled to seek out more adventure in the jiu-jitsu world and to trust my spidey sense, I visited David Ruiz's academy in Denver and Mauricio Zingano's in nearby Broomfield. Much to my relief, I was heartily welcomed in both places, where I had fun, safe, collegial training experiences with skilled instructors and friendly students. Amal's words were always in the back of my mind, but I decided to use them as a guidepost rather than a barrier.

Between the training and the ruminations, I hiked with Lacey and Tallulah, indulging in a small celebration of my 36th birthday in Crested Butte. I drank one of the state's own beers. I felt rugged, flanked by the Rockies, and a little lightheaded, at an elevation of almost 9,000 feet.

- - - - - - - - - -

Then it was time to move on. When I think back to that summer, particularly late July and on into August, I am reminded of those montages in older movies and TV shows that mark the passage of time and distance with the animation of a chugging locomotive or a line being drawn across a country map while postcards that say things like, "Greetings from New York City!" in colorful bubble print zip in and out of frame. Only in my case, as I went farther and farther west, the greetings were from Salt Lake City! Hailey and Boise, Idaho! Tumwater, Washington! The line went generally westward, but sometimes traveling it felt like walking the stairs that go nowhere in the M.C. Escher lithograph *Ascending and Descending*.

I fell into a routine that consisted of creating an agenda for each individual day. Some days I drove for hours, farther and farther from where home had been, clueing into that fact because each state out west seemed never-ending, unlike the smaller clusters of states in the northeast. Some days I cased yet another jiu-jitsu joint in preparation for facing the unknown that waited inside, armed with my usual discomfort and now a new tendency to scour my intuition for any potential pitfalls or dangers.

Some days I was catching up with old friends, feeling apprehensive when I pulled into the driveway, though I need not have worried. To a person, these fixtures from my past welcomed me so unconditionally that I daydreamed about just falling into step with them for good. We marveled at how different and how much the same we were after many years of separation, like I had done with Lacey and Darin and Linh. Then, far too soon, it was time for the inevitable and I was tearing myself away, adding another goodbye to what seemed like an endless series of losses. Everywhere I went, friends and strangers, jiu-jitsu people and non-grapplers alike, told me, "I hope you find what you're looking for."

I hoped so too and worried that I would not.

One day the postcard on my video montage said Vancouver, British Columbia. Vancouver is the reason I got to say I traveled the continent instead of the country, because it is the only place I went to that was outside the domestic border. I visited two academies there. One was run by Marcus Soares, whom I knew had been a student of Carlson Sr.'s. He was out of town when I arrived, so I did not get to meet him, but his students were very welcoming, including Stephan Kesting, of whom I caught a glimpse when he had to come by and unlock the gym for us. Stephan is the proprietor of Grapplearts, a popular online repository of information—interviews, videos, articles—about Brazilian Jiu-Jitsu.

I also connected with my friend Brandon. He had been following my blog, and when he found out I was going to be passing through Vancouver, where he lived, he reached out to me, inviting me to get together and train. In the intervening time, he had gotten injured, but he directed me to his instructor, Tim, at Gracie Barra Vancouver, an affiliate of Gracie Barra, a longstanding and venerated jiu-jitsu lineage associated with the Barra neighborhood of Rio de Janeiro. Brandon and I still planned to connect in the evening after I trained. He decided not to go to class because it was too depressing for him to watch and not be able to participate, so we chatted beforehand to make some plans.

"Okay, what time do you want to meet up?" I asked, juggling my phone and my car keys.

"Well, there's been a slight change of plan," Brandon said.

"What change?"

"See, my friend from work is moving away, and he wants to get together for a farewell happy hour. Do you mind if we meet up with him and some of his friends?"

"Not at all," I said. "The more the merrier. The only thing is, are we going to meet somewhere where there's food? I'm sure I'm going to be starving."

"Oh, well, funny you should mention where we're going to meet," Brandon said, drawing out his words as if he did not want to actually say them. I imagined him pulling on his collar or biting his fingernails.

"What's funny about it?" I asked, my interest piqued.

"Well, um, so, yeah. My friend wants to go to a strip club. It's kind of a famous one in Vancouver, and he won't be able to get back there for a while."

"Because he's moving away," I said.

"Yeah, exactly!"

My knee-jerk reaction was one of indignation. I did not go to places like that. I had always had the impression that strip clubs were unsavory breeding grounds for sexism and violence against women. I had never actually been to a strip club, though, so this impression was unfounded and, I realized, unfair. In my professional life, I always gathered data before drawing a conclusion. It dawned on me that I was being hypocritical by not doing the same in this situation. My traveling persona decided to make my social scientist persona put her money where her mouth was.

"Brandon, how dare you? I am a lady!"

"I'm sorry! I'm sorry! I just thought, well, I didn't mean, I mean, I'm sorry!"

"Brandon, Brandon! It's okay, it's okay," I said, smiling. "I forgot. You don't know me very well. It's fine. I'm kidding. I mean, I've never been to a strip club before, but there's a first time for everything."

"Well, you'll be with us, and it'll be fine."

"Listen. Do they have food?"

"Yeah, they have pretty good food, actually."

"Okay, relax. I'm in. What's the address?"

"Hang on. I have it right here," Brandon said, breathing an audible sigh, presumably of relief. I made a mental note to call him a pervert when I saw him.

When I hung up with Brandon, I thought for a moment. I had made a good show of enthusiasm for him, but I was still a bit uncertain. I reminded myself I was collecting new experiences, and this certainly fit the bill.

Adding to my consternation was the fact that I was absolutely grimy. I had just trained for several hours. My hair had become drenched with sweat and had dried in ropes. My skin had been equally drenched and had dried sticky. I did not have time to shower before I met up with the group, so I had wiped myself down as much as possible. I had also changed my clothes, but it was like putting clean cotton material on a deep-fried mannequin. I had tried to dress for the occasion by upgrading my shirt to one that did not have any words or pictures on it and my shorts to ones that did not have a drawstring. My ever-present flip-flops were still present.

When I arrived at the club, I found Brandon and his friends in a booth in the back of the spacious room, directly across from the stage where the strippers did their thing. The group consisted of Brandon, his friend who was moving, and two cute, slender blonde women who were probably ten years younger than I. Brandon's friend was handsome and exuded confidence. Unlike me, the other women were perfectly coiffed, had impeccable manicures, and were dressed to the nines. I was tempted to put my hands in my pockets, as they were rough and covered with cuticles from grabbing the coarse material of countless gis.

"There you are," Brandon said. He introduced me around to the group. "This is Val, everyone. And that's Chris, Jenny, and Evelyn[18]."

"Hi. Nice to meet you."

"Hey."

"How are you?"

I was in my typical post-grappling haze, exhausted, a bit brain dead, a bit out of it. Part of my exhaustion had to do with my hunger, which was at threat level midnight. When my water arrived, I downed half of it in one gulp and read the menu as if its contents contained the secrets to my salvation.

Then, there it was. The holy grail of post-training meals, Canadian style: a burger with cheddar and Canadian

---

[18] Not their real names.

bacon. I put my finger on the description and kept it there until the server came to take our order. The conversation around me at the table sounded like it had been muffled behind a glass partition as all of my attention was consumed with the idea of eating.

"So what's the allure of this place?" I asked, trying to engage in the conversation.

"Oh, it's been around for a long time, and I have enjoyed coming here," Chris said. "I wanted to kind of say goodbye, if that makes sense."

"Thanks for letting me come along. This is my first time at a strip club," I replied.

"Oh really? What do you think so far?"

I looked around. Female servers in spangly and suggestive costumes took food and drink orders while the women onstage divested themselves of what clothes they had started with, climbing on poles and gyrating suggestively on the floor to the rhythm of sexy, back-beat-heavy music. Many of them appeared to have had breast augmentation, and they had seen to other body areas as well. I felt weird noticing, but I told myself it was for the experience. The patrons were a mix of men and women. Some of them fixated on the show while others were engrossed in conversation and seemed completely oblivious to the titillation. If I had been facing away from the stage, I would have thought I was in any other boisterous happy hour spot.

"It's surprisingly tame," I said. "It seems like every other restaurant. Just with more skin showing."

Chris laughed. "Yeah, they run a tight ship around here."

"It's kind of weird how not weird it is. 'Can I get you anything else? Ketchup? Another drink? More nudity?'"

Jenny and Evelyn chuckled.

Brandon said, "See? It's not so bad."

"I guess not."

I am still ambivalent about strip clubs. I have been to several others, always at someone else's suggestion, and they are varying combinations of depressing, bemusing, and odd, depending on the day and the clientele. I do not have enough data to draw any definitive conclusions, but I do know they are not my first choice when considering a place to socialize. However, I only know this because I decided to have the experience, something I never considered doing before I left on my jiu-jitsu travels. Just as with this journey in particular and Brazilian Jiu-Jitsu in general, I was apprehensive and reluctant at first, but when it was over, I was glad I had pushed the limits of my comfort zone.

If I had it to do over, I would change one thing: I would find the chef who made my burger and prostrate myself in gratitude.

- - - - - - - - - -

Soon enough, it was time to leave again. I had swooped in, left some breadcrumbs, and was now preparing to swoop out, moving on to the next place where it might be— that thing I was looking for. I left Vancouver armed with some new fun techniques to try, some new acquaintances, and a slightly more informed perspective. I headed for the United States, and in my mind, I noticed that I said, "Time to go home."

Sometimes you get lucky at the border and can sail right through in a matter of minutes, but sometimes it is lousy with cars and the crossing can take closer to an hour or even far more. The day I crossed back over into the United States after my trip to Vancouver was a picture-perfect, sunny specimen in the heart of the summer, which may have been one of the reasons the border that day looked like a menorah lying on its side, as dozens of cars traveling from the multi-lane highway tried to insert themselves into the narrowing part of the funnel.

As I approached the checkpoint itself, which was laid out like a row of toll booths with a cluster of cars descending upon each booth and eventually sorting itself into a tidy-ish line, I sighed once or twice, wanting to get the show on the road—literally—but steeling myself for what, in my immediate family, we call the Worthington Curse. Whether it is a line at a supermarket, the bank, the gas station, a port-a-potty, or even the border of the country, we Worthingtons will invariably choose the slowest one. Even if we think we are being sneaky by joining the end of a line that has fewer people in it than the one adjacent, those fewer people in front of us will happen to be the ones to write a check instead of paying with cash or credit, have multiple transactions to complete, forget which side of the car their gas tank is on and have to turn around—so sorry, get some kind of Montezuma's revenge, or do God knows what that raises the suspicions of the border guard. By the time we realize we have done it again, it has usually become impossible to maneuver into a different line—which would surely slow to a standstill anyway.

Whether the Worthington Curse is a self-fulfilling prophesy or an actual measurable phenomenon—my vote is probably obvious—is somewhat beside the point, as my experience of it is real and infuriating. Join me in a line and I will show you how the seconds and the people on either side seem to pass smoothly and inexorably by while the members of Team W become fossilized in the amber of our temporal destiny. Just make sure you have a few minutes to spare.

That day I just chose the first line I came to, predicting that the ones I had not chosen would move along while the one I did choose would grind to a halt. This was neither the time nor the place to allow my frustration to translate into snippiness, though. I reminded myself that there were worse places to be than behind the wheel of my beloved car with the sun warming my left forearm and shoulder. I knew where I was going, but I could have gone anywhere, and there is not much that is more freeing than that.

"Passport, please," said the border guard, when it was finally my turn.

I handed over the dark blue and gold-embossed booklet.

"Where in Canada are you coming from?"

"Vancouver," I responded, resisting my usual tendency to connect to people through stupid jokes, and my habit when I am nervous of talking more than is necessary. Not the time for that either.

"And what brought you there?"

"I was visiting some friends," I said.

"From Florida, eh? You're a long way from home," he said, indicating my license plate, which he could see from his vantage point thanks to a camera feed that was projecting an image of the rear of my car onto a computer screen in front of him.

"Yes, I am on a little road trip," I said. "I figured, if not now, when? Summer is a great time to have an adventure, you know?"

"I hear that," he said. "What's with the bumper stickers?"

By this time, I had covered around a dozen states, visited around a dozen academies, and encountered hundreds of jiu-jitsu people. I had seen many tough-looking logos on many academy doors, as well as others that advertised gear, supplements, and other grappling-related products for sale, from companies run by some of these same people, on t-shirts, patches, and stickers. Some of these people had graciously given me these t-shirts, patches, and stickers, and I did with them what you do with such things: I wore them and I stuck them. As a result, my car's rear bumper, like my body, had slowly become covered with a pastiche of indicators that I had embraced the grappling lifestyle but good.

"Oh that," I said. "Well, I train a martial art called Brazilian Jiu-Jitsu, and those are stickers from some of the places I've trained at."

"Oh, I know jiu-jitsu!" the border guard said excitedly. "The ground game, right? You see the last UFC? That was crazy!"

"Oh, do you train?" I asked.

"Well, I've done some boxing, and I wrestled in high school," he replied.

So, no, I thought, though I smiled pleasantly, both because at that point I would try to talk the ear off a brass monkey when I had the chance to discuss jiu-jitsu, and also because, more cynically, it occurred to me that a happy border guard was less likely to use his authority to make me an unhappy border-crosser.

"Yeah, I used to train muay Thai, but I don't do it anymore. I love kicking and punching, but *getting* kicked and punched? Turns out that's not nearly as enjoyable. But I'm working on my wrestling. Gotta improve my takedown game."

He chuckled. "Yeah, I've gotten my bell rung a couple times for sure. But jiu-jitsu ain't no joke. You must be pretty tough."

"Well, such as they are, I use my powers for good," I said, as I often did.

He guffawed. "Oh man. I would love to get more into grappling, but, you know, life gets in the way. Now, I don't mean any offense, but are there a lot of other females that train? It's kind of a rough hobby, isn't it?"

"None taken," I said. "You're right. There aren't nearly as many women as men, so I'm always outnumbered. There are some, like me, for instance, and I see more and more getting into it, so that's good. I visited a place in Vancouver that had a few women. They were brand new, but they really seemed to love it, and I was happy I came along when I did because I think it helped them to see that there is room for them. It's healthy for everyone to work out their aggressions, you know? Male and female, and this is a pretty safe way to do it, relatively speaking."

"For sure!" he exclaimed. "I loved the camaraderie of wrestling too, you know? People helping you push yourself and work on your discipline and stuff. Wrestling is one of the things that kept me from becoming a total knucklehead."

"Yeah," I said. "I feel like jiu-jitsu helps me work on being a better person." Then I added, "Plus, it's just cool. Even when I'm the one getting my butt kicked, it's always so awesome. All the positioning and submissions and the whole back and forth. There's always so much more to learn."

"Well, some people might think it's weird instead of awesome, but I'm with you. I never miss a UFC. Maybe I'll get back to the gym soon and do a few rounds. I'm way out of shape."

"That's just temporary," I said. "If you want to get back to it, it's always there, and your conditioning will come back. It will just suck at first while you work on it."

"Very good point," he said, handing back my passport.

"Okay, enjoy the rest of your trip, and keep on training! You're all set."

"Thanks a lot," I said, "and good luck with the boxing if you decide to go back."

"If not now, when, right?" he responded, grinning.

I smiled as I drove away, watching through my rear view mirror as the guard's facial expression molded itself back into an impassive mask before he beckoned to the next car in line. My weird hobby had made the world feel a little warmer. This guy may not have gotten the day-to-day of training, but he got the allure. He had reaped the benefits of similar pursuits in his own life. Though he could not have known it, he had also restored a tiny bit of my faith in jiu-jitsu and in myself, at least until the next rude awakening.

Oh crap, I thought, glancing at the digital clock set into the dashboard. We had to have been chatting for at least 10 or 15 minutes while I idled at his booth and he retained my passport. The guard had obviously not been in any kind of hurry, and I certainly had not been inclined to do anything other than follow his lead. Afterward, as I accelerated away from Canada and toward some graduate school friends and then some college friends in the Portland area, readjusting the sun visor and fiddling with the radio while I did so, I realized the other lines must have been moving the entire time we were talking, dispatching travelers back into the United States with slow but steady regularity. My line, on the other hand, had practically begun to gather dust, standing motionless like a horse that has been worked to death, but this time, I was not the one liable to pull my hair out from the waiting and the uncertainty about the reason for the delay. Apparently the Worthington Curse was still in full effect, but today I had been the perpetrator rather than the victim. Did this mean I was freed? Had I passed on the damnation to someone else? If so, I would have felt bad, but on the other hand, maybe it was someone else's turn. Maybe my hours of waiting in the slowest line were over forever.

As it turns out, they were not—in the intervening years since my encounter with that border guard, I have discovered time and again that the Worthington Curse is still in full effect. For instance, just a few days before the time of this writing, I waited, with as much patience as I could muster, while the lady in line in front of me at the supermarket wrote out a check for her groceries and fumbled for two forms of ID for what felt like thousands of seconds but was probably only 30.

In that moment, though, driving back into the States from Canada on a beautiful summer evening after an unexpectedly energizing and validating conversation, I had something almost better than the actual dissolution of the Curse—and almost better than the actual answer to my questions about life and what in the hell I was looking for: I had hope.

- - - - - - - - - -

My next stop was Monmouth, Oregon, home of my friends Mark and Tanna, a married couple I had known in graduate school in Michigan. Mark was in the cohort that graduated two years after me, and Tanna worked in our department as an administrative assistant to help with their family expenses. Their first child, a daughter, was born during their first or second year. As I crossed paths with them during the first weeks they arrived in town, I decided I liked them and invited them to go with me to the dairy store on campus. The dairy store was run by people in the food science program at the university and featured site-made ice cream, cheese, and cheese curds. While I did not make it there nearly as often as I would have liked, it made me happy to know it was on campus, and I thought Mark and Tanna might want to know about it too.

It turns out they were not such big fans of cheese curds but did appreciate good ice cream, and on this promising basis an abiding friendship developed, the kind that is not harmed by distance, time, or lack of communication. I soon confirmed this when I arrived at their place one July evening. I had not seen Mark for at least a couple years, longer for Tanna. The house was located on a rural stretch of land, with many farm accoutrements and machines, and was occupied at that point by only the family dog, Poochie. The rest of the family was out of town until the next morning, but they had left instructions for me to go inside and make myself at home. As I learned when the sun came up, the only living creatures for miles besides me, the family, and Poochie were the cows in the barn.

It turned out to be a good thing that I was visiting for a few days in the summer, when Mark had less work to do at Western Oregon University, where he was an assistant professor of education, and when Mark and Tanna's kids were on vacation from school. This meant they were better able to work around my jiu-jitsu schedule, and, I was gratified to observe, they were more than willing to.

"Hey, the kids and I thought we'd take you to the coast today to check out the rock formations and the water," Mark said after we said our hellos the next morning.

"Hm, how long will that last?" I asked. "I definitely want to do that, but there's a class at a place called Straight Blast Gym in Portland that starts at 5 that I want to check out, so I have to leave here around 3." Monmouth was about an hour and a half drive from Portland. Plus I needed my 30 minutes for vaguely creepy recon.

"Oh, then we shouldn't go today."

"Well, tomorrow there's a class at a different place that doesn't start till 8, so I'd have till 6. Does that work?"

"Sure, we can make that happen."

"I'd be back late, probably around 11 or midnight. After the kids are asleep, I'm sure."

"They'll survive. Then maybe today we can hang around here and do some sightseeing in town until you have to go. Then, when will you be back tonight?"

"Oh, 8 or 9, I guess."

"Okay. We'll hold dinner for you till you get back."

"Well, what time do you usually eat?"

"Don't worry about it. We won't starve."

"Are you sure? I know this is kind of a crazy schedule. It's not fair for me to impose it on you, and yet, here we are."

"Val, we have kids. Our crazy schedule could jiu-jitsu the

crap out of your crazy schedule."

I laughed. "My schedule wants to know if we can't just all get along. Thank you for being flexible."

"Plus, we knew what we were signing on for when we asked you to come visit. This is a jiu-jitsu odyssey, after all, not a chase after rats with Poochie odyssey."

"That could prove to be pretty awesome, actually, but now you might see why my non-jiu-jitsu friends have mostly given up on me," I continued after a moment. "I'm banking on my family being legally unable to disown me, but I have alienated more than one friend because I'm always training at 'normal' times. 'Sorry, I can't go out because we don't have a sitter,' people get. 'Can we shift our dinner back an hour or two because I have a work meeting?' Nobody faults you for that. But 'I'm busy till 9 or 10 every night this week including Friday because I'm going to be beating people up and getting beat up myself. How about Sunday? I can meet you in the afternoon after that beat-up session, though I will probably be sub-verbal due to exhaustion and in limited control of my table manners due to hunger.' Somehow, that doesn't compute. It seems perfectly normal to me, but for some reason, it's off-putting," I smirked.

I was laughing, but that exchange with Mark also, through no fault of his, dredged up some feelings of anger, guilt, and shame I had had about similar plans-making scenarios in the past, depending on the person and the situation.

I tended to feel anger if the person I was trying to make plans with said, in a manner I always interpreted to be condescending, "Well, you did that stuff the other night. Can't you just skip a day?" and was unable or unwilling to see that the fact that training jiu-jitsu was perhaps an unusual priority did not make it any less important for me. Once or twice I made the mistake of responding to that question with, "Well, you parented your child/went to work/hung out with your spouse the other night. Can't you just skip a day?" but that backfired, either because it insulted the person to think that this strange hobby could be as important as their home and work lives, or because it simply did not compute. Plus, I did not like being snide, though I am good at it.

Sometimes I felt guilty when the person I was trying to make plans with really was putting forth an effort to meet me halfway, only to have me show up late ("Sorry, class went over") or looking like a hurricane had picked me up and deposited me at the designated meeting point ("I didn't have time for a shower. Stand downwind of me.").

I felt shame because it was at those times that I noticed how odd my life seemed in comparison to others' lives. I was reminded that I was not prioritizing the goals I had convinced myself I *should* prioritize—should *want* to prioritize—but did not. I knew this because for many years I had tried to, and I had made myself miserable with the effort. It was comparably uncomfortable, though, to prioritize something different, especially since I was hard pressed to explain to anyone's satisfaction, much less my own, the allure of this pastime that had prompted me to embark on my current path.

Mark was genuinely trying to plan around my schedule, and I managed not to go on the defensive against some slight I had created in my mind. Historically, I was not always so successful—sometimes the slight was real, and, though I am loath to admit this, sometimes I deserved it.

I had thought my stress around wanting to do what I wanted to do while still recognizing how odd it seemed to others would resolve itself a little on a walkabout devoted to jiu-jitsu, but, as I discovered during the latter part of my stay in Oregon and beyond, it did not.

"Well, we already knew you were weird," Mark continued, deadpan.

"It's not like I hide it well. I do appreciate you working with me on plans."

"You just have to let us show you some real Oregonian coastline, let us feed you, and not teach the kids too many moves they can use against me."

"All of these things can be arranged."

"Now, have you heard of a thunderegg?"

"The fact that I have not is a travesty. It sounds like a turbo-charged breakfast food, like something my jiu-jitsu friends would want to eat to get a competitive edge."

"Well, not quite. But it's still pretty cool. We'll find some when we go to the coast."

"Remember that band in grad school that was made up of students and professors in the college of education, and they used to play at big campus events and professional conferences? They should call themselves Thunderegg."

Mark stopped abruptly. We had been walking toward the barn, me slightly behind him, so I almost walked into him. "I will make it my personal life's mission to ensure that happens. In the meantime, have you ever milked a cow?"

In the next two days, I did learn what a thunderegg is: a rock formation that resembles a geode but is even cooler, and that is common to Oregon. I poked around the coast with Mark and his kids and their cousin. I hung out with Poochie, though I did not catch a single rat. I drove a tractor. I trained in several places, enough to recognize a few faces here and there when I returned for second visits.

I also got used to seeing Mark and Tanna and being part of their routine, if only for a couple days. When it was time to say goodbye, it was yet another case of too soon, and I again felt ripped from a place of familiarity just as I had started to feel comfortable and comforted. I could have stayed another day or two, but that would have only delayed the inevitable. Also, I had to train, of course. Bad things would happen if I did not. So, as with all the other friends and family I got to see but then had to say goodbye to on this trip, I hugged and thanked and hugged some more, and then I waited until I had driven out of sight before I let myself cry. This time, even I was questioning my sanity in pursuing Brazilian Jiu-Jitsu so voraciously.

When I try to explain my attitude about training to people who do not share it, I am unable to communicate it to them unless and until I discover something they are passionate about. Then the comprehension explodes into existence like the birth of a star. Video games, playing the guitar, spelunking, collecting action figures—it does not matter. Once I realize the person I am talking to has a passion of his or her own and understands what it feels like to be so compelled to do something that it is always at the top of your to-do list, then the specific thing does not matter. What matters is being able to recognize that, just as their thing is irresistible to them, my thing is irresistible to me.

My father is a retired counseling psychologist and college professor who specialized in counseling for clients with drug and alcohol addictions. Like him, many of his students were not in recovery themselves, which meant they were going to be working with people who were experiencing compulsions and challenges that they themselves had never experienced, at least not related to the substance of choice. Among other things, if these would-be counselors did not have issues with alcohol or drugs, it would be dangerously easy for them to think it would be appropriate and even helpful for them to say, "Well, just don't drink. It's all about will power." To an addict, though, that would be as sensitive—and as helpful—as saying, "Well, just don't breathe. It's all about will power."

To help these students develop the kind of comprehension and credibility they would need in order to be effective and trustworthy therapists, he did the next best thing: On the first day of class, he asked them to identify an aspect of their daily routine they could not live without. Whether it was having a morning cup of coffee, taking a cigarette break at lunch, or watching the evening news, each student had to share with the class some habit or practice they engaged in *every day without fail* that brought them pleasure. Then he instructed them to give that thing up, for a week, until the next class session. No substitute was allowed: no tea, no Nicorette gum, no radio broadcast. Not the same habit at a different time or a different location. Just a gaping hole where the thing usually was.

Wouldn't you know it, at the next class session, when my father canvassed the room, a large number of students had "forgotten" to complete the exercise, or had tried it once or twice and then stopped. It was left to the students who actually had followed through to describe what it was like to abstain from their ingrained habit, even for a week. Verdict: It sucked. It left these students feeling out of sorts, disoriented, irritable and frustrated, and for some, those feelings about not being allowed to engage in the behavior exacerbated their desire to engage in the behavior. They would catch themselves initiating the behavior until they remembered it was verboten. Some reported picking fights with loved ones or strangers, escalating minor or non-existent issues to the point of argument because they were so addled by not being able to do the thing. They started to see a glimmer of what an addict might be up against, and how their therapeutic actions would have to account for the established dynamics of addictive behavior, not their own biases about it.

They began to realize that although they might not ever be able to imagine having an unhealthy preoccupation with drugs or alcohol, that preoccupation was as real and at least as all-consuming—and probably much more so—to the people they would be counseling as their own need to engage in the behavior they had tried to give up.

I must clarify that I do not use the analogy of addiction lightly. I understand, intellectually because of my father's professional work, and personally because of several experiences from my past with people I loved who appeared to me to be struggling with addiction, the cruel toll it can take on the individual and on the people who love that individual. Further, from the perspective of someone even just a bit closer to the end of the spectrum where the addict resides, since my early teens I have struggled with my orientation to food and its influence on my feelings about my body and, by extension, myself. I understand the difference between an avid interest and a true addiction, but I also believe these categories are not always clearly delineated, that instead there is a spectrum. I believe this because of how I reacted to the prospect of not being able to train when I went to visit my friends Jon and Alison in Portland, Oregon, on the next leg of my trip.

Jon is a good friend I met in college. For as long as I have known him, he has always been off on some adventure, even choosing to spend the winter of our senior year in South America. While study abroad programs were plentiful and popular at our college, it was rare for students to participate in them during the last year of school. Participants were usually sophomores and juniors, but the program Jon wanted was only available every other year, so he went when he could, not seeming to give a second thought to the timing. Later, he met his equally intrepid and well-traveled wife, Alison, when they were both in medical school in Portland. They had gotten married some years prior to my jiu-jitsu journey over a beautiful summer weekend, holding the event at the Timberline Lodge, a resort at the top of Mount Hood.

When I chatted with Jon about possibly paying him and Alison a visit on my way through town, we talked about my other travel plans. When I mentioned I was going to Alaska, he waxed nostalgic for the trip he had taken to climb Denali and talked about Talkeetna, which is a staging area for Denali expeditions. Not surprisingly, then, I always associate Jon and Alison with adventure and the outdoors.

For these reasons, it should have come as no surprise that when I contacted them to see if they were available to get together on the weekend I was planning to pass through on my way to southern California—the mecca of BJJ in the United States—they told me that while Alison would be in town, Jon would be leaving that Friday to take his annual rafting trip down the Deschutes River, an excursion involving about a dozen of his friends, two nights of camping alongside the water, food and cocktails, and, true to Jon's nature, adventure in the outdoors. Alison would be working during the days but getting together with friends at night, and I could stay at the house and hang out with her if I wanted.

"Why don't you come on the trip?" Jon asked when we talked. "It's a great time, and I'd love for you to meet some of my friends from med school and the hospital."

"Oh man, it sounds great, but I was planning to train at a couple places this weekend. There's lots of jiu-jitsu in Portland." I had already been to Straight Blast and a place called New Breed Academy and was planning to go back to both of them. I also wanted to check out Team Quest. All of these were located within the city limits.

"Oh yeah? Well maybe you could stay an extra day or two and do that when we get back. It's going to be awesome, and the forecast is really good. You're in Portland at the perfect time—the rest of the year is cold and rainy. You have to take advantage of the good weather while we have it!"

I hesitated. "Yeah, I think I'm just going to stick with the original plan, but you don't leave till Friday, right? I arrive on Thursday, so we can hang out then."

"Okay, but if you change your mind, there's plenty of room for you."

As I hung up the phone, I thought, "I will not be changing my mind."

When I arrived in Portland, I still had not, and yet, sometime between my Thursday evening reunion dinner with Jon and the Friday evening class I was planning to take at Straight Blast, I found myself in a car, speeding south on Interstate 5 toward the embarkation point for the rafting trip.

At some point that Friday, I was standing outside Jon and Alison's house, chatting with them. I had spent Thursday night there after dinner in town with Jon, and over breakfast, Alison and I had made a plan for me to meet up with her and her friends that evening after I trained. Jon had finished his packing for the trip, and we went outside to wait for his ride. It really was beautiful out. Presently, two cars appeared, each one ferrying some of Jon's friends.

That is when things went sideways. A car door opened, and a man got out and approached me, hand extended. "You must be Val. I'm Steve[19]. I understand you are planning to skip the rafting trip in favor of staying inside all weekend doing some weird wrestling stuff."

I shook the proffered hand. "Nice to meet you. Yes, that's the plan." I did not respond to the judgment. I was used to it, and I always tried to assume the best of people, that they were teasing but not really disapproving. Still, it always annoyed me, but it was not worthwhile to get into it here. That is the mindset I started with, at least, though know what

---

[19] Not his real name.

they say about the best laid plans.

"Well, that is completely unacceptable. This is the trip of the year. It is epic, and it can't be a coincidence that you're in town on the weekend it happens. You must come with us. We are a ton of fun. I promise!"

My hackles started to rise and my body started to tense. I felt like a dog whose leash was being yanked just when it had found something particularly fragrant to sniff at. Like that dog, I dug in, standing my ground. "It sounds lovely, but like I told Jon, I already have plans." Plans that matter to me.

I did not say that last part, but I thought it as loudly as I could.

I looked at Jon, and he shrugged, grinning mischievously. I would learn later that Steve was known in their circle of friends for being good-naturedly contentious about everything. He had never met an argument he did not like, and he hated losing as much as he loved sparring.

More people emerged from the cars and stood around Steve, encouraging me to ditch my plans and come along.

"Yeah, come on an overnight trip in the wilderness with complete strangers. It's not at all like *Deliverance*!"

"You'll get to use all of nature as your toilet!"

"We saved the middle seat in the back of the car just for you."

Dammit. Now I had a veritable posse of outdoorspeople on my scent. Even if I could have escaped, they would have been able to track me.

This is the part of being a defender of BJJ that I have always disliked: I find it difficult to explain the significance of it in my life to people who do not consider it significant—or consider it at all—in their own lives. Then again, you could also argue that I was angry because these people were disrupting a potentially addictive behavior I had come to rely on. It was probably a little bit of each.

I divined that I had a choice between escalating the fight until I was puffing like a grampus or capitulating. I think it was the realization that my actions would reflect on Jon that finally prompted me to manage, "All right, already. I'll go, but I need to pack." I seemed to be the only person aware of my own consternation. I am not a great actress under the best of circumstances, and here I was what you might describe as "under duress."

The assembled gathering burst into a smattering of applause. "No problem. We have plenty of extra gear," Steve said. "Just get some warm clothes and whatever toothpaste and stuff you need."

I fished around in the trunk of my car and hastily assembled some belongings, looking wistfully at the pile of neatly folded gis that occupied one corner of the interior. Those friends of Jon's I had not yet met came up to me to introduce themselves and say things like, "So glad you're coming! It's going to be great. Jiu-jitsu can't hold a candle to us!" I tried to respond in kind. I probably failed. I felt like I had just eaten a giant, soaking-wet sponge.

I do not believe I have ever told Jon or Alison how completely I flipped out during that exchange in front of their house and afterward, or how long it took for me to calm down even somewhat. The better part of the weekend, as it turns out. I nodded and smiled and shook hands, struggling to display a modicum of social grace. I did this glassily, though, on autopilot, with one-word answers and a smile that could be better described as a "rictus." In later years when I recounted the story, I probably joked and downplayed, deflected and self-deprecated. At the time, though, most of my energy was directed toward suppressing the disquiet—an exquisite combination of fury and abject panic—that was roiling around in my gut and threatening to shoot out from my every pore. I was beside myself at the thought that I would not be training for three whole days. "Three whole days" may sound snarky, but believe me when I tell you that at the beginning of it, it felt like an absolute eternity, during which untold disasters would surely come to pass.

If I and my skewed sample of my own family, friends, and acquaintances is any indication, human beings absolutely hate to miss out. It feels like Murphy's Law that whenever you cannot be present for something, that is when the magic happens. The party you cannot attend turns out to be the blowout that defines an era. The episode of that popular show you slept through just happens to be the one where all the plot lines come together in an explosion of "oh *my* GOD! Nobody could have seen that coming!" and then, for days, weeks, months to come, you are left out of every conversation that starts, "Hey, remember when...?" Nobody goes out of their way to make you feel left out. In fact, those in the know always take great pleasure in explaining to you what you would already be in on if you had bothered to make the effort. It is all you can do not to tell them to shut up about it, can't we talk about something else? You refrain, though, because letting fly would only confirm your bitterness. You can pick up bits and pieces after the fact, but that is not the same as having been there or seeing it firsthand. You slacked, buddy, and now you are paying the price. There are even Urban Dictionary and Wikipedia entries about this phenomenon, called Fear of Missing out, abbreviated FOMO.

A similar dynamic is at play for me in jiu-jitsu, and I suspect I speak for some other grapplers as well when I admit the following fear: The day I miss class is sure to be the day all the mysteries of jiu-jitsu will be explained. It is on the day I do not attend that that technique, that modification, that principle I have been waiting for all my grappling life will be revealed. The one that will solve every problem and get me out of every jam. Catapult me to mythic levels of skill and comprehension. Even solve all the other, non-jiu-jitsu-related problems in my life. Yes, yes, I know there are hundreds, nay, thousands, of jiu-jitsu classes going on in the world at any given time, and I cannot attend all of them, but are my chances of solving jiu-jitsu higher if I attend one of those classes or if I attend zero of them? Let us not concern ourselves with the flaw in the original idea that there could ever be a solution.

"Anyone need to stop? Bathroom break?"

"Sure, why not? We have some time. What do you say, Val?"

"I don't care."

That was the most I had said since we had left Jon and

Alison's house, probably an hour prior, and I said it borderline rudely. We were about halfway to the place where we would get on the rafts. The Goddamn rafts. This Goddamn weekend. What in the actual hell had just happened here? I was still trying to process it. What *had* registered, with the rushing force of that first enormous drop on a roller coaster track, was that I really was not going to be training tonight. Or tomorrow. Or the next day. And what if they decided they were having so much fun that we should stay through *Monday*? Holy shit. Jesus God.

I sat in the back of one of the cars, behind the driver, my arms folded across my abdomen as if I had been kicked in it. It was not far off from how I felt.

Here is just a sample of the thoughts that leapt around in my mind like exploding popcorn kernels while our little caravan sped away from Portland, from jiu-jitsu, and from, it was becoming increasingly clear, my sanity: "Jesus Christ, what am I doing here? I need to train...I need to train...that person just asked me a question AND bumped into me...what did she say? If she bumps me again I'm going to scream...I can feel it...Okay, just chill the hell out. There are two cars in this caravan. Maybe that other driver would let me pay him to take his car back to Portland...they could just cram all the stuff in that car into this one...I'd be taking myself and my stuff, so there would be room, right? It could work...How much should I offer? I could offer like a couple hundred dollars maybe...Jon could vouch for me that I'm not going to steal it...I just need to train...this is stupid...they would think I was crazy, and they'd never let Jon live down having a friend like me...but I need to train...shit...I'm not going to train this weekend...can I do some drills on the beach when we're stopped? That would look weird too...maybe it's not such a crazy idea to get them to let me take a car back...we're stopping for gas, so now is the time to ask...shit...shit...goddammit...fuuuuu...what can I do?"

What I did do was continue to roil silently in the back seat until we arrived at the embarkation point along the river. I dutifully helped unload the cars, bring the supplies to the pier to which our rafts were tethered, wrap the supplies in waterproof plastic, and hand them to Jon and Steve, who arranged them in the rafts, which resembled giant rowboats. Unlike everyone else in the group, I did not engage in small talk or laughter or even smiles of anticipation about where we were headed. I was busy roiling.

Jon caught my eye as he helped me into the raft. "You okay?"

"Yeah, I'm fine," I replied, settling myself into a seat along the perimeter of the raft. "Just a little shell-shocked at the change of plans."

"It's going to be great, Val. I'm really glad you decided to come along."

"Yeah, me too." I smiled, though I did not feel like smiling.

"Okay, food, check. Luggage, check. Two rafts, check. People to put in the rafts, check. Oars, water bottles, everyone in a life vest, check, check, check. It looks like we're ready to go! Any last words before we shove off?" Jon asked.

Our group whooped and cheered. I kept the smile pasted to my face that I had flashed at Jon.

Away we went. The river was swift and blue, sporting the occasional bit of froth. The riverbanks were about fifty feet apart, which provided enough room for our two rafts to race each other as we headed downstream, Jon steering one and Steve steering the other.

"I guess I'm doing this," I thought to myself.

One of Jon's friends dug around in the waterproof food containers, found beers, and handed them out, saying, "Here. It's happy hour somewhere in the world." The rest of the group nodded and murmured agreement.

I passed the beers, not intending to take one.

"No, Val, that one is for you," she said. I opened my mouth to protest, and she cut me off. "Go on, take it."

At first I accepted the beer to appease her, but then I noticed it looked refreshing. I took in the rest of the group that was on the raft with me. I scanned the cloudless sky and saw the occasional bird. I listened to the plapping of the water under the raft, the banter of Jon's friends, and my own breathing, as it slowed and deepened. I felt the rocking of the raft on the water, the warmth of the sun, and the cold of the beer in my hand. The speed of my racing mind started to decrease, and I found myself slightly more aware of my surroundings. It felt like a fever plaguing me had just broken.

"Here's to a great weekend!" Jon's friend said, clinking beers with the people on either side of her. The clinking expanded to include our whole raft, and then we hollered to the other half of our group in the other raft, toasting them as well.

With the first swallow of my beer, I started to admit, grudgingly, that it was a gorgeous day and that there were worse places I could be than with an old friend spending a summer day on the water. There were numerous other families and groups of friends preparing to set off down the same route we were going to follow, and they were laughing and smiling. I wanted to stay stressed out, but the good will was infectious.

"We'll make a little time, and then we can find a place to stop for lunch. In the meantime, check out the ropes that are hanging off the boat. You can hang onto them and float in the water," Jon said.

From the other boat, Steve hollered, "Boy, I'm glad I'm out in nature instead of being inside chopping and kicking some random people."

I sighed inwardly, smiled, and raised my beer in salute.

"Hey Val. How does sleeping on the riverbank under the stars sound?" Jon asked.

"It sounds pretty damn good," I said, realizing I actually meant it.

Rickson Gracie is a well-known member of the Gracie family, itself a cornerstone of the Brazilian Jiu-Jitsu phenomenon. He is featured in the 1999 movie *Choke*, which chronicles his preparation for the 1995 Japan Open, a vale tudo ("anything goes") event he had won the previous year. The movie, as well as his accomplishments in grappling and vale tudo, have secured his iconic status in the hearts and minds of many jiu-jitsu and MMA practitioners.

Rickson is credited with coining the phrase "Flow with the go" to describe how he engages with opponents. Some have speculated that in speaking the words, he transposed them from the more common English phrase "Go with the flow." Others believe he meant something different. Either way, he discusses the need to stay relaxed and to recognize that we cannot anticipate what is going to happen, which is true in life as well as in jiu-jitsu. I learned this firsthand on that summer weekend in Portland. My best laid plans had gone out the window, and all I could do was flow with the go. As evidenced by my visceral reaction, I was not good at it, but since then, I have had many opportunities to practice.

Also, I trained like a madwoman when I got back to Portland.

6

The next place the animated line and chugging train of my journey took me to was Alaska, by way of Seattle. I had purchased a round trip plane ticket from the Seattle-Tacoma airport to Juneau, where my high school friend Debbie lived. Later in my trip I planned to go south to California, so going north meant a bit of backtracking, as I had to drive north to Seattle from Portland and then, when I flew back from Alaska, south from Seattle back through Portland and on into the Golden State. I figured I could visit some schools in Seattle after I returned from the Land of the Midnight Sun.

When I departed for Juneau, I parked my car in the Seattle-Tacoma International Airport long-term parking lot and, with much trepidation, bade it goodbye for the first appreciable length of time since I had left Chicago. I was surprised at how difficult it was, but perhaps I should not have been, given all the car had come to represent to me: home, familiarity, safety. My separation was made easier by the fact that I was headed to visit a dear friend.

Juneau is the capital of Alaska, located at the foot of Mount Juneau, in the southeastern corner of the state. There are no roads connecting Juneau to the rest of Alaska and the rest of North America, only planes or ferries, so people who drive what the locals call "out the road," away from the city center, only get so far. Juneau is a port city that is on the itinerary of numerous cruise lines. A strip of stores, bars, and restaurants that flank the water where cruise ships and tourist boats dock provide a place for passengers to disembark and contribute to the local economy.

Debbie lived in a hilly part of town somewhat away from the water, within walking distance of the Silverbow Bakery, which offered big tables, bagels, electrical outlets, and wi-fi. I did some blogging there during the times when Debbie had to work. She was, and still is, a doctor of naturopathy and a midwife, providing medical care in an area where it is not plentiful. She did rearrange her schedule to take advantage of my visit, and we crammed many sight-seeing opportunities into the time I had. We took a whale-watching trip, during which we "got some tail," as we put it, which amused us so much it almost compensated for the fact that we did not see a complete whale. We hiked along the Mendenhall Glacier, taking in Juneau's beautiful mountain scenery.

Debbie's boyfriend Shane gave me shooting lessons at the local gun club with a rifle and a shotgun (that poor milk jug never saw it coming), let me pretend to drive the bulldozers and tree uprooters he had on his expansive property outside of the city, and fed me frontier-style fajitas full of elk and bear meat that he had caught himself. There were also many friendly neighbors and acquaintances who commiserated among themselves about the "crazy heat wave" Juneau was experiencing—could we believe the temperature had risen as high as the low 70s (Fahrenheit), for goodness sake? When would the insanity end?

I also got the opportunity to catch up with Debbie and get some insight from someone smart who knew me well.

"So you're done with Chicago, eh?" she asked, as we rested in her apartment one evening after a day of sightseeing.

"I think so. I don't know. I don't know much of anything lately," I replied.

"What do you mean? You're taking an awesome trip and getting to have adventures. Plus, you get to see me."

"Well, that is obviously awesome. I just, I feel like the rest of it isn't what you'd call normal, and I'm not headed for normal anytime soon."

"What do you mean?"

I scratched my head. "Well, I had this life that looked really good on paper, and I hated almost all of it. Or, it didn't make me happy, at least, not the way I thought it should. I felt really stupid that I was living this unsatisfying life and like there was something wrong with me that I didn't like it. So I kind of went crazy."

"Okay. To be clear, you were unhappy because you were surrounded by things you didn't like and then you beat yourself up about not being able to force yourself to like them? That part does sound kind of crazy, but then you acknowledged what you didn't like and tried to change that. It sounds like that's what you think makes you crazy, when I think that's the part that makes you awesome."

"Well, it's kind of the way I went about it. I mean, who does the stuff I did—cutting and running around all over the country?"

"Um, Val? Have you noticed where we are right now? Is it 'normal' for a Jersey girl to end up in Alaska?"

"I don't know, but you seem to have established a great life for yourself. You are well-respected and you are needed."

"Well, so are you. You're just in the process of figuring out some things. Welcome to being human."

I sighed. "I guess. I just wish I wanted what I had, you know? It would have been a lot easier."

"Think about it this way," Debbie said. "You probably know a lot of people who don't want what they have, but they try to convince themselves they do, which just makes them more miserable, or more deluded. What sounds crazier to you, that, or what you are doing?"

"When you put it that way, you make it sound like I actually have a master plan." I replied.

"Man. I don't know if any of us has that," Debbie said. "But at least you are doing something to make yourself happier."

"I worry too much about what people think." I hated admitting it, but it was the truth. "I have this impression that everyone is sitting in judgment on me and finding me lacking. I should have my shit together by now."

"Here's the thing, Val. Everyone does have an opinion, and some of those people will be more than willing to give it to you, whether you want it or not. I mean, how many times do you think I've had to explain why I decided to get an ND rather than an MD? Even how many times people tell me that I actually mean 'MD?' Not to mention how often I get questions like, 'And what is a midwife again? I have heard of it, but isn't that something people used to do before there were doctors?' That doesn't mean you have to accept what they say."

"Easier said than done," I said.

"Of course, but it's necessary, if you're going to figure out what makes you happy instead of what you think should make you happy, based on what someone else told you."

"True."

"And on the flip side," Debbie continued, "no offense, but while it's true that lots of people will want to tell you what to do, lots of other people couldn't give two shits about what you are doing. In fact, they are so self-absorbed they will forget what you tell them almost as soon as you stop talking."

I laughed. "Yes, I know those people. I usually am those people."

"The point is, there will always be people who judge you, people who disapprove of you, and people who don't care about you. There will also be people who do care about you, who will go along with whatever you do even if they don't understand. That's what you did when I told you I was moving to Alaska."

"I remember," I said. "I was really excited for you and glad for me because I'd have someone to visit."

"That's why I told you—because I knew you'd support me even if you thought what I was doing was weird, and that is what I needed."

"So what you're saying is that I need to pay attention to

the people who give me atta girls and ignore the rest."

"That's a big part of it. The other part is, do what you feel is right for you. No one else can tell you it isn't. They can say it doesn't seem right to them, but you're the one who lives your life."

It seemed such an obvious point, but it started to hit home. When I was a kid, my parents and teachers told me what was and was not acceptable. In college and grad school, I could rely on professor comments and grades as a way to determine whether I was on the right track. I had to make academic decisions, but I learned what was more and less effective. At work, I got regular feedback from supervisors and colleagues, raises, and performance reviews, and they were generally all positive. From all of these sources, I developed a sense that I was living my life "correctly." Unfortunately, I also apparently developed a sense that others' opinions about what was right for me, in all areas of my life, superseded my own.

Particularly on this journey, I did not have any sense of what success meant, and my conversation with Debbie was driving home the point that there was only one person who might have a clue. No wonder I was terrified all the time. It was just me and my own opinion. I had demonstrated I could protect myself when I decided to leave the academy in Kansas because I got a bad feeling, but I was not yet confident that that skill extended to making optimal decisions for my entire life. I realized I needed to pay more attention and take more ownership of my choices, even if I crashed and burned as a result of them. At least I would be crashing and burning on my terms.

After a few days with Debbie and Shane, I returned to the Juneau airport to make my way to Anchorage for a side adventure. I had bought a round-trip ticket there because I reasoned that since I had no idea when I would be back that way again, I might as well take the opportunity to see what there was to see. While not smack dab in the middle of the mainland, Anchorage was roughly 1000 miles northwest of Juneau, uncharted territory for me. I made arrangements to rent a car there so I could venture out to see some of the surrounding area. This I imagined to be desolate but beautiful, wild and woolly, and full of colorful characters.

True to form, however, I loved the idea of visiting Anchorage when it was abstract and distant, but as the time for me to travel there neared, my reluctance kicked in and I seriously considered not going.

"You are welcome to stay here as long as you want, of course, but I do think you'll regret it if you don't go," Debbie said.

I knew she was right and wished she was not. "I know. I'll go. I just have misgivings about it now."

"I bet you'll love it once you're there."

"This is what you mean about being supportive when I do crazy things, isn't it?"

"Well, in this case, crazy would be not going."

"Stop making sense."

"Okay, David Byrne. You'll have fun in Anchorage. Now get out."

As if to justify my reluctance, I wasted no time in worrying about what would happen if I ran out of gas out in the middle of the frontier—why put off until later fretting about something that will probably never come to pass when you can start now? At least I was in the area during the summer, when the skies stayed light long into the night, I thought. So if I did end up stranded on the side of the road and was subsequently attacked by a band of marauding caribou— because that was even more likely than running out of gas— at least I would be able to memorize their faces, increasing my chances of identifying them in a lineup. This was pretty much my exact train of thought: equal parts real fear and smart-alecky overcompensation.

Of course, one of the reasons I planned to go to Anchorage was jiu-jitsu-related. I knew there was an academy there, called Gracie Barra Anchorage, which was another affiliate of the famous Rio academy.

When I arrived at the airport in Anchorage, I picked up the rental car I had reserved for driving around town. I had rented a room in a hotel in town that looked more like a largish, cozy house run by friendly proprietors. As I was checking in, I noticed there was a festival going on in a nearby park, with booths featuring arts and crafts, a stage on which different dance troupes and musical groups performed, and food stands, so while I was closer to the end of the earth than I ever had been, it did not feel as desolate as I had been expecting it to. Also, as luck would have it, when I had made my plans some weeks or months earlier, I had timed my visit to coincide with an amateur MMA event to be held at a venue in town over the weekend I would be there. Of course that was at the top of my to-do list, along with training jiu-jitsu myself.

Before any of that happened, I took a trip to the foot of the tallest mountain in North America. After listening to my Portland friend Jon talk about his Denali expedition, I decided to take a day trip to visit Talkeetna. I was not up for a trek to the top of the mountain, but in theory I was comfortable committing to getting a little closer to it and encountering people who were. When the time actually came to head out, though, I started to balk—for someone on a road trip, I really did not seem to want to go anywhere—so I made a deal with myself that I had to stay for an hour and then I could come back.

Talkeetna is located a roughly two-hour drive north of Anchorage. While I have participated in many hiking and camping trips over the years, I am a dilettante, depending on the kindness and knowhow of friends when it comes to pitching tents, starting and cooking over campfires, and distinguishing in the scary, fraught dark of night between the growl of a bear and the labored breathing of a portly man in a nearby tent. (Actually, that last one seems to be a challenge for even those friends of mine who are seasoned campers.)

On this side trip I had other goals in mind, but it occurred to me that the mountain was kind of a metaphor for my own journey. I still was not sure what I was looking for, but I knew I had to keep looking. Similarly, I suspected many people felt compelled to summit this peak but might be hard pressed to explain why. I felt a sort of kinship with the mountain, and with the people who climbed it.

The day I made the drive from Anchorage was chilly, probably in the mid-50s Fahrenheit, and marked by a persistent drizzle—just your typical summer day in mainland Alaska. I wore a proto-version of what became my winter uniform. I was breaking in my new Merrell hiking boots from the REI in Juneau. I also had on jeans and my too-big blue-gray windbreaker with a layer of t-shirt and fleece shirt underneath, which still left room for me to shield any stray puppies or kittens I might come across.

The drive itself was uneventful, on a desolate stretch of highway flanked at different times by trees and bodies of water, but with relatively little evidence of human presence. This was more of what I had been expecting when I pictured myself in Alaska. I had triple checked that I had a full tank of gas before I left, due to my chronic nervous Nelly-ism. If the surrounding environs did not do enough to drive home to me how close to the edge of the world we seemed to be, hitting "scan" on the radio and then watching the numbers on the digital readout cycle through the possible stations at a dizzying speed, stopping on a total of three signals on the entire spectrum from 87.7 through 107.9 put a period at the end of the sentence. The AM dial was not much more populated. The stations I could receive there were concerned with weather, wildlife sightings, and fire warnings. When in Rome, I thought, listen as the Romans listen.

Eventually I neared my destination and made my way toward a gravel parking lot demarcated by railroad ties. I parked my car there, still full of gas, though I reflexively looked around for a filling station. The lot looked out onto a road flanked by rows of buildings closer to the lot and large white event tents like the kind used at weddings farther down. As I approached, I could see that the buildings were low and wooden, housing restaurants, general stores, and the like. Some of the tents were full of kitchen equipment, sizzling noises, and cooking smells.

Others contained long rectangular white folding tables on which flat display boxes of jewelry, folded scarves, and other souvenirs had been carefully arranged. Still others contained the same types of folding tables, only these were occupied by pairs of people who appeared ready to discuss civic and town issues. Their tables featured clipboards and pamphlets.

The rain continued, and yet this strip of buildings and tents was alive with people: families, couples, lone wolves like me. All of them were dressed in some variation on the theme of waterproof jackets and hats or baseball caps, jeans or carpenter pants and hiking boots, and backpacks. Occasionally people wandered by wearing big black plastic garbage bags. There was a preponderance of facial hair on the men, lending the younger ones an "earthy crunchy" vibe and the older ones a familial resemblance to Grizzly Adams.

The coif of choice tended to include some permutation of dreadlock or cornrow, at least among the young adults of both genders. The whole tableau smacked of a combination of a Grateful Dead show, a Phish show, a county fair, one of the big weekends at my undergraduate alma mater that tended to attract "randoms" from other nearby colleges, and another Grateful Dead show. Plus rain. I did not know what I had walked into, but I liked the vibe. Much as it pains me to use that particular word, it well describes what it is I liked. People were laughing and chatting, and, as I noticed when I happened to make eye contact with one or two passersby, smiling at strangers.

I decided to explore the scene (another of my least favorite, but in this case most accurate, words) systematically, working my way down away from my car along the row of buildings on one side of the lane and going into or at least stopping to read the signs on each one. Then I intended to investigate the tents before I worked my way back toward the parking lot. There was a general store, at which I bought some postcards. I could add "Greetings from Talkeetna!" to my map of my journey. I stood outside a bar-slash-restaurant, weighing my options as I listened to the noises inside.

After a tour of the rest of the relatively short row of permanent buildings and businesses on the one side, I turned toward the tents. They were open on one side, with flaps reaching to the damp grass on the opposite side, as kind of a backdrop against the rain that continued to angle toward the ground.

"Yeah, it's been raining all day. All week, in fact," I heard someone say as I approached the closest tent. There did not seem to be anything "official" in it, just a small knot of people I took to be locals, standing with their hands in their pockets and chatting about weather. I predicted it would be a pretty short chat. This group was standing near more long white tables, and a few people, some families, some not, were seated at them. Some were eating food they had apparently purchased from the kitchen set-ups nearby. Others were drinking beer. Still others were doing both. None seemed at all fazed by the steady downpour.

I approached the counter that stood in front of the stoves and ovens and perused the menu. I was tickled that when I saw elk sausage listed, I was able to say to myself, "Hmmm. I had elk on Thursday." I smiled as I looked down, the way people do when they appear to be trying to share a secret with themselves.

I laughed again when I got my order, a reindeer sausage, because it was probably a foot and a half long but only about half an inch in diameter. It looked like something the less artistic among us might make with Play Doh, rolled out thin and long between the palms. It was served on a plate in a bun, but the ends of the sausage stuck way out of the bun on either end, to the point where it would have been useful to have another one to take care of the spillover.

Just as I was contemplating how I might actually go about ingesting my purchase, I heard a voice behind me say, "If you cut it in half, you can put the two halves next to each other on the bun. Then you just have to wrap the bun around both pieces."

I turned around to face the owner of the voice, a tall-ish, slender white man maybe a few years younger than I, which would have put him in his early 30s. He looked like he belonged at a jam band concert. He wore a wool ski cap, scruffy hair of both the head and the facial varieties, Carhart-type pants, and a windbreaker. He was handsome.

I laughed. "You've obviously done this before."

"Figured out how to eat weirdly-shaped food? Yeah, I'm pretty resourceful when it comes to mealtime, and I don't discriminate on the basis of structure."

"Well, I appreciate the suggestion. I'm a good eater myself, but this had me stumped. But now I know, and knowing is half the battle. Do you think I need a knife, or can I just tear it in half? In a ladylike fashion, of course."

"I think you can do that. When I tell this story later, and I will, I will emphasize how proper you were when you broke that weiner."

"Yes, I'm sure we can agree that manners are one of the things that separates us from the rest of the animal kingdom," I said, smiling.

"Most definitely," he responded. "Speaking of manners, would you like to have a seat?" He was leaning on one of the tables, and he moved over to make room for me on the bench in front of it.

"Thanks," I said, occupying the place he had vacated. "A lady always eats her freshly-snapped reindeer sausage with elbows off the table and, ideally, accompanied by music from a string quartet." I looked around, observing that no such musical group was to be found in the tent. "I guess the background noise will have to do."

"Well, I just met you, but you strike me as the kind of person who will endure," he replied. "What brings you to Talkeetna, anyway?"

I told him my story around mouthfuls, feeling that familiar self-consciousness as I did so. Thirty-six years old and shoveling gamey (but delicious) entrails into her body at the end of the world instead of dandling a newborn or heading up the new R&D division.

"Oh wow, what a fantastic adventure," he responded, with obvious enthusiasm. "You must be very brave. Or very medicated."

I laughed, pleasantly surprised at his reaction, though I supposed we were not at Mommy and Me classes or in the boardroom, where I already knew the reaction was likely to be somewhat different. "Or both," I replied. "I basically have no idea what I'm doing, but so far, I've managed to have some cool experiences. What about you?"

"Kind of a similar story, except without the jiu-jitsu" he said. "I'm from Virginia, and I had a job that required a lot of travel. I realized I liked the travel, but not so much the job. So I kept the one and got rid of the other. I am working on a business idea with some friends, but I make a point of continuing to go to places like this one. I mean, I just got the opportunity to share some important culinary knowledge with a fellow traveler. That's pretty cool, and not something that's going to happen that much in an office building, you know?"

I did know. And I marveled at how matter-of-factly this guy, whose name was Jake, told his story, as if doing what he and I had both done was the most typical thing in the world. I probably even stopped eating—which does not happen often, if ever—because I was digesting something more important: There were others like me. Some people— this guy—viewed what I had done as normal, even desirable. Maybe people like him were harder to find, because they were on the move, but they were "out there," and they understood why I had done what I did, because they were doing similar things themselves.

I do not remember his business idea. What I do remember is sitting with him for a couple hours, as if that had been the plan all along. During that time we sometimes chatted with other passersby, who easily came into our circle, hopefully feeling welcomed by us because they were. Then those people just as easily departed, leaving us comfortably alone together, as if he and I had a tacit understanding that we were a team, for as long as we both chose to be. I remember being focused on our conversation, our surroundings, and those moments as they happened, not because I had made a point of doing so, but because, for those hours, they were all that existed to me. Csikszentmihalyi would have approved.

In many domains I am reasonably intelligent, but in matters of the heart, I am a slow learner. Throughout my life I have misread signals as if it were my job, such that I have not realized members of the opposite sex have been interested in me until much later, either because the person finally told me or because someone else told me, at which point the moment, if I had eventually decided I wanted there to be one, was usually gone. On the flip side, I have, more times than I like to remember, read into a man's actions and words a level of interest in me that did not turn out to exist. In those cases, I have also turned into a contortionist, trying to fit my opinions and preferences to his, hoping that the interest I thought I detected would gather strength if I could figure out what he was looking for and be that.

I never actually realize that is what I am doing at the time. It is only after the fact, when I learn that the man is not interested, that along with a powerful sense of disappointment, I also notice a sensation of unclenching, as if both my physical and my psychic selves had been confined to an economy-sized airplane seat for too many hours and were now finally being allowed to stand up and stretch. To reassert themselves.

Arguably, it is better when I do not know that someone is interested than when I misread the signals. In the first case, I simply act as much like myself as I do around anybody, as opposed to trying to act, if only temporarily, like someone more enticing than I actually am or have the energy to try to be. In Talkeetna, the dynamic between me and my fellow traveler Jake was either the first-case scenario, or there was no attraction on this man's part at all.

I did not stay long enough to figure out which, though. Instead, precisely because I was not viewing this as a potential love connection, I acted in a way that was, for me, normal—which is to say, obsessive—about getting to training on time.

After he and I had spent a few hours together, I could feel myself coming out of the flow, first thinking that I might want to check the time, returning to the conversation, noticing my mind wandering back to thinking I should check the time, refocusing on my new friend's voice and presence, and then finally checking the time.

"Got someplace to be?" he asked, noticing my unsuccessful attempt to be furtive.

"Well, I had made plans to train in Anchorage this evening, and it's a two-hour drive," I replied. "Class is at about six, which means I should leave a little before four." I did not reveal that "about six" actually meant "at seven," because he didn't need to know about my habit of casing every BJJ joint I trained at before I trained there. He and I seemed to have a connection, but that did not mean it was time to invite him into my lunacy.

"Oh, that's cool that there is jiu-jitsu even in the Great White North," he said.

"Yeah, it's everywhere!"

"I see. So what time do you have to leave, again?"

The thing is, though, I did not have to leave. I did not have to do anything. I felt like I had to leave, and I felt wistful that I could not stay, because I really believed I could not, but that was my old conditioning layered onto my new obsession. I chose not to stay, though at the time it did not feel like a choice. It felt like the only possible course of action.

Don't get me wrong. I had a great time at Gracie Barra Alaska, where the guys were very friendly during training and took me out for pizza afterward, to a place called Moose's Tooth. One guy even shared bits and pieces of his own life in a way that made me think to myself, "This is what this trip is about, meeting people like this," alluding to a past "down south," somewhere in the lower 48, that was colorful enough to encourage him to find a more remote place to call home.

He did not come right out and say he was on the lam, but he mentioned several times that he made a living doing a series of odd jobs here and there, that he always paid for his purchases and arranged to get paid in cash for the work he did, that he that he had not seen his family in many years though he missed them, and that he might be moving to Fairbanks, which is located some 350 miles north of Anchorage—which would put him still farther away from the bulk of U.S. civilization. Just getting to hear that story was reason enough for me to leave Talkeetna when I did. I had already made a memorable connection with somebody there, which exceeded my expectations about what might happen before I had set out that morning. It was time to strike out and add to the pile in a different place, right?

My answer to that question has gradually shifted over time from an emphatic "yes" to a more wistful "maybe, maybe not." I am not saying this man and I would have danced off into the sunset together if I had stayed and that my choice to leave may have short-circuited the growth of something lovely.

However, I am also not *not* saying that.

As I have spent more years training, I have become more aware of the tradeoffs I make to be able to train as regularly and intensely as I feel I need to in order to continue to improve. This man, and my encounter with him in Talkeetna, is the representative example of the many times I have chosen jiu-jitsu over other alternatives, alternatives I now realize could have been just as rewarding. Maybe even more so.

This man, though I cannot even picture his face clearly anymore, is who comes to mind when I consider the cumulative effect of the countless times over the years that I have made a choice on a given day between training and the rest of life. If I do the math, it would probably come as a surprise to no one that jiu-jitsu has consistently won by a landslide. Nowadays, though, as my formerly imperceptible march toward declines in both physical capacity and psychic hunger has become increasingly perceptible, he is the question I ask myself when I, for the umpteenth time, contemplate the choice.

These realizations are happening in fits and starts and in hindsight, these epiphanies that even choosing my passion with corresponding passion carries all manner of potential consequences, not all of them positive. At the time I am making my jiu-jitsu decisions, I find it difficult to see past the decisions themselves to the potential long term impact. Or, more accurately, I may catch a glimpse of the potential impact but continue in the same course of action anyway.

For example, during my many contemplative hours of driving during the summer of my walkabout, I came to realize that I had habitually short-changed my non-grappling friends and family by fitting them in around training. Since, as a result of musings like those, there now existed in my brain the faintest of impressions that could be labeled "jiu-jitsu lifestyle cost-benefit analysis," I may have sensed a small fluttering around the edges of awareness that was trying to signal that my encounter with my new Talkeetna acquaintance had the potential to be momentous.

At that point in my journey, though, the voice of jiu-jitsu was still the loud, strident one, insisting "Train now! Train *now*! Train NOW!" In contrast, the voice of intuition and dawning realization was quiet, suggesting in a whisper, "See where this interaction with this person takes you. It may take you nowhere, but it may take you someplace amazing."

At the time, though, all I apparently heard from my intuition was "nowhere."

I should have stayed longer in Talkeetna.

That I did not is something I now regret, both in terms of my jiu-jitsu walkabout and also more generally. Though if I had stayed, I would have regretted not leaving. Maybe my life would not have turned out to be radically different, which is to say happier, but then again, stories like Ray Bradbury's *A Sound of Thunder* and movies like *Sliding Doors* suggest that it could have, that choosing a different node on that seemingly insignificant branch of the decision tree of my life might have been significant after all. Unfortunately for me, while some quantum physicists posit the existence of parallel universes, in which all possible outcomes to all possible actions and reactions are available for us to know, I only know the outcomes of the actions I have taken, not the ones it was possible for me to take but did not.

Maybe you can never completely avoid having to wonder "what if," given that any decision necessarily closes off countless others—even a small decision. We cannot know for sure which decisions—even which small ones—could have resulted in meaningfully different paths if we had followed a different node, but I think sometimes about going back to Talkeetna and trying to find the exact location where I made the decision I now regret, as if doing so would give me closure or even a glimpse into what my alternate universe might have looked like if I had chosen to stay.

As I have tried to piece together why I left Talkeetna when I did, more than anything else it is the experience of the rafting trip in Portland that helps me better understand. My reaction to the discovery that I would not be training that weekend was visceral and all-consuming, and it violently stripped me of most of my self-control. I may not ever be able to articulate fully why I train, but this was a particularly strong indication that I can't not, as a friend of mine put it when I asked him why he trains. Syntactically awkward though this sentiment may be, it hits the nail on the head.

Over time, I have improved at occupying a more balanced point along the jiu-jitsu spectrum that skews toward healthy fulfillment and away from naked compulsion, though it is a lesson I must relearn again and again, via successive approximations. I have discovered that my relationship to food provides a good analogy for helping me understand how I orient myself to jiu-jitsu. I can never fully abstain from eating, and it is highly unlikely that I will ever fully abstain from training—all things considered, I still know in my heart that having jiu-jitsu in my life is far better for me than not having it. This means I will always have to reckon with both. From the time I was a teenager, food and eating have been minefields fraught with incendiary devices of self-loathing, fear, and negative impact on my well-being.

I have to work at eating in a healthy way, eating the right amount, and loving myself even if I fall short. I have improved, though I will always have to put in effort and pay attention. I often think about food when I am not eating, either because I am anticipating when and what I will eat in the future or because I am contemplating what I have recently eaten. These thoughts are often filled with self-judgments, usually hateful ones. I have my work cut out for me when it comes to this most basic of human needs.

On the other hand, there are plenty of people, in the

western world, at least, who do not give a second thought to the nature of their relationship to food, eating when they are hungry, stopping when they are full, and, even if they do sometimes eat too much or too little, and/or for reasons other than hunger—celebration, community, sadness— doing so only occasionally and very quickly righting their course once again. Similarly, there are plenty of grapplers who are able to strike a healthy balance between their desire to train and the rest of the priorities and responsibilities in their lives. I am evidently not one of those grapplers. I have to work at balance, and I have to reckon today with the consequences of compulsive decisions I have made, like leaving Talkeetna when I did.

- - - - - - - - - -

"In Anchorage. Heading into an MMA show," I texted my friend Andrew (Goatfury). "Have no idea what to expect."

He texted back a few minutes later. "Yes you do. Crap."

While MMA was becoming more popular, many of the regional shows still had a veneer of inexperience about them, particularly with respect to the skill levels of the practitioners. Andrew's text was a comment on the fact that the show I was about to see was likely to have relatively low production values. I was looking forward to seeing it anyway.

When I entered the venue for the Anchorage MMA show, I was reminded of a giant cafeteria, or a space that would typically be used for bingo or a Kiwanis Club fundraising event or the like. The rectangular room was dark, lit only by the spotlights shining on the raised platform that supported the roped off square of canvas where the Pacific Northwest's best and brightest—or, at least, the Pacific Northwest's willing—would face each other in combat, using just their bodies and their cunning to try to defeat their opponents. As my eyes adjusted to the dimness, I noticed there were several concession stands along both long walls of the rectangle that offered pizza, soft pretzels, nachos covered with neon orange liquid cheese, candy and chips, soft drinks, and, of course, beer. For seating, there were long, rectangular tables arranged in rows, the arrangement interrupted by the ring in the middle, as well as a pathway on either side that had been constructed to permit fighters to process into the ring from doors in the center of each long wall.

Groups of spectators who had come together and found places at the tables faced each other before the show started and between match-ups, chatting and horsing around, but when the action was going in the ring, the group members whose chairs faced them away from it turned them around so they could see, putting their backs to their tables and their friends on the far side. The venue was not close to being at capacity, with some full tables close to the ring, and more and more sparsely populated ones farther from the action.

After a quick survey of the room, I sat down at an empty table, about halfway between the door and the ring, in a chair facing the ring and toward the left-most side. I felt self-conscious that I was alone, wishing yet again that I had a partner in crime on this trip, someone to nudge in the ribs when something particularly awesome happened, and, truth be told, someone to tell me sometimes that it was all going to be okay, but I did not. I smiled and reminded myself that for every time I wished for company, someone I knew probably wished for solitude. I remembered that I was Prancing and Sucking.

I took in more of my surroundings. This audience was skewed mostly male, though I did not know whether that was because of the demographic that tended to like MMA back then or because Alaska itself seems to have more male than female inhabitants. There were some women in attendance, but none in a single-sex group, though I saw numerous cadres of just men. There were also no other women by themselves, and I scanned the room every now and then to keep track of the men who appeared to be alone and who looked particularly over-served and/or creepy, ready to make an escape if they noticed me and decided to make an approach. There were a few of those, but for the most part, they stayed against the wall or in a corner, and everyone else seemed focused on their own group and excited for the show. The crowd reminded me of what I grew up seeing at amusement parks in New Jersey: big hair, flannel (yes, it was summertime, but it was summertime in Alaska), intricate manicures, concert t-shirts, liberal use of the seven dirty words from comedian George Carlin's famous list.

Eventually I noticed that a table slightly in front and to the right of me was particularly boisterous. This table was packed with twenty-something guys, most of whom had availed themselves of the beer selections at the snack bar. They did not seem dangerous or menacing, just upbeat and a little slurry, a bunch of armchair quarterbacks who had decided to bestow their powers of drunken analysis on this relatively new sports phenomenon.

Then the lights over the empty ring dimmed, shifting the entire venue from semi-dark to almost entirely dark. On this cue, the chattering crowd began to cheer, clapping and whistling in anticipation of the upcoming spectacle. The announcer spoke. "Welcome to Anchorage! Are you ready for some exciting MMA action?"

The crowd went crazy.

"We are pleased to present some of the hardest working fighters in the area, coming to us from as close as down the street and as far away as Vancouver and Washington State! Are you ready to get this party started?"

More cheers and whistles.

The venue went dark again, and the strains of a heavy metal song blared out from the loudspeakers, bass thumping in every chest in the room like a second, overbearing heartbeat. After a three-count, a spotlight appeared on the left-hand side of the venue, revealing a fighter standing in the doorway on that side. He wore a fighter's robe, hood covering his head and part of his face, and red satin shorts with a wide, elastic ribbed waistband. He was flanked on either side by his corner men, who were there to coach him during the fight and regroup with him during the breaks between rounds, feeding him sips of water and icing his neck to keep him cool. Those men kept to the side and a step behind as they walked the width of the room from the wall to the ring, ensuring the attention would fall on the fighter and seeming to like it that way.

As they approached the ring, one of the corner men busied himself with equipment: towels, a bucket, a water bottle, athletic tape, and ice. The other helped the fighter remove his robe and stood beside him while he engaged with the referee, who checked the fighter for a mouth guard and asked the fighter to demonstrate that he was wearing an athletic cup in a move sometimes described as the "jock knock."

The corner man held open the two middle ropes on one side of the ring to make a space through which the fighter climbed, stepping onto the battlefield he had probably pictured in his mind many times before. He ran around the inside of ring, throwing jabs at an imaginary opponent and then, when he had completed a circuit and returned to his corner, bouncing on the balls of his feet, swinging his arms, and slapping his face and body. His corner men kept up a steady patter, talking up to him from their positions on the floor while he nodded and bounced, keeping his eyes on the middle of the ring.

The room went dark again, accompanied by more hooting and screaming from the audience. Another spotlight shone, this time on the right side of the room, and this time falling on a different fighter, though one who was similarly built, who had the same goal in mind, and who was accompanied by a corner team of his own. Another song rang out, another thunderous backbeat assaulted the chest cavities of the assembled masses, and another procession started. This fighter savored his moment in the spotlight just as his opponent had done and took his own opportunity to parade around the inside of the ring. As he passed his opponent, the two bumped fists, a silent, "Props for agreeing to let me try to kick your ass."

The second fighter returned to his corner, turning his back to the center and his opponent across the ring. He draped his arms over the topmost rope as he received some last-minute coaching and encouragement from his corner guys, leaning down to hear them as they looked up at him from their positions on the floor next to the raised platform.

The announcer took the mic again. "Okay, it's time for some action! In our first matchup, in this corner, is a fighter from Fairbanks, Garrett D'Angelo[20]!"

There was a smattering of polite applause and some cheers, including a lone woman's voice screaming, "Kick his ass, baby!" The fighter stepped forward, punching the air and continuing to bounce up and down.

"And in this corner, a home-grown fighter from right here in Anchorage—Jerry "The Ogre" Kittering[21]!" The Ogre shadow boxed and then made the sign of the cross, kissing his fingers and looking heavenward.

More polite applause, a whistle or two, and then:

"The Ogre? Seriously? The *fuck*?" snorted one of the guys at the table to my right. "What a douche." His friends laughed and agreed.

"Haha. Totally."

"If that guy's an ogre, I'm a runway model."

"You are a runway model. A plus-sized one."

"Shut up, dummy."

I smiled a little to myself. This probably was not the time to remind those guys that, according to Theodore Roosevelt, it is not the critic who counts, but the man who is actually in the arena. I was kind of glad old The Ogre probably could not even hear his corner guys that well over the general sounds of humanity in the room, let alone the alcohol-fueled, derisive color commentary from the audience.

The fighters bounced up and down in their corners, watching the referee, who pointed at each of them in turn, asking them, "Are you ready to fight?" and then, when both of them had nodded, signaled that it was time to do just that. The crowd roared again as the fighters assumed defensive postures with fists protecting their faces, closed the distance between them, and began to wallop each other.

---

[20] Not his real name.

[21] Not his real name.

I, along with the rest of the audience, watched silently for several moments. I was reminded of my own striking experience, which is limited to the two years of Muay Thai I trained at the same place where I took my first jiu-jitsu class with Julian. In that case, "training" in Muay Thai entailed kicking, punching, kneeing, and elbowing a heavy bag sometimes and a set of pads that my partner held for me sometimes, neither of which ever struck back. I did "fight" in Muay Thai once, a single match against my friend Michelle that occurred during a regular class. Julian had decided it was time for those of us in the class, all relative beginners, to participate in a real bout and surprised us one day with the opportunity.

While I was waiting to fight Michelle, I experienced for the very first time the pure, naked panic that the anticipation of competing inspires in me and that I went on to spend countless hours and endless effort trying to tame. During our match-up, Michelle and I flailed at each other with our gloved hands and shin-guarded legs, landing tentative, wonky punches that injured us only in that they knocked our protective headgear around, requiring us to retreat at different times to readjust it so it was not blocking our vision. By the end of the match, two interminable minutes, my limbs felt leaden, I had to bend over and place my hands on my thighs to try to catch my breath, which was not forthcoming, and my chest felt fiery and full of something syrupy and mentholated. I coughed up that syrup for hours.

Both Michelle and I found that experience to be so traumatic that we joked after the fact about going to find some General Foods International Coffee and talking about our feelings. I had not yet learned how to compartmentalize, to view the same person as a friend one minute and a foe the next, depending on the context, and then to act accordingly. When Michelle and I were fighting, a filter dropped over my senses that turned everything suddenly very menacing and very serious. When she landed a shot, my kneejerk reaction was one of fury, both that she was able to penetrate my defenses and also that she would dare to try to hurt me in the first place. What the hell? When my aim was true, I gloated, feeling—no, *knowing*—I was the shit. It was not until the fight was over that I thought to worry about her well-being.

Neither of us had inflicted any damage because we were padded up and, as it turns out, awful at Muay Thai, but I was surprised and ashamed at how little I cared in the heat of battle about this person who was supposed to be my friend. Coming to terms with that, to be able to live with my contrasting feelings about Michelle, turned out to be as tiring as the physical demands of the fight had been. It did not happen overnight. As a competitor in straight jiu-jitsu, I have been uneasy about competing against my friends. As I have done it more, I have improved at living with the dissonance, and with recognizing that anyone who squares off with me on the mat is actually helping me by allowing me to discover how what I think I know about jiu-jitsu measures up to what I actually know.

Though I was not a great striker myself, I had observed enough halfway decent boxers and Muay Thai practitioners and had developed a good enough intellectual grasp of effective movement and positioning on the feet to feel confident in my assessment of the striking games of The Ogre and his adversary, which was that they were terrible. I observed wild punches, knees aimed toward Timbuktu, and elbows that looked to be more apt to incapacitate the person who threw them than the intended target.

The Ogre and his opponent swatted at imaginary flies. They performed double axels that would probably have scored them perfect tens if they had been on a skating rink. They kicked at sand that only they could see. They chest passed invisible basketballs into each other's torsos. They may even have hulaed—for the fences, of course. ("Swinging for the fences" is common MMA parlance for hitting as hard as you can, with the goal of finishing your opponent.)

What does Roosevelt know, anyway?

Then it happened. The fighters went to the ground.

I would like to be able to say that one of the fighters put the other one on the canvas with a precise, deliberate takedown that showcased elite skills. However, it would be more accurate to say that one of the fighters, The Ogre, appeared to trip and lose his balance, and the other one appeared to trip over The Ogre and fall on top of him.

Ooh, here we go, I remember thinking, choosing to ignore the writing on the wall. I always liked it when MMA fights went to the ground, because this is when fighters had to jiu-jitsu each other. I had a better sense of what I was watching. I liked it better. Maybe they would be better on the ground than they were on the feet.

They were not.

They hugged it out. They skidded across each other like bars of soap on a wet floor. They clamped on each other's heads like they were trying to crack open a lobster tail with their elbows. They stuck out their arms and necks invitingly, in a way that a more skilled grappler would have made them pay for. They went for submissions they had probably had the opportunity to practice a few times at most—this was made obvious by the space they left, enough to drive a truck through.

On one hand, I did want to side with Mr. Roosevelt. It takes serious stones to put yourself out there the way these guys were, not only testing your mettle against someone who wants to make sure your bloodline stops with you, but also leaving yourself open for ridicule from people like me and my rambunctious fellow audience members who probably could not do any better if they even had the guts to try. I know from years of experience that if you want to get good at something, you have to be willing to be terrible at it first, for a long time.

On the other hand, though, this was painful to watch. It reminded me of cringe comedy television shows like *The Office* and *Curb Your Enthusiasm*, which are designed to make viewers uncomfortable. In this case, there was no joke for anyone to be in on, no way to alleviate the discomfort. There was just earnest effort that fell far short of the mark. It was like settling in to watch a student film that had been touted as that person's magnum opus but then realizing you could see the zippers on the costumes and that the parts that were meant to be deadly serious were instead laughable. I started to wonder about the difference between pushing yourself and fooling yourself. Not every filmmaker was going to be Francis Ford Coppola. Should those also-rans, like me, continue to pursue their dreams for the sake of the pursuit, or should they consider finishing their degree or finally taking their in-laws up on that standing job offer in the family business? Was this display a necessary step in the evolution of martial arts into a more mainstream pursuit, or did it set the endeavor back several generations? Crap. Was this jiu-jitsu thing not going to work out for me? Oh God. What if I had to go back to work?

I was jolted out of my depressing reverie by my pals at the next table. "Stand those faggots up!" one of them yelled, his voice carrying into the next county. "Nobody wants to see two grown men hugging on each other. Let 'em duke it out!" His friends whooped and snapped their fingers in agreement, presumably because clapping would have required two hands, meaning they would have to put down their beers.

"Stand them up! Stand them up! Stand them up!" the Boy Scouts chanted, pounding the table on each word. Then the referee, as if obeying, did just that, calling time, instructing the fighters to stand and go to their respective corners, and then signaling the restart. A restart frequently happens when the action on the ground has ceased to be active. The referee will warn the fighters one or more times that they have to move, and then if they do not, will stop the fighters, instruct them to get to their feet, and square them off again. This can shake up the energy between the two fighters and jumpstart the action.

Within seconds, The Ogre's opponent threw a punch that connected, surprising the fighter himself probably as much as it did the spectators, hitting the sweet spot on The Ogre's jaw and causing him to crumple to the canvas. A collective "Ooooohhhhhhh!" went up from the audience, followed by shouts of "Finish him!" "Go! Go! Go!" and "Get him!" The Ogre's opponent jumped on top of him to administer a flurry of blows, but the referee threw himself between the two fighters, waving his arms to show he had decided in a split second that The Ogre was done for the day. One section of the audience went wild with claps and cheers. The fight was over. The same woman's voice screamed, "Yeah, baby! That's my baby!"

The Ogre stayed put, and his corner men rushed in to examine him. The other fighter danced around the ring, clenching his fists and yelling. He then ran over to check on his downed opponent, confirmed that he was going to be fine, and continued carrying on.

Presently, the fight announcer took the mic and cleared his throat. "Ladies and gentlemen, how about that for a fight, eh?" The crowd whooped. The frat table grumbled and chugged. I clapped halfheartedly. "And your winner is...Garrett D'Angelo!" The applause increased in volume as the referee raised the fighter's hand into the air and pointed at him. He danced around the ring some more, hugged his corner guys, shook the hands of The Ogre's team, and grinned wide.

By this time, The Ogre was stirring, being helped to his feet by his guys. A ringside doctor had checked his reflexes and his vision, had spoken to him and elicited some verbal responses, and had concluded that he was, if not good as new, at least capable of exiting the ring. His corner men threaded him through the ropes and lowered him to the floor level. Then they flanked him, draped his arms over their shoulders, and began to walk him out of the venue toward the door through which he had entered.

"Ladies and gentlemen, there is no fight without two people. Let's give it up for The Ogre for putting on a great show for us tonight!" entreated the announcer.

Before anyone else could say or do anything, a voice rang out. You can probably guess whose.

"The Ogre sucks!"

I was wholly absorbed, wanting to laugh and cry at the same time. I felt sorry for the Ogre, and at the same time, the situation was admittedly a little absurd. Sam Sheridan, author of A Fighter's Heart, explains why I might be so taken with the experience: "We are drawn to the spectacle of violence for hereditary, genetic reasons, but here, too, I think there is something more, and it's not easily accessible—you have to watch a thousand bad or mediocre or even good fights before you see one that is truly great, truly transcendent...Fight fans keep watching, hoping for the great one, that fight that transcends and becomes art."[22]

As Sheridan describes it, fighting enables fighters to access something primal in themselves, which in turn enables them to access something evolved. The spectator gets to experience that simultaneous expression of the profane and the sacred through the efforts of the fighters. It was Sheridan's articulate explanation that helped me realize I was attempting that expression in my own small way through jiu-jitsu.

I am sure my attempts put me about as close to transcendent as The Ogre and his partner. Andrew was right that what I saw at that amateur MMA event was pretty crappy, but Roosevelt was right too, that at least the competitors were trying, and maybe if they had read Sheridan's book, they would have seen themselves in the description. Maybe they would have decided they were willing to strive for transcendence even though the likelihood was low that they would ever achieve it. Maybe, like me, they couldn't not.

---

[22] Sheridan, S. (2007). *A fighter's heart: One man's journey through the world of fighting*. New York: Atlantic Monthly Press.

7

After my visit to Anchorage, I returned to Juneau and spent a little more time with Debbie and Shane before initiating another wistful goodbye, flying back "down south," as Alaskans refer to the lower 48 states. My car was right where I had left it in the Sea-Tac parking lot, and I was as happy to see it as if it were human. After pit stops in Seattle at Marcelo Alonzo's academy and Gracie Barra Seattle, it was time to saddle up again and head south, back through Washington, back into Oregon, and on into California. My next major destination was southern California, at the time probably *the* Mecca for Brazilian Jiu-Jitsu outside of Brazil.

The UFC had heightened the popularity of jiu-jitsu in the States, the weather in that part of the country was similar to what you would find in Brazil, and though the cost of living was higher, there were opportunities to make a living. These considerations brought many an actually *Brazilian* Brazilian Jiu-Jitsu black belt to that swath of land occupied by the counties of Los Angeles, Orange, Riverside, San Diego, and even Ventura, Santa Barbara, San Luis Obispo, and San Bernardino. Obviously some practitioners from Brazil had landed in other places. Otherwise I would not have had the opportunity to train with Carlson Sr. and Carlson Jr. in Chicago. In my jiu-jitsu-fevered imagination, though, "SoCal" had an academy on every corner, each one run by a larger-than-life grappling figure, each grappling figure sure to be the one to solve all the jiu-jitsu mysteries that were perplexing me. Who knows, maybe one of them would recognize in me my penchant for greatness, my destiny as a towering figure in the grappling world, whatever that meant, and make it his personal mission to help me realize my full potential. (Ego, please.)

Before I arrived there, when I thought "SoCal," I, like the east coast native I was, vaguely pictured Los Angeles County. That is where I landed, though I also became familiar with some of the surrounding cities and towns as well. I also assumed when I passed through Portland for the second time that I was much closer to SoCal than I was, forgetting that although on the east coast when you drive for six hours in any direction you have probably passed through six states, on the west coast when you drive for six hours in any direction, you have probably passed through six hours' worth of California. In other words, it took me far longer to arrive in SoCal from points north than I anticipated, though I did not mind.

My eventual arrival in Southern California was officially kicked off by my first ever trip to In 'n' Out Burger, where I was accompanied by tour guide Jimmy (forum name "Wutang"), a long-time devotee who lived and trained in Los Angeles, and fellow first-timer Chrissy ("Clinzy"), of "always bring a towel" fame. We met in the parking lot of a franchise somewhere in LA County before going in for taste testing. In 'n' Out Burger is a regional fast food chain, at that time located mostly in California and Nevada, that had been praised in story and song by many of my west coast forum acquaintances as the best burger chain in the country. I know of at least five guys who might think differently, but that being said, my double-double was pretty tasty. I was not as impressed with the fries.

Chrissy was in town for a work event. Brian ("Brain"), her husband, arrived later that day, so he did not get to share the In 'n' Out experience, but he did make it in time to attend a barbecue forum member Johnny ("Rude Boy Johnny") was hosting that coming weekend. He had invited any and all forum members who were in the area. By the time I left on my walkabout, we forum members had all invested countless hours in building our little online community, so the opportunity to see how the real people compared to their virtual personalities was too good to pass up.

Thus began my relationship with California, and, more substantively, my relationship with Brazilian Jiu-Jitsu in California, where I shifted my training into overdrive. I figured I would have to stay for two whole weeks to get in as much training at as many places as I wanted, as opposed to the day or two I had been budgeting so far at each stop on my journey. Two weeks eventually turned into six months, and on and on until five years had passed. Though I may not have become a Jedi Master of grappling during that time, I did find guidance from more than one Yoda. I cannot say exactly when I knew I was staying for longer than just a couple weeks, but I do know it had much to do with my introduction to New Breed Academy.

During our conversation at the barbecue, Chrissy invited me to come with her to a jiu-jitsu school in the area that she wanted to visit, which was in a small town in Los Angeles County called Santa Fe Springs. Like many of my jiu-jitsu friends, she was not going to let a work trip derail her training, and there was no shortage of academies in the area. Of course I was game to join her. She chose this place, New Breed, because it was under the umbrella of BJJ Revolution, the same organization that provided lineage to her own academy and her own instructor. (The California New Breed was the main academy location with which the affiliate of the same name in Portland was associated, at which I had trained earlier in the summer.)

BJJ Revolution was the brainchild of Julio "Foca" Fernandez and Rodrigo Medeiros, and between the two of them, they had created a bi-coastal affiliate organization, with Foca providing leadership on the east coast from Vermont and Rodrigo holding down the fort in San Diego. Chrissy and her instructors had rank under Foca, while Rodrigo was the instructor of the two black belts who ran

New Breed: Johnny Ramirez and John Ouano.

In a happy coincidence for me, both Foca and Rodrigo had been awarded their black belts years earlier by Carlson Gracie Sr. so this would be a sort of homecoming, or at least an opportunity for a game of "Do You Know?" We were all in the same extended jiu-jitsu family, so we had probably crossed paths with at least some of the same people, in addition to the Carlsons, of course. John was also the owner of Ouano International, a jiu-jitsu gear company. He and his employee, a young guy named Sean who eventually became a good friend of mine, ran the company from the back rooms of New Breed.

Chrissy and I planned to go to New Breed in the week following Rude Boy Johnny's party, after Brian had gone back home to Virginia and before she had to get to work. Class was mid-morning, so we figured we would be all right if we allowed an hour to take the roughly 25-mile trip to Santa Fe Springs, where the academy was, from the hotel in Pasadena where Chrissy's company had put her up and where Chrissy had in turn put me up. We decided to head east on the 210 and pick up the 605 at its northernmost point, which would take us south to the Telegraph Avenue exit. (I found it odd that Southern Californians referred to their highways with a "the." I eventually got used to it.) Turn left shortly after the exit onto Jersey Avenue, and the academy would be on the right. Easy peasy. Plenty of time, right?

"Welcome to LA, I guess," Chrissy said, craning her neck from the driver's seat of her rental car as she merged into the glacial, bumper-to-bumper traffic. We were going to be late. I knew this because I kept doing the math on how far we had to go compared to how much time we had to get there, wondering every time I glanced at the dashboard clock whether it was on the fritz given how quickly the minutes were ticking by.

"Yeah," I mumbled. "Where are all these people going?" We had just made it onto the 605, which meant we were at least 15 miles away. It was 30 minutes till go time, and we were not moving anywhere near 30 miles per hour, which according to my math was the slowest we would be able to go if we were going to get there on time, let alone early. This was not at all my usual M.O. There would be no casing of any joints today.

"Well, it is jiu-jitsu, after all. Chances are even if we're late we'll be early." As a subculture, Brazilian Jiu-Jitsu has historically been more than a little bit laissez-faire when it comes to time such that it is not uncommon for classes and events to start and end late, with "late" covering a broad spectrum.

"You're probably right." I was antsy anyway, and no matter what anyone said, that guy was driving like a moron.

The miles crawled, and the time flew. "Uuuuuuuaaaaaaaarrrrrrggggggghhhh! I hate this! And throwing a tantrum about it isn't fixing it!"

Chrissy laughed. "No, but it's amusing me."

"You're welcome!" I shouted. Then I went back to fidgeting.

By the time we turned onto Jersey Avenue, it was probably 20 minutes after the start time of the class. There were several cars in the parking lot, but the building, a short, squat, white brick affair with iron bars on the windows, sounded ominously quiet. "Should we bring our stuff in?" Chrissy asked.

"Let's go in first and see if we can even join the class," I said. Through osmosis in my travels, I had divined that it is not a bad idea, even in the "whenever" world of BJJ, to test the waters when you are late to class to see if the instructor is feeling magnanimous that day. Sometimes an irritated instructor might choose to make an example of a presumptuous student, particularly one who brought a sense of entitlement. A devil-may-care attitude about time was acceptable. A mentality of "You're welcome that I have deigned to grace you with my presence" was not, though there is a surprising amount of that, even and especially among lower belts. You can read it in people's body language as if they were shouting out loud.

If the instructor allows it, there will always be those people who come to class late accidentally on purpose so they can miss the warm-up and even sometimes the technique section of class because they "just want to get in some rounds." Those people are not late due to work obligations, like some people. They do not hurry to get on the mat like the other type of latenik. They walk in slowly and spend an eternity taping up and "stretching," because they do not want to do what the rest of the class is doing. I understand the allure of just wanting to roll around. Drilling can sometimes feel like work, and straight rolling usually feels like freedom, even if you are getting crushed, but how can you have any pudding if you don't eat your meat? Anyway, we anticipated New Breed would be friendly territory because of the familial connection, but we were still unknown quantities to them and did not want to come across as the entitled kind of late.

We got out of the car and both tried to position ourselves so the other person would have to go inside first. You would think that at this stage of my journey, after having visited a bunch of academies, I would not give a second thought to going inside. You would be wrong. Every entrance was stressful and intimidating, and that feeling has only increased as I have moved up the belt ranks. I still feel that way sometimes even when I go into places where I am a known quantity. It is that trepidation, every time, about facing the unknown.

I lost the jockeying contest and found myself leading the charge into the building. (Well played, Chrissy.) To my left was a half-wall, kind of like the wall that separates the kitchen from the dining area in some classic diners, beyond which I could see the mat space. Class was in full swing, with eight to ten guys in those familiar heavy pajamas doing jiu-jitsu, including one man wearing a black belt.

The other belts ranged from white to purple. In front of me was an entry room, and I went to stand at the reception desk, coming face-to-face with the impassive-looking guy seated at the desk. He looked up from a magazine when he saw us come in. He said nothing and did not smile.

Great. A real happy pants.

"Uh, hi. We thought we allowed enough time to get here

for class, but we ran into some traffic," I began, already over-explaining, "but we wondered if we could get on the mat anyway."

He stared at us, for what felt like many, many seconds. Just when I started to consider saying something else to fill the horrible silence, he replied, "It's up to John."

"Okay."

More silence as we continued our stand-off. Finally, I ventured, "Can we *talk* to John?"

He looked at us for roughly a skedillion seconds before slowly raising himself out of his chair and going to the wall across from the desk that had the window in it.

He leaned on the ledge and said, "Hey, John. Can these two train? They are late."

John came to the window while the students in the class continued to drill a takedown of some kind. He smiled at me and Chrissy and said, "Sure, come on, come on. Plenty of time! I'm John. I see you met Eben."[23]

---

[23] On April 19, 2015, between the time I completed the first draft of this manuscript and the time I went on to edit it into a second draft, a black belt in Brazilian Jiu-Jitsu named Eben Kaneshiro was taken into custody on child sex abuse charges involving a boy in Deschutes County, Oregon (http://www.oregonlive.com/portland/index.ssf/2015/04/update_portland_police_seek_in.html). Subsequently, on April 26, 2015, Eben committed suicide in custody (http://www.oregonlive.com/pacific-northwest-news/index.ssf/2015/04/martial_arts_instructor_accuse.html) while awaiting court proceedings. He left behind a series of notes indicating where authorities might be able to find information about additional victims (http://www.oregonlive.com/pacific-northwest-news/index.ssf/2015/04/portland_martial_arts_instruct.html#incart_river).

Eben Kaneshiro is the Eben described here. He was the first person I met at New Breed, and he was one of my coaches for several years thereafter. I knew, or thought I knew, Eben from the first day I walked into New Breed until the day he died. We had lost touch in the intervening years, but I, like everyone I communicated with after this news broke who had thought they knew Eben, had no idea he was capable of what he was accused of. This is probably a common refrain among people who thought they knew someone and then

It was yet another time I wished I could raise one eyebrow sardonically. Instead I cursed my genes and said, "Uh, yeah. He's quite the Welcome Wagon." I said it with a smile to

---

learn something about them that does not fit with what they thought they knew.

I will not presume to say that I "agonized" over rhetorical decisions involving Eben and this book. There are plenty of things legitimately to agonize about in this entire awful situation, and my story is not one of them. I did give some serious thought to the ramifications of mentioning Eben here. Regardless of what I thought I knew of him, the things he is accused of doing—that the evidence strongly indicates he did—are now the only things I can think of when I think of him. These are things I cannot fathom anyone doing, things I denounce. Things it was sorely tempting to distance myself from, by not including Eben's name in the book.

I did include him, and the reason is simple: To deny that I knew Eben would be a lie. Cynically, the grappling world is a small one, and it would not be too difficult for anyone so inclined to make the connection between me and him. The truth is that I knew Eben—or thought I did—and it is also the truth that the main concern in this situation is and should always be those people Eben hurt.

The fact that Eben turned out to be someone different from who I thought he was does not change the fact that the person I thought I knew was in my life during the time I was in California. I cannot change that, and I cannot change what he did, though if I had the choice, I would certainly change the latter.

I also decided to include mention of Eben in this narrative because, unfortunately, his story and his actions are not unique in the grappling world. The nature of grappling as an intensely physical, hierarchical, and aggressive activity makes it a prime environment for people at the top of this hierarchy to manipulate and exploit their students if they so choose. I am thankful that there are many in positions of power and respect in the BJJ world who strive to act with integrity and to use BJJ as a mechanism for good. I hope I fall in this category. It is incumbent upon those of us who are committed to using BJJ this way to do our part to identify and stop those who use jiu-jitsu as a mechanism for evil, and the first step is to talk about it.

blunt the sarcasm. Not that Eben seemed to notice.

"He doesn't mean anything by it. He's probably not awake yet! He's fun to train with, though, right Eben?" John pounded the window ledge.

Eben had resumed his seat at the desk. He did not respond. Instead, he pulled two white paper forms, which I knew from prior experience to be waivers, out of a hanging folder in one of the desk drawers. He placed them next to each other on the desk along with two pens. "Fill these out and sign them."

Chrissy and I leaned over the desk and each took a pen.

"Changing room," Eben continued, pointing toward his right, which was to our left, "bathroom," indicating the room two doors down from that, "entrance to the mat," which was farther down and to the left.

"Thanks," Chrissy said.

I said, "We have to go get our stuff. We'll be right back."

Eben looked at us, and then looked back at his magazine. If the novelty key chain that says, "You've Obviously Mistaken Me for Someone Who Gives a Shit" had been made into a person, it would have been made into Eben.

Chrissy and I exchanged glances. "Yeah. Thanks."

We suited up in record time and stepped on the mat, bowing before we approached John. I extended my hand and said, "Hi, I'm Val."

Chrissy said, "Chrissy," smiling and shaking John's hand as well.

"Welcome! Okay, here's what we're working on." John took us through the details of the single-leg takedown variation he had showed and that the other students were drilling. Chrissy and I gripped up with each other and started through the sequence as John kept chatting. "So, where are you from? Mike, keep your head up."

Chrissy and I exchanged glances, with Chrissy starting her response while looking at me and then turning her gaze toward John. "I live in Richmond, Virginia, and I train with Andrew Smith. We're part of BJJ Revolution on the east coast, but I'm in town for work, so I thought I'd look you guys up!"

John broke into a big smile and said, "Hey, that's great! I just saw Andrew a couple months ago. We had an instructor meeting out here at Rodrigo's place. Hector, you have to circle to the inside."

"Yeah, he came back with a bunch of fancy new tricks," Chrissy replied.

John looked at me. "How about you?"

I hesitated. "I'm kind of along for the ride," I began.

"Val is on a jiu-jitsu walkabout," Chrissy put in. "She has been driving around the country training jiu-jitsu all over the place."

I offered a small smile. "It's true. But my rank is under Carlson Sr. and Carlson Jr. I was living in Chicago right before I left on my trip."

"That's awesome!" John said. Then, more pensively, "I think about Junior a lot. It was so sad when we lost his dad."

I sighed. "I know. That's one of the things that prompted the trip. I guess I wanted to see as much as there was to see, jiu-jitsu wise, to make the most of it, you know? Now I want to stay in the area for a while so I can visit a bunch of places."

"Where are you staying? Pinch your knees!"

"What? Oh, *him*. Well, Chrissy has a hotel room in Pasadena through tomorrow, and I'm staying there with her. Then she leaves and then I'll probably get a hotel somewhere in the area."

"No, you should stay here," John said.

"Where?" I replied.

"Here. At the academy."

"Stay here?" I looked around. Reception area, mat, bathroom. Definite industrial and slightly bunker-ish feel, enhanced by exposed ceiling girders and bars on the windows that looked out onto the nearby residences, some of which sat behind thick white walls that were taller than my head. Strangers on every corner, most of them young, male, and Latino. Nary a thirty-something white woman to be seen, besides me and Chrissy—and Chrissy was leaving. Yet, I knew I would take John up on his offer.

"Sure. Johnny sleeps in that room off the reception area

and Sean stays in the back. You can have the couch." I remembered now that when Eben had leaned on the ledge to talk to John he had been standing to the left of a couch that sat along the same wall. "They won't care. There's no kitchen, but there's a shower and a TV, and a grocery store and all kinds of take-out right around the corner. Then you can train whenever you want."

I hesitated. "Well, that's really nice of you. I do have a sleeping bag, but I would like to train at other places too."

John shrugged. "I don't care. I doubt Johnny will either. If he does, well you can tell him I said it was okay. He's out of town for a couple days, but I'll tell him you're moving in!"

"Johnny's the other instructor here, right?"

"Yep. I also run Ouano International. Sean is another student here. He works for me too, and he and I hang out in the back. Okay, guys, water break." The students fist bumped their partners and headed for their water bottles, many of which were lined up on the window ledge, cracking jokes as they went.

"Wow, thanks, John!"

John patted my back. "You are welcome here." I could tell he meant it.

I looked at Chrissy. She opened her eyes wide and turned her mouth down at the corners as if she were trying to stifle a smile. "You're home!" she said.

We waited along with the other students for what was coming next, me probably more than anyone.

I survived my first night as a resident at New Breed, training that first evening in John's class—arriving unnecessarily early, of course—and meeting Sean, the blue belt John had mentioned, in the process. Then, around 10 or 11pm, after class had ended and most everyone had left for the evening, I showered, unpacked—which consisted of bringing my sleeping bag in from the trunk of the car and taking my dirty laundry out to it—and then lingered uncomfortably in the general vicinity of Eben and Sean, who were sitting on the edge of the mat shooting the breeze.

I wanted to be friendly but non-intrusive. They belonged here, while I had my nose pressed against the window. I needed to at least be able to get along with them.

I poked my head around the corner and waited for them to look up. They did. "I'm going to go get something to eat. You guys want anything?"

"No thanks," they both said. Eben added, "But if you want a suggestion, Yoshinoya is good and cheap. And they have good chocolate cake."

"Thanks," I said. "Do you live here too?" I asked him.

"Fuck no," he said.

Sean laughed. "Eben needs his time away from the gym."

"Don't we all," I said. "I have a feeling there isn't much privacy around here."

"What have you heard?" Sean demanded, though he was smiling.

"Oh, just a feeling I have," I said, smiling back.

"By the way," Eben said. "That couch. You're brave to sleep on it."

"What do you mean?" I responded, though I had the feeling I already knew.

Sean put in, "He wouldn't shine a black light on it, is what he's trying to say."

"Lovely," I said, disturbed, but also disturbed that I was not more disturbed. Bodily fluids—or the threat of bodily fluids, I guess—apparently did not have the same effect on me that they used to and that they probably did on those in polite society. The dirtbag was strong in this one. I had apparently become inured to some of the grosser effluvia the human body was capable of. When you spend enough time rolling around in other people's sweat, hair, band-aids, mucus, toenails, and even tears, doing so stops being disgusting and starts being some kind of normal. "Though I shouldn't be surprised. It's not like this is a tea party. Maybe I'll just wrap myself in plastic before I lie down."

I did make sure the sleeping bag was between me and the couch as much as possible, including my head, for the six months I ended up sleeping on it.

After that small but promising start, I met and worked on winning over more and more people at New Breed: students, parents, spouses. It had only been a couple days, but I had already fallen into a routine that persisted throughout the months I lived there: John came in around 9am each day yelling "Good morning!" and rapping gently on my forehead if I was still asleep. I usually was, because the guys were never in a hurry to leave after evening classes were over, so they shot the breeze in the reception area— MY bedroom—till all hours of the night. I learned later that most of the students had no idea I was staying at the academy, so they must have wondered why I was hanging around, screaming inside my head for them to go home so I could get some sleep. Particularly since Johnny turned out to be a night owl of mythic proportions, this usually happened around 3 or 4am, and sometimes even later.

In the mornings, which always came too soon, I rolled up my sleeping bag and stowed it in my car trunk, grabbing a granola bar or some dried fruit from the stash I kept there among the rest of my worldly possessions. I turned on my computer and dinked around, blogging or surfing, occupying my time until students started to trickle in for the morning class that started at 11am. Then, people who did not know me expressed interest in who I was, and people who did know me smiled and chatted. Sometimes, as I got to know them better, I went in the back and hung out with John and Sean as they busied themselves clothing the world in Ouano gear.

I finally met Johnny for the first time one afternoon in late summer 2006, several days after I had moved in to the academy. Eben sat at the desk. Vince, a purple belt and another fixture at the academy, was picking on me. A few stragglers were showering up and kibitzing after the morning class, and I sat in my place on the couch with my computer on my lap, trying and failing to ignore Vince.

"Haha, hey Eben," Vince said, starting in on me. "I told Val I was half Egyptian and half Italian, and she believed me."

Eben shot me his I-just-smelled-a-turd look, but I swore I saw more amusement behind it this time. "Are you blind or something? That dude is 100% Mexican."

"Yeah," Vince laughed. "She's all, 'Oh, that's so

interesting. Do you have family in either of those countries?'" He straightened his posture while he talked and then cracked up behind his hand.

"Hey," I shot back. "I just meet some guy and he offers up his ethnic heritage. How am I supposed to know? Even if I didn't believe you, I wasn't going to call you out on your own background. 'No, man, that's bullshit. You're going to have to prove it.' I was trying to be polite."

Everyone kept laughing, including me, Vince shaking his head and Eben sniffing his turd.

"Okay, fine," I said. "Congrats on being Mexican. Way to go. Nobody gives a crap."

"Are you mocking my ethnicity, Val? Oppressing me with your whiteness?" Vince asked, feigning hurt and indignation.

"Not right now, but I can get to it later. After class tonight?"

Vince smiled. Eben didn't frown. I felt happy.

Just then, the door opened to the room that sat between the changing room and the bathroom. A figure emerged, one I assumed was Johnny's. He had obviously just awakened. It was 3pm.

"Well, look who's up," Vince said.

Johnny wordlessly went into the bathroom.

"He's a real ray of sunshine in the morning," Vince said. "Even when the morning is almost dinnertime."

"This is the first time I'm laying eyes on him," I responded.

"Really? Wait till I tell him how dumb you are."

"Believe me, you don't need to. It's not like it's any big secret."

"So I've noticed."

"Shut up."

Johnny emerged from the bathroom.

"Johnny, this is Val," Vince said.

Johnny cleared his throat. "Yeah, I heard you were coming," he said in a voice rattly from sleep. "We're scheduled to go to R1 tomorrow and Tinguinha's the next day, and then maybe over the weekend we can hit Rodrigo's in San Diego."

I blinked. "What?"

"Well, John said you wanted to train in different places. I know people around here, so I made a few calls."

"Wow, really? You did that?" I was bowled over.

"I've been meaning to get out and visit some people. This will be a good excuse. We'll bring Vince. He needs a field trip."

"No way. I'm not going if Vince is going."

Johnny did not hesitate at all before replying, "I feel the same way, but we can't leave him alone here. He'll get into trouble."

I looked at Vince, smiling.

He nodded. "It's true."

I still marvel at how simply and matter-of-factly the people at New Breed took me in, allowing me to stay at the academy, including me in their excursions, teaching me jiu-jitsu. At first I stayed longer than the couple weeks I had been planning on because there seemed to be a never-ending list of academies to visit in the area, and after visiting a few, I decided I wanted to make some return trips. Eventually I stayed longer because I started to feel at home there, not in California necessarily, but at New Breed. Over the weeks and months I became more invested. I loved the training, the people were fun and welcoming, and the routine became predictable. This last was particularly enticing after my time on the road.

During the fall of 2006, Johnny, Vince, and I, along with other interested students, took field trips to numerous academies in the area. Depending on how far away a given school was, we woke up, found some kind of breakfast, left around 10 or 11 in the morning, participated in class, lingered to shoot the breeze with the instructor and have "lunch" at 4pm or thereabouts, and then endured rush hour traffic as we tried to get back to New Breed in time for Johnny to teach and for me and Vince to take the evening classes. I continued to be exposed to a variety of teaching styles and technique sequences, contributing to the pastiche of my jiu-jitsu education.

The difference, though, was that Johnny was now in the picture. He helped me make connections between what a given instructor was sharing and what I tended to do in my own rolling that I would not have seen on my own. Over a plate of grilled chicken and salad, or on one of the the highways en route back to New Breed in his car, he said things like, "That framing sequence we worked on today fits in with where you like to be in half guard. You tend to end up on your back, but you need to think about staying on one shoulder, and you can use that sequence to get there."

He did the same for Vince, and over time, I realized he was doing the same for everyone he taught, whether at New Breed or at the places we visited. I nodded dopily, recognizing how useful his insight was and wondering why I had not seen it myself. I saw a lot of dopey nods from a lot of students when he shared his observations.

Slowly but surely, Johnny became my coach. He became more familiar with my game, helping me do the same, and also helping me find language to explain and understand how I moved and why, where I capitalized effectively, and where my weaknesses were. We discovered that our personalities meshed in a way that supported that coach-athlete relationship. We developed genuine affection for each other, too, and yet were still able to snap into work mode when necessary. This means that sometimes I wanted to punch him, like when he delivered particularly difficult home truths ("Your stand-up is not where it should be") or made me drill again ("That was almost perfect but not quite"), but then he pulled me back from that brink by promising me that he could help me get to where I wanted to go ("Lots of people are in the same boat. We'll work on a couple go-to takedowns for you.") and actually following through or offering a perfectly-timed word of encouragement exactly when I needed it ("That way, Val. All day."). Much as my ego hated to admit it, Johnny was but the messenger, and I was lucky he was willing to deliver the message. What I did with it was up to me.

A la Allison and Claire in The Breakfast Club, I asked him on more than one occasion why he and everyone at New Breed were being so nice to me, a virtual stranger. His response? "Because you're here and you need it."

Over time, I became steeped in the environment of New Breed, to the point where I continued to visit other academies in the area, but now only every once in a while instead of every day. I kind of liked it where I was. Just like in any academy, there were loudmouths, quiet students whose calm demeanor belied the fact that they could systematically dismantle most anyone they faced on the mat, weekend warriors, precocious kids, gangly teenagers, know-it-alls who actually knew very little but said what they needed to in order to save face in their own minds when they got schooled. There were spouses and significant others—usually wives and girlfriends—who waited for their loved ones, there were weird smells and blue language, there was sweat and exertion, frustration and triumph, and people of all colors, both belt and skin. There was posturing, armchair quarterbacking after the latest UFC, supplements and recovery drinks, nicknames and arguments, some joking, some more serious. There was testosterone by the bucketful.

As the weeks passed, there was a growing acceptance of my presence, seeded by idle curiosity about what had caused me to appear and what was keeping me coming back, and fueled by my attempts to fit in and contribute. I slowly chiseled through the benign neglect I have seen so many seasoned grapplers show to so many would-be members of the inner circle, as with each day on the mat and each night on that dubious couch, it became clearer to everyone, myself included, that I was going to be staying for a while. Add to that the fact that I was in class every day, twice a day, save for the times when I went on field trips, and that when I was there I was working hard, and people started to see the writing on the wall.

There were multiple turning points, like those moments that accumulate to transform your work friends into your friend friends. I started to hang out with some of the New Breed denizens in between class, getting lunch here, tagging along for a movie there, though I always remained cognizant of the fact that a lot of these guys were kids—10 or more years younger than I, and, when they were not preparing for competition, interested in the stuff young guys are interested in. I am fairly fluent in young dude-speak, which contributes to the occasional existential crisis, but which helped me at the time. Still, I knew the boundaries, and I took calculated risks to ingratiate myself, building on the success I had had in ball-busting with Eben and Vince, though making sure never to cross the line into full-fledged Anybodys.

For example, there was John (different from John Ouano), also known as Big Ugly, one of the aforementioned loudmouths. This guy was formidable, dangerously smart, and angry at the world for real and perceived injustices. He routinely blamed me for the things that ailed him, with the percentages of serious to joking usually hovering around 60-40. After we had gotten to know each other better, I teased him about the fact—and it was pretty much a fact—that he could not stand that he could stand me, and that he actually grew to like me. He never denied it, choosing instead to deflect the conversation toward my background or my education (though I did not tell him, somehow he found out about where I had gone to school and for what), and for as long as I was at New Breed, he reminded me that my status was precarious, tapping his nose in the international symbol for "snob."

The first time I met him, he was complaining about his nickname, which was apparently new, but had apparently stuck. I said, "I agree with you. Big Ugly is a terrible nickname for you."

"See? Thank you," he said, exasperatedly looking at the assembled group, which had just been busting him about the name.

"You're really not that big," I finished. Everyone laughed as he flashed me a look that, true to form, was about 60 percent murder and 40 percent respect.

In the interest of full disclosure, I have to admit that Big Ugly busted me as often and as effectively as I did him, and usually better, but I will never cop to it when he is within earshot. Not when he used to say things to Johnny like, "Hey, man, this chick is disruptive. You should kick her to the curb.

Why are you letting her stay here?"

Fortunately for me, Johnny replied, "Because she keeps coming back."

I remember a conversation I had with a friend who is a formally educated pianist. During her undergraduate years, she was spending four and five hours a day playing, and more than that thinking about playing and structuring her rehearsal time. Listening to music. Discussing piano with her friends and colleagues. As a result of that attention to her art, her playing was sharp. It was on point. She was acting and reacting effectively, and she also felt she was improving quickly. In other words, she was doing what she needed to in order to be the best she could be in light of the amount of natural talent she had been given combined with her existing level of experience.

This is how I started to feel with my training, which, of course, was the reason I was at New Breed. I was not better at jiu-jitsu than the people who had more experience than I did, and, painful though it is to admit it, the fact is that no matter how much time I invest, my innate ability level limits how good I can get.

At that time, though, when I was training regularly with the tutelage I got from Johnny and John and the feedback I got from the guys who were becoming my regular training partners and therefore learning my game, I came closer to being the best purple belt Val it was humanly possible for me to be. My timing improved, as did my ability to capitalize on opportunities made available by others' mistakes or their own infinitesimally slower timing. Since I was so steeped in training, there were always things I wanted to work on, both offensively and defensively, so I got smarter about how to take advantage when there were opportunities to drill on my own. I started to distinguish between types of rolls and types of training. I learned different speeds and how to manage my energy better. I learned that I did not have to fight as if my life depended on it in every session, though of course that was necessary sometimes. It is a combat sport, after all, but I became better able to appreciate the value of different intensity levels and different purposes for a given training session. My understanding of jiu-jitsu expanded and became more sophisticated. Now that I, the student, had become ready to do this, it was clear the teachers had appeared.

Each passing day brought with it opportunities for me to "leave my ego at the door," which is a central tenet of the Brazilian Jiu-Jitsu mentality. The idea is that any jiu-jitsu practitioner must be willing to be humbled on a regular basis. We can only improve at what we are first willing to be bad at, and at every training session I discovered another aspect to jiu-jitsu that fit the bill. I spent hour after hour absorbing instruction and critique from people who, it was not lost on me, were often significantly younger than I and who probably did not give a crap about what I had accomplished in the for-profit, proprietary education field. They knew more than I did about the thing I wanted to excel at. Further, though I was not fully divested of the markers of my professional life, they had receded far into the background, as they had no relevance here. The replacement, my identity as a full-blown grappler, was slow in coming and felt awkward and clumsy as I painstakingly built it piece by piece, technique by technique, epiphany by epiphany.

One major hole in my game was take-downs. As its name implies, a take-down is a sequence of movements one partner employs in order to take the other partner off his or her feet and bring the action to the ground. In the academy, training with a partner frequently starts from the knees due to space considerations, but in competition, opponents square off on the feet. This means that, while there are ways around it, a solid take-down game, both offensively and defensively, is important for the would-be competitor as well as anyone who wants to have a well-rounded understanding of jiu-jitsu.

I had neglected my takedown education prior to landing at New Breed, through my own laziness and my belief that since I was not going to be competing, I did not need to focus on it. At New Breed, though, it was impossible to avoid working on takedowns. I told myself it was good for me.

Among other things, I practiced a wrestling move called "running the pipe," hating every minute at first because, for a full month I could not execute it, not even on a non-resisting partner. I struggled and strained, clutched onto my various partners' legs, leaving them standing on one foot while I tried to apply irresistible pressure to their hips, forcing them to sit to the ground. While I wrenched and pulled, drove my shoulder down and spun in circles, my partners regarded me the way a cow might a passing car, standing stock still or hopping emotionlessly with no indication that they were even a little off balance, and reporting in response to my questioning that no, they did not feel the pressure on the hip that would force them to the ground, in fact they did not feel much of anything, Goddammit. (Blasphemy mine.)

Then, as if by magic, on a fateful day more than a month after I first tried, I hit one, watching my partner go down but not believing my eyes. When I asked my partner, he confirmed that yes, he had been forced to go to the ground and had not just fallen down to be nice. Of course, he had also not been resisting at all, and as with most things jiu-jitsu-related, the more I learned about running the pipe, the more I realized how little I knew about running the pipe, but hey, baby steps.

I learned that, not coincidentally, takedown instruction at New Breed went hand-in-hand with discussions about competition strategy. Here in SoCal, where there were many jiu-jitsu academies per capita, there were also many local, regional, national, and international tournaments, which provided many opportunities for grapplers in this area to throw their hats into the ring. Part teaching to the test, and part recognition that a solid set of takedown skills is a vital component of a well-rounded game, most of the classes at New Breed started with some kind of judo or wrestling practice before we worked technique on the ground. This had been the case at many of the other schools I visited as well. There was also always talk about progression, progression, progression. How could a practitioner advance position off a takedown? When we ran the pipe, for instance, we were instructed to establish the takedown and then immediately think about how to maintain the upper hand we had created by directing the action to the ground and ending up on top, building on it to increase the likelihood of scoring and, in an ideal world, pulling off a finish. In this way, I started to learn the languages of competition, both the spoken and the physical, though I had no intention of competing myself. I had competed once or twice as a blue belt and told myself it "wasn't for me." It was not competing that was not for me, though. It was putting myself in a situation that scared me that I had no interest in. I just did not yet recognize it as such.

Because I was game, and because I was proving myself to be dependable, during the fall of 2006 I started to help other New Breed students prepare for competitions, adding myself to the warm bodies that came in fresh and helped to push to their limits the students who were getting ready, a la the gauntlet I observed back in Kansas. These gauntlets did not scare me, however. Or rather, they did not scare me in the same way. I never worried for the safety of the people pushing themselves because I intuited that, young though some of them were, these were experienced coaches who knew when to call a timeout. Rather, I felt a sense of foreboding when I participated in these gauntlets because the thought of being on the receiving end was enough to make me wish for an adult diaper and a Lorazepam.

Regardless, it did not take long before Johnny said to me, "You should think about competing. You have been working hard, and I think you'd do well against some of these girls who are at your level."

"Nah," I said. "Competing isn't for me."

Johnny shrugged, but I could tell we were not done with this conversation.

A funny thing happens when you work closely with people to prepare them for something like a competition: You start to become invested. You become protective of them while doing everything you can to jiu-jitsu the crap out of them, and you realize these are two sides of the same coin. You start to strategize, as well as you can given your

195

skill and experience levels, about their games, and you start to check in on their mental state to see if you can help them get to where they need to be in order to bring it to training. I started attending the competitions I had helped my new teammates prepare for, wanting to support them and see how they did. I noticed just how many tournaments there were in SoCal, at least one within driving distance almost every weekend, it seemed. SoCal had also become the permanent home of two major international tournaments: the PanAmerican of Jiu-jitsu and the Mundial (which means "world" in Portuguese).

Run by the IBJJF, these tournaments had been going on for many years in Brazil and had in recent years relocated to the States. Winning a gold medal in them conferred bragging rights of the highest order. My performances at the PanAms as a blue belt had been nothing to write home about, but I knew even then that the competition itself was a relatively big deal.

It is when I started attending tournaments that the questions started in earnest. "When are you going to join us, Val?" "Ever get the itch to jump in yourself?" I smiled and shrugged it off. The tournament promoters, always hungry for female competitors in those days, said things like, "We've got some tough girls, and we'd love to have you participate." At the mention of "tough girls," my stomach clenched and I said lame and vague things like, "Oh, I don't know. I've got my hands full just training." Every now and then, Johnny would catch me watching matches intently, or asking one of the guys how he dealt with nerves, and when I saw him looking, he would smile. I would roll my eyes and say something like, "Don't get any clever ideas, pal," and he would smile some more.

I do not know exactly what changed my mind about competing, but I think it hinged on a few things that combined to tip the balance. The first one was something a friend of mine has always said, and which has become a mantra I try to live by: She makes her decisions about her life out of love, not out of fear. She strides toward instead of shying away. Whenever we discuss this, I am reminded of

Doug Hastings, a character in the spectacular movie *Strictly Ballroom*. At a pivotal moment in the film, Doug shouts a game-changing line to his son, Scott, whom he is trying to encourage to dance the way he (Scott) wants to instead of following rules he finds stultifying. Doug yells, "We had the chance, but we were scared. We walked away. We lived our lives in fear!" Both in my mind and in the movie, the last line reverberates a little.

It was becoming more and more evident that I was refusing to compete *not* because it "wasn't for me," but because I was petrified of it. I was definitely shying away, not striding toward. When pressed, I could not come up with a plausible reason to explain why I was not competing, and eventually it dawned on me that everyone knew I was being lame except me. They were just being nice about my lameness—they did not for a second believe that I "just didn't need to compete." Gah. Now, writing those words, which I used to say with such abandon, makes me squirm with awareness. Eventually it dawned on me that I was afraid, plain and simple, and, as always happens when I realize that I have to do something that scares me until it no longer scares me, at some point in there I probably thought to myself, "I have to fricking compete, but only after I spend some time in the fetal position."

Another thing that prompted me to drag myself onto the competition train was my need to back up my claims that I was dedicated to my jiu-jitsu education. There are plenty of people who never compete, and it is possible to become very good at jiu-jitsu that way. However, there is evidence that competing helps you improve more quickly. Further, being an effective competitor also requires the development of a skill set that is distinct from straight jiu-jitsu acumen, though of course it is related. It includes skills like focusing on the task at hand and blocking out extraneous stimuli, listening for the sound of your coach's voice and taking corresponding action, regulating your own state of arousal (preventing the dreaded adrenaline dump) and mental preparedness (controlling anxiety—a big one for me). I got to the point where I had to concede that, hey, dummy, you chucked it all for jiu-jitsu. You have a chance to pursue it all. You have people who can help you, you have competitions coming out your ears, and the only kind of person who would not see this as an amazing opportunity and jump on that noise is a chickenshit chicken person—a person who lives her life in fear.

There was a third thing that probably contributed to my reluctant change of heart: If I am being completely honest, proximity to the people, energy, and spectacle of competition started to get me a little fired up. My friend Natasha, the one who had broken the news to me about Carlson Sr.'s passing, and who competed quite a bit in the years we trained together, used to joke about how she liked competing because she "had an anger inside that can't be taught," and she could funnel that into her matches. That was never my thing.

I remember the very first time I competed I was just so happy to meet other women who trained that in a split second I had decided my opponent and I would become friends and support each other in the trials and tribulations of the woman who has chosen the jiu-jitsu path. I had kind of forgotten that we were going for all the marbles. In the next split second, as this opponent-who-was-not-my-friend rushed at me with the force of a rabid kangaroo, I realized that I might not live past the next five minutes, and that if I did, she might try to finish me off later in the parking lot. I should have known from the sour expression on her face that she was not interested in camaraderie.

I, on the other hand, did not have a deep reservoir of anger or frustration at the world to draw upon. My anger and frustration were saved for me. I did start to notice that there was something about competing that was compelling to me, though, some twitch I got when I watched my teammates putting it out there that made me want to try it. It was the same mechanism that had prompted my flustered indignation when Michelle dared to kick and punch at me in my one and only Muay Thai "fight." It became a buzzing sound in my brain that I found highly disturbing but that I could not push out of my mind. When I realized this, I sighed, said "Goddammit" a couple more times and went to Johnny.

"Ok, you win. I'll compete," I said. I swallowed bile and frustration and dread.

When he realized I was serious, he hugged me and said, "All right, now we're talking!" He looked at me with the same expression Rocky gives Adrian in *Rocky II* when she wakes up from the coma and says, "There's one thing I want you to do for me...Win. Win!"

From that moment, my life became a montage of chicken chasing, meat punching, and raw egg drinking. I may even have run all the way across the country to the City of Brotherly Love and sprinted up the steps of the Philadelphia Museum of Art. I also did a lot of panicking. That last started immediately after I spoke the words, and drowned out Johnny's excited chatter such that I only caught bits and pieces: "schedule...dial in your diet...drilling...minutes of takedowns a day...practice tournaments...prepare for the bigger ones..."

Ones.

Ones?

Oh God.

Ones.

8

Training at New Breed gave me a grappling home once again, as well as the opportunity to improve my jiu-jitsu. As summer turned to fall and I realized I was done traveling for the foreseeable future, I threw myself into training with even more vigor than I thought I had in me. Before too long, participating in "two-a-days" and adjusting to the increased demands of preparing for competition started to affect me physically and mentally.

First and foremost, my increased training schedule put me directly in the path of a bullet I had previously dodged for many years: After I had maintained my new, more intense New Breed schedule for a few weeks, my right ear slowly became sore and squishy as it filled with fluid. Much as I tried to pretend it was not so, I was getting cauliflower ear.

Cauliflower ear is a condition caused by undue rubbing or other trauma to the cartilage of the ear. Frequently, the trauma can disrupt the blood flow to the affected area, forming hematomas. If the ear is untreated, the cartilage can fold in on itself and become deformed as it heals. Wrestlers, football players, and rugby players, as well as grapplers, are prone to it because their ears are also subjected to grinding, twisting, and other sorts of traumatic physical contact, usually with other people's body parts and rough clothing. Many of these folks actively cultivate their cases of The Ear by training hard, rubbing the ears in various ways, not draining the resulting fluid, and even making a point of getting punched in the ear—or of punching others there. They are trying to identify with the grappling lifestyle, and displaying The Ear is one of the quickest, most prominent, and most permanent ways to display that connection. The "cauliflower" part of the name is just one option that could accurately have been chosen, because on most people I know, the condition looks more like a fist or a lima bean. At any rate, I was not one of those people who wanted any sort of ear disfigurement, so when it started to happen to me, I took action.

One night after the evening class, I could no longer deny that my right ear was sore and swollen and filled with fluid. It had been bothering me the entire training session, though I tried to ignore it, and I realized I had to take care of it. I had acquired some syringes, which are relatively easy to procure in a grappling environment because while some people do cultivate The Ear, others are as interested as I am in keeping it to a minimum. I had most of the necessary equipment, but I was lacking the most important piece: the stones. I could not bring myself to act as both doctor and patient, being neither a fan of needles nor confident in my ability to keep my hands steady. So, that night, post-training, while non-jiu-jitsu people from my past were probably tucking their children into bed or painting the town red with their significant others, I asked the guys who were lingering at the academy, shooting the breeze after class, whether any of them would be willing to stick a needle into my ear and remove whatever was in there that was making it squishy and painful. Jason, one of the students at New Breed, readily volunteered.

"Okay, let's go over here," I said, moving from the mat to the entry room.

I perched distractedly on the chair located next to the desk in the entryway. It was against the same wall as the entrance, and when I sat in it, my right elbow rested on the desk. My knee bobbed up and down as I agitated my foot nervously. My ear throbbed and my heart pounded. I do not like needles.

Jason tore open the packaging of a syringe and examined the needle. I tried to avert my eyes, just like I always did when I donated blood or had to give samples at the doctor's office for testing. The needle looked big. Like, many gauges. Jason put on a pair of purple latex gloves, knelt down next to me, and flashed me a huge, shit-eating grin. I pooched my lips out and furrowed my eyebrows as I cleaned my entire ear with an antiseptic wipe and tied back my hair.

"Ready?" Jason said, a bit too gleefully for my taste. In response, I took a deep breath, pressed my eyes shut, and squeezed the armrests of the chair.

"Just get it over with," I said.

Jason had a pretty big target to aim for. The top part of my ear, just under the ridge on the inside, had given rise to a macaroni shell-sized, viscous lump that was painful to the touch. His job was to aim for the heart of the lump and use the syringe to remove the fluid inside that was causing the viscosity. Aim he did. He did not have the same misgivings about Makeshift Plastic Surgery for Dummies that I did, probably because it was not his ear. I felt a pinch as the needle struck home, and a weird pressure-y sucking sensation as Jason, in a skillful-seeming manner, filled the syringe once and then twice with yucky, thick yellow fluid. As the syringe filled the first time, the guys who had stayed behind to see the show crowded around to get a closer look, grossed out and fascinated in equal measure.

"Sick, Val!"

"It looks like snot!"

"Lemme see!"

"How much is in there?"

"Dude, that was in your ear meat?"

It probably goes without saying that at least two or three of the guys pretended to drink the drained fluid, directly from the syringe, and since I was not paying the closest of attention, it is possible that at least one of them succeeded. I do think most of it went directly into the bathroom sink. That is my hope at least. I regarded my tender, deflated ear in the mirror and poked gently at the visible hole where the syringe had gone in and from which fluid was still slowly oozing out. I soaked it up with a paper towel from the academy bathroom.

Once the oozing had stopped and it appeared some kind of proto-skin had started to grow back over the hole, I clamped a piece of SAM splint onto my ear to keep it from filling back up, as cauliflowered ears are wont to do, wincing as the pressure from the splint squeezed my ear. A SAM splint is a thin sheet of spongy material attached to a thin sheet of metal, the idea being that due to the metal you can bend it around ears, among other things and it will keep the shape you have put it in, but due to the sponge it will not be too uncomfortable. Both premises are somewhat faulty, but that is probably more because of my lack of coordination than because of the nature of the product.

In the leaky aftermath, I thanked Jason for his handiwork. "You must be an old pro at this, eh?"

"Oh no," he said. "I've never done it before."

What concerned me is that I was not more concerned about that, as evidenced by the fact that I had Jason perform at least one or two more ear procedures on me in the next few months, when my right ear flared up and when my left ear decided it wanted attention as well. That night, post-op, I tossed and turned because my ear kept throbbing. I laughed yet again at the state of my life. I spent the next couple weeks of class wearing headgear, the kind wrestlers wear, and of course I kept training.

Over the next few months, I continued to live in the New Breed fraternity house, sharing space with a rotating cast of temporary roommates who were friends of friends or who were passing through and trained elsewhere in the country or the world, though Johnny and Sean were fixtures like me. Then, when the lack of privacy and the late hours finally got to me, I made a big-for-me commitment to stay in California indefinitely. I found a one-room apartment in nearby Whittier that was equipped with a Murphy bed and a kitchenette, renting it on a month-to-month basis. While that gesture did not exactly indicate that I was pledging my troth, it did make a statement—to myself and to the guys at New Breed—that I was less of a flight risk. In fact, in December of 2006, when I left California to drive back across the country to Florida so I could spend the holidays with my family, I stopped in Chicago to see friends and to talk to Carlson Jr. I had gotten his blessing to take my jiu-jitsu road trip earlier that year, and he gave me his blessing again, this time for me to cast my lot with New Breed officially, which meant that John and Johnny took over promoting me through the rest of the belt ranks.

This was a very big deal in the jiu-jitsu world, to move to a different academy, even on the up and up. It was a bittersweet conversation, with Carlson Jr. saying I had to do what I had to do, but with both of us feeling sad because of what me doing what I had to do signified. It was the beginning of something exciting, yes, but it was also the end of something precious. It was situations and people like this that made me wish Chicago was still the right place for me, but I felt I had work to do in California.

Work I did, when I got back to California in early 2007. I spent the year becoming ever more steeped in the competition scene, even competing in places as far away as Turkey and actually meeting with some success. The fear stayed with me, though, throughout 2007 and on into 2008. That January, activity at New Breed kicked into overdrive as those of us who cared to started preparing for the PanAms and the Mundial. Some of my competition anxiety was focused on these tournaments because I knew I would be participating in them, but most of it was aimed at the more immediate competition-focused training sessions at New Breed.

During that time we continued to have regular class, but for those of us preparing for these tournaments Johnny also reinstated the periodic sessions he sometimes ran that were more competition focused. These were the sessions I had begun to help out in earlier in my stay at New Breed, but now it was time for me to be one of the people getting forged in the fire. One day post-holiday season, in one such class, Johnny decided to teach very specifically to the test.

"Okay, guys. The PanAms and Mundials are not that far away, and there are a bunch of smaller tournaments coming up that we can use for practice. So here's what's going to happen today. You're starting from the feet, with only one pair going at a time. I will referee and your teammates will coach you. Each of your matches will go for regulation time for your division, and you will get that amount of time to rest in between."

A blue belt broke in. "I don't understand that timing. Can you explain?"

"All right, take you for example. You're a blue belt, adult division, so your IBJJF matches are five minutes long. That means your training matches in this class will be five minutes, so you can feel how much time you have to get your work done and how long you need to be able to make your energy last. Then you get five minutes to rest, and then you go again. In the actual tournament, you may have more time to rest between matches, but the more you win, the fewer people there will be, so there will be fewer people in the bracket to get through. You will always get the duration of one of your matches to recover before you have to fight again, though. Think about it this way: If you only get five minutes, that probably means you're close to gold!"

The blue belt blinked, trying to understand. I knew how he felt.

"Every time we do this, each person will do five matches," Johnny continued. "Some of you may have fewer than that at the actual tournaments, depending on the number of people in your division, but it's not likely that you'll have many more. We can keep track of the event registration and adjust closer to when the tournaments happen if it looks like anyone will have more than five matches for gold. The point is, you'll have to turn it on and off. Regulate your energy and your focus. This is all part of it, guys. It's not just how well you do jiu-jitsu. It's how well you play the rules, pace yourself, all that stuff. Pay attention to all of it."

In the short time I had been regularly attending

tournaments to support fellow New Breeders, I had rarely, if ever, seen a women's division big enough to result in more than two or three matches for the opponents. The PanAms and Mundial were bigger of course, but even so, for me, completing five matches was likely an example of being as prepared as possible and then some. After Johnny's explanation, I assumed the pencil-dropping position I had spent so much time in when I told my realtor I wanted to sell my condo, though I was able to pass it off as stretching. It seemed long ago.

"Now that competition season is starting, we're going to do this kind of training from now on during this class, so we'll be able to get everyone the same kind of prep. This time, we're going to have two of you in the hot seat. Val, and Vince, how about you? You're both purple belts, so we can do seven-minute matches. You'll take turns going and resting."

Crap. I had started staring intently at the mat as soon as Johnny started speaking again, more interested in not being selected than the kid who has not done the homework. Why do people persist in looking away in an attempt to make themselves invisible? It does not work.

Vince nodded in agreement. Johnny looked at me, waiting for a response. I nodded. "Okay."

"Okay?"

"Okay." Louder this time, with conviction I did not feel.

"Okay. Let's take a water break guys, and then we'll get going."

For Vince, this was another day at the office. He had wrestled throughout high school and college—in California, a state whose wrestlers consistently ranked among the highest in the country. Those in the know will understand how much better equipped this made him to handle the stresses of jiu-jitsu competition than someone like me, who had no such experience.

This session was going to be a walk in the park for him, at least in terms of the mental aspect. For those who do not understand, watch a wrestling match. Imagine yourself being one of the wrestlers. Notice the intensity, the surroundings, the expectations and eyes on you, and by extension, the judgment. It is easy to say you do not care what other people think until you are surrounded by people who have nothing to do but watch as you try to be good at something. Vince had done this every day in practice, every week in competition, throughout high school and college, working his weight-cutting ass off for years to improve. He barely noticed any of these stimuli anymore, so experienced was he at filtering out the extraneous ones.

For me, on the other hand, this whole scenario was another threat to my control over all my marbles. Yet again, I wished I had started jiu-jitsu earlier and that I had worked my stand-up much, much more. Then I wished I would get struck by lightning. Johnny came up to me.

"We can get someone else to go this time if you want," he said.

"You're killing me," I said. "Yes, I want that."

He smirked, but not unkindly, and waited.

"What are we waiting for? You know I'm going to do it. In fact, I'm going first," I snapped, like the pre-teen I was channeling.

He looked at me for a moment longer, saying, "Okay guys, bring it in!" Then he turned to the group. "Val's going first. Kevin, I want you to go with her. Vince, you're warming up, and Paul, you're going to go with Vince after Val's first round. Everybody else, you're coaching, keeping time, and keeping score, and remember, you're on deck. In fact, James, you're with Val next, and Roberto, you're with Vince after that. Got it?"

Everyone nodded. I moved toward the middle of the mat, shrugging my shoulders, rotating my fists, and lifting my knees up and to the side one at a time to get the blood flowing throughout my body, because it felt like it had pooled in my feet, leaving me lightheaded.

In the limited experience I had gained in competition, I knew these things actually did help me loosen up and prepare for battle, but when I did them, I still felt the way I had when I first started doing them: like I was still on book in a big stage production. The alternative was for me to stand

and wait, slack-jawed and tense, so I went through the motions.

Kevin was a blue belt, in his late teens, taller than me and thinner. We were probably about the same weight. He and I had always had fun rolling together, and over time he had overcome his natural shyness, so I considered us pals. This was the first time we were being pitted against each other in a "real" competition situation, though. Normally we just played, and even if things got intense, it was not on display the way it would be here. I could feel ambivalence, sour in my throat. I did not want to lose, but I did not want to have to grind Kevin down to win, if I got the chance and he fought it. I suspected he felt the same way. I flashed on my one Muay Thai "match" with Michelle. This was not going to be a friendly roll.

Kevin and I faced each other in the middle of the mat. Johnny stood between us as if he were the officiant in a motley commitment ceremony. I could not tell if Kevin was nervous, and then I realized my mind was wandering and I needed to focus.

Johnny put a hand on each of our shoulders and reiterated the rules. "Seven-minute match, starting from the feet. All the rules for your division apply, so only straight ankle locks below the waist. If the match goes the distance, we'll figure the points. Submission stops the match. Capisce?"

We both nodded. I stole a glance at Kevin to discover he was stealing a glance at me. We smiled tiny, shy smiles, and then at the same time, we stopped smiling and went impassive. Johnny started the timer, and at the dingdingding, we were off.

Kevin and I circled each other warily, making sure not to cross our feet, but instead doing a step-glide, step-glide, all the better to maintain our balance. He reached a hand out to make a grab for my collar. I side-stepped and reached for his sleeve. He re-grabbed my sleeve and used the grip to find the lapel with his other hand, immediately swinging himself down to the mat, landing on his right hip and pulling me into his half guard, so named because he trapped just my right leg, instead of both of my legs, between his legs.

I was comfortable here. For some reason, I frequently ended up in many partners' half guard when I was rolling, so I had learned how to settle in and make it work for me. From his back, Kevin tried to control my hips with his legs while keeping my torso and arms at bay, but I swiveled my arms and my chest to bypass the frame he was making with his hands and arms. I managed to get chest-to-chest contact, trying to stay heavy, and then I fished my arms in for the crossface/underhook, where my left arm cradled his neck and my right arm scooped up under his left arm. I needed to keep this underhook as a way to prevent Kevin from getting up on his right side and moving around to my back.

Kevin continued to try to make space and to switch the underhook so that his left arm was under my right arm, and I continued to try to keep the close contact I had established. I had a "go-to" sequence from here, known as an arm triangle, which is a choke that traps the arm and the head of the person being choked inside the arms of the person doing the choking. I began to set it up. Our heads were close together at this point, and I could hear us both breathing heavily. I tried to breathe in through my nose and out my mouth.

The first thing I needed to do to set up the arm triangle was to put my forehead on the mat between Kevin's right arm and his torso so I could start using my head to force that right arm above his head, eventually notching his bicep and shoulder under his chin and using my head to eliminate space. I moved my left arm out from under his neck and pinned his right wrist to the mat with my left hand at a 45-degree angle from his head. I put my forehead in the space I had created so he would not be able to close it off again by bringing his arm to his side. Kevin had other ideas, and he tried to push his arm lower. I angled my pressure out toward his elbow, where he was weaker, and soon his arm went up and folded itself in toward his face.

Then I moved my right arm from under Kevin's left arm and shoved it under his neck. I clasped my hands together, keeping my head tight against his right triceps. Then I moved my head closer to his right arm, pushing it further into his neck, tightening the noose. Breathing in through my nose and out through my mouth. Listening to his breaths become quicker and shallower as he became more and more trapped—and more and more aware of it.

I worked on freeing my right knee from his guard, piking on my feet, elbows, and forehead. I turned my hips to my left, which turned my right knee in the same direction, and I slid my hips to the ground next to Kevin, using the weight to free my foot, all the while trying to maintain constant pressure on his head and arm with my arms. I turned back and put additional pressure on Kevin, closing off the blood to his brain with the pressure of my arms and chest, forcing him to tap.

"Time!" Johnny yelled.

I let go and separated myself from Kevin. He lay on his back for a second or two, and then he sat up, at which time I hugged him and we got to our feet, to the sound of applause from the other students. I had not heard any coaching from them, if there had been any. Only the sound of Kevin's and my breathing and the crashing of my heartbeat.

"Good job, guys," Johnny said. "Kevin, we'll work on that guard pull to get you in better position. Val, nice finish. Watch your base when you are freeing your knee." I nodded, still breathing heavily, and walked toward the rest of the students, who were standing and sitting against the wall with the paneless window. A small group had assembled on the other side, leaning and observing.

I sat down and tried to control my breathing, in through the nose, out through the mouth, until my heart rate slowed. I drank some water. I looked at Kevin as he slid down the wall to sit next to me.

"Thanks," I said.

"I wish I could say the same," he said, though he was smiling.

I had been training jiu-jitsu for longer than Kevin, but I still understood how it could cause a little cognitive dissonance when a woman physically dominated a man. I experienced some of it myself. To Kevin's credit, he shrugged off the loss, certainly better than some other guys I have observed, and certainly better than I have done at various times.

We watched Vince square off against Paul. I did not pay much attention, because I was trying to get back into some kind of zone. Next up for me was James.

James was a blue belt too, but significantly bigger than Kevin and also possessed of a judo background, which means he was more comfortable and experienced with takedowns than I was. I say this not as an excuse for what happened next, but because those facts set the stage for what happened next—and for my reaction, which is mine to reckon with.

"Okay, Val, James, are you ready?"

I nodded. When there was about a minute left in Vince's match with Paul, I stood up and started moving around again, practicing my lines, so to speak. Vince had hit a takedown and passed to side control, where he spent the rest of the match trying for a finish, but Paul fended him off, so the match ended with Vince winning on points.

James stood up, and we bounced on the balls of our feet to the center of the mat, shifting our weight back and forth from foot to foot and smiling wanly at each other as Johnny went over the drill again. We fist bumped and slapped hands, and Johnny said, "Fight!"

James and I circled each other the same way I had just done with Kevin. I reached for his collar with my right hand, though I did not have a real purpose behind doing it other than that I knew I needed to do something.

This turned out to be a terrible, horrible, no-good, very bad idea. James went two-on-one with both his hands on my sleeve and freed himself. He kept his grip on my sleeve with his left hand, and before I knew what was happening, he fitted himself underneath me and executed a perfect drop *seoi nage*, a judo throw in which the thrower uses sleeve and collar grips as entry points to drop to his knees, facing the same direction as his opponent, and toss the opponent over his shoulder.

In this self-referential age and with the technologies that facilitate that self-reference, I have no doubt that there is plenty of video out there of people being judo thrown, from the perspective of the throw-ee. I do not need to see it. In that match between me and James, I *was* that video. This particular throw was a doozy. I had the presence of mind to land correctly—chin tucked, exhaling, slapping the mat with my free hand—but that could probably more accurately be described as "presence of reflex."

James landed on top of me, in side control, which means that I felt the force of his weight on me in addition to the shock of contact with the ground. I was the filling in a rock-and-a-hard-place sandwich that had been pitched out of a third-story window. By the time all of this registered, James was establishing his position, working for the crossface/underhook and separating my elbows from my body, something I absolutely did not want.

"Where are you, Val? Get in it! Defend the mount!" I heard someone yell. It might have been Vince.

I obeyed the voice. James had landed on my right side, so I put my right foot on my left knee to create an obstacle to try to prevent James from snaking his right leg over my body and establishing a mount position.

James, probably partially paying attention to the voice too, timed his counter perfectly, and as I tried to move my right leg into position, he redirected my knee toward his right, across my body, and followed it over with his own knee. James had taken the mount.

For those of you keeping score, James had earned two points for the takedown and then four points for the mount, for a total of six. He had not landed in my guard at all, so he did not have to pass to side, which would have garnered him another three.

Regardless, I was still way behind the eight-ball, both score-wise and mentally. James was on top of me, one knee on either side of my body, maintaining his base. I, on the other hand, tried to focus and breathe, and then I set about trying to unbalance him. I worked on getting to my right side, which would reduce James' stability on top—but not too much, because I knew if I overexposed my back, James would be able to put his chest behind it, and roll me to my stomach, keeping me there with the pressure of his body weight. This is the absolute worst position to be in in jiu-jitsu.

I tried not to think about how much I would need to do to get back in the game, or how heavy James felt, or how close his gi top was to my face. I failed.

Fighting back panic, I fished for James' left leg with my left foot, which I had brought over toward the right side of my body when I turned to my right. I tried to slide my right foot under his left foot and drag it back toward the center line with my left heel, but James shoved my right knee down with his left hand, which created room for him to free his foot. Then he buried both feet under my hamstrings, which were off the ground because I had placed my feet on the mat and bent my knees. I was trapped again.

I heard someone say, "Good, James! You're up by points! Time to look for a finish!"

Someone else said, "Val, you are still in this. Do not give up!" I could feel tears assembling. I was almost glad I was hidden under James' gi, because I am sure my game face was completely gone, replaced by an expression of pure panic.

James went for a collar grip, inserting his right hand, four fingers in, in the lapel that was, from his perspective, on the left side of my neck. I knew he would try to secure an overhand grip on the other side of my head with his left hand, as close to my neck as possible, in an attempt to set up a cross-collar choke.

Before he could do that, I grabbed onto his right hand and forearm with both of my hands and planted my left foot on the outside of his right foot. In one explosive movement, I lifted my hips and bridged over my left shoulder, attempting what is known as a mount roll. If I had been successful, this movement would have forced James to his back, and my connection to him combined with the momentum would have brought me on top, in his closed guard.

I was not successful. I heaved and strained as hard as I could, but James managed to free his hand, post out on the mat with it, and maintain his position. I fell back on my back and inched closer to despair. I had used a lot of energy trying to overcome the inertia of James' significantly larger body, and I had not advanced my position at all. I felt the same claustrophobia I had felt on that first day of my jiu-jitsu career. This time I did not tap, but I was sorely tempted. All that work and all those years, and I was still only a scary situation away from my basest instinct.

James continued to attack my collar, and I continued to divide my attention between defending his attack and trying, more and more desperately, to snare his foot between my feet to recompose half guard, and then to snare his arm, to try to set up another mount roll, back and forth between the two, but James had established a top position that put pressure on my hips, making it harder for me to both move and breathe. I had less and less energy to use to try to maintain my composure, let alone move strategically. Nothing I tried was working, and as I continued to try and fail, I could feel myself weakening mentally. My adrenaline had long ago dumped and seeped into the earth.

We continued to see-saw back and forth, James grabbing my collar to set up the choke and me unbalancing him enough so that he had to let go, but not enough to reverse him. Then he grabbed my collar again and I tried for the mount roll again. I kept my shoulders hunched and my hands at my throat, and James alternated between keeping the pressure on my hips and stomach and switching his weight to his knees so he could move around my body. When I felt the pressure lessen, I could move, but not effectively, and this only contributed to my distress. I imagined this must be what a chicken feels like in a factory farm enclosure.

I continued to try to move, at this point just trying to make it to the dingdingding before I screamed.

Then, dingdingding. James and I both let go of our respective grips on each other. He relaxed. I would have collapsed, had I not already been on the ground. He got up and reached out a hand to help me to my feet. I took it and hugged him, fighting back tears. I wanted to run off the mat, but we had to finish the ritual of competition, so I stayed, walking around in a small circle, tying my belt and fixing my hair, breathing in through my nose and out through my mouth, this time to prevent the switch from flipping. James did the same, though his hair looked fine. When we had put ourselves back together, Johnny stood us all in a row with himself in the middle, holding my right wrist and James' left. He faced us toward the wall with the unpaned window, against which the rest of the students in the class sat and on the other side of which some people were leaning.

He raised James' hand, at which point everyone clapped, including me, in a gesture of respect to James. I had to bring my left hand to my right one, as Johnny still had a grip on my right wrist. James and I hugged again, and he walked toward the wall and slid down it. I hurried off the mat and into a second, smaller bathroom that was down the hall toward John's offices, shutting the door behind me. Only then did I allow the tears to come.

I cried out of self-pity and ego. I had gotten trounced, and it was embarrassing, and I felt sorry for myself, but those were only two of the reasons. I also cried due to the frustration borne of complete ineffectuality. I had tried—really tried—to advance my position. I had expended serious energy in the effort, and it had gotten me nowhere. Both during the match, where I had strained as hard as I could only to end up in exactly the same place, and afterward, where I replayed those efforts in my brain until they were burned there, trying and failing felt worse than not trying.

I cried a little out of fear. I was not afraid of James, and I knew without a doubt that he would have stopped immediately if I had tapped, even if there had been nothing tangible to tap to. Yet in that match I got a small taste of what it feels like to be completed physically controlled, to have your every move countered and neutralized, to realize that unless the other person let up, I had absolutely zero control over what would happen to me next.

I cried for existential reasons. There in the bathroom, I had no satisfactory answer to the recurring question of why the hell I was doing this, because I was failing, and it felt awful. I had put all my eggs in this basket, and then I had been made to watch helplessly while someone else snatched the basket from my hands and stomped the eggs to goo.

I cried because I was tired and because I still had three matches to go, and there was nothing I wanted to do less than go back out there and face everyone with eyes red from crying, let alone throw down again. I savored the idea of just staying in the bathroom, sitting on the floor, which was another place in New Breed that should probably not have a black light shined on it. I must have been pretty upset, because I knew that, and yet there I sat.

When I heard a muffled voice out on the mat yell, "Two minutes to go!" from behind the bathroom door, I got up, wiped my eyes, and willed myself to look like I had not been crying, though of course it was obvious. When James saw me, he did a double take and stood up, stricken. I walked over to him and hugged him.

"I'm fine," I lied. "You helped me. Thank you." That part was true.

He hugged me back but looked concerned.

"I promise."

The rest of the students shifted uneasily. I clapped my hands several times. "I'm ready." More lies. I looked at the mat.

"One minute!" someone yelled. Johnny saw me emerge and shot a questioning glance at me.

I gave him the thumbs up, though I could not smile. I went through the same warm-up ritual I had performed before the first two matches, trying to keep the waterworks off and sometimes succeeding, but not always. This was a place where sweat came in handy—I had an excuse to wipe off my face with my gi sleeve, and I could surreptitiously dab at my eyes at the same time.

Dingdingding.

"Val," Johnny said. "Are you okay?"

"I'm fine. Let's do this." I hoped I was a good actress.

"Okay. You and George."

"Okay."

After I competed against George, I went back into the

bathroom and cried again, though this time I leaned against the wall instead of sitting down, and then I did it again after my fourth match. When I heard someone yell "One minute!" or when the match was cut short by a submission and I heard "TIME!" I wiped my eyes, straightened my gi, and walked outside to fight again.

By this time, the group had figured out what was happening, but to my relief they ignored the elephant in the room, instead focusing on coaching me, keeping time, and cheering me on. I did not fare as poorly in the rest of the matches as I had with James, though after each of the final three, I still beat a hasty retreat, each time making it to the sanctuary of the bathroom before the tears came. I cried as quietly as I could.

After my final match, I kept my composure long enough to shake hands and thank Johnny in his role as the ref, and then I went back to the bathroom. I stayed in there long after class had ended and the other students had headed out, but eventually I had to leave my disgusting lavatorial sanctuary. I was starting to shiver as the sweat cooled but, particularly on my sports bra, did not dry. Plus, the longer I stayed in my nasty training clothes, the more I smelled like Hot Pockets.

I did not want to come out, this time because I was embarrassed at having to face everyone. I had cried over jiu-jitsu before, and I would again, but I had broken my own cardinal rule that I would never do it on the mat. I waited until things became quiet and it sounded like most everyone had left. Then I slowly opened the door and tiptoed out into the reception area. Johnny was sitting behind the desk, still in his gi, and Vince was sitting in the chair on the other side of the desk, wearing a t-shirt and his gi pants.

They looked up when they heard me, and I smiled a small smile. "Hi," I said.

"What's up, Val?" Vince said.

I took a deep breath, hoping apologetic words would form in my brain and then come out of my mouth in some coherent way.

Before I could get anything out, Johnny looked at me,

put down the pen he had been holding, and said, "Nice job today. I'm proud of you."

That was not the reaction I had expected. "But—"I felt the tears coming again.

"Val, you came back, and then you came back again. And again. That's a victory. Do you see?"

I saw. "I didn't feel like I had a choice." I wiped my eyes again and half-laughed, half-coughed.

"Well, good," Johnny said, laughing.

"Did James leave?" I said. "I need to explain."

"He's fine," Johnny said. "I talked to him. He gets it."

"I need to make him see how much he helped me," I said.

"He does."

"You guys did too."

"Don't you forget it," Vince said.

"I won't. I promise."

"We know."

Over the next several months, I participated in many local and regional tournaments. I won some, lost more than I won, and learned something each time—something about my game or something about how to compete more effectively. I still loved to hate it. It gave me nightmares, waking and sleeping, and as early as a couple weeks out from a tournament, I would start in with self-loathing and contemplate yet again the question that had no satisfactory answer: "Why am I doing this?"

Since I competed at least every few weeks, I was in a constant state of physiological stress. Heaven help the server who got my order wrong or the teammate who joked about something I would normally be able to see the humor in—my age, my state of origin, my jiu-jitsu skill, anything else about me. While I was getting used to the demands of competition, I had less available for social graces. Much like I had done on the rafting trip in Portland, I could see myself behaving boorishly but seemed unable to curtail the behavior. I seemed to have been reduced to my basest human impulses.

When I spoke with my non-training friends or relatives, I

started responding to their observation that I "always seemed to be training," with the feeble, joke-adjacent line, "Well, yeah, jiu-jitsu is my career, but since I don't make any money at it, making a living is my hobby." In terms of how much time and energy I devoted to each of these things, this was pretty accurate. I went to sleep and woke up thinking about jiu-jitsu, I trained twice a day for at least two hours at a time, I sat and stretched or just stared at the wall to recover from training jiu-jitsu for minutes on end, I ate as if I had a tapeworm, but as much from exertion as from compulsion, I hung out with other people who trained, I complemented my training with strength and conditioning workouts, and I maintained my blog. I was the same person I had been when I left Chicago, and I was vastly different.

I spent my remaining time and energy, of which there was precious little, thinking about money—how much I had left, where it was going, and how I could earn more. This was almost an afterthought, though, so entrenched had I become in a jiu-jitsu way of life. It was almost magical, the way I had a fear about money or the future but then realized it was time to train and got lost in the session for several hours. The fear did not surface again until later, and when it did, it had less impact, as if the training session had temporarily raised my outlook metabolism in addition to my physical one. In truth, I was also usually exhausted, which means I was not capable of expending as much energy on being worried or planful.

Eventually I did work out a way to make a living, but it was something I definitely fit into the spaces of my life rather than vice versa. In this way, I took to its logical conclusion my wish when I was working full-time that I could just train all day. I realized that getting this wish made me both happy and beleaguered.

A black belt friend told me recently that during the years in his life he spent training to the almost complete exclusion of everyone and everything unrelated, it was not so much that he was addicted to BJJ. Rather, he was addicted to avoiding his problems, and jiu-jitsu had turned out to be a terrific avoidance tactic. The part about being addicted to avoiding my problems rang true for me when he and I discussed this, though in my case it was not either-or. When I was in competition mode, the fact that I was simultaneously able to distract myself from life issues was just a happy by-product of my fixation on jiu-jitsu and getting better at jiu-jitsu. The afterglow and the pleasant enervation were a nice complement to the almost intoxicated feeling I got after class when techniques and alternatives roiled around in my brain, leaving little room for other things. I was not even in the neighborhood of the transcendence Sam Sheridan describes, but with each training session, each competition match, even each frustrated breakdown, I moved a millimeter closer.

"Valerie Worthington, please report to mat coordinator number 8. Valerie Worthington to mat coordinator number 8."

I whipped my head around toward the disembodied voice that beckoned me to my immediate future, fleetingly wished I was not Valerie Worthington, grudgingly admitted that I am, and reported to mat coordinator number 8. He was a kindly looking, slender man in his 40s, wearing a blue, heavy cotton bib with the number 8 stamped in canary yellow on the front and back. He carried a clipboard that contained the brackets for his mat, brackets like the ones you see on sports shows and in Sports Illustrated around NCAA basketball finals time.

Only these brackets were for Mundial competitors, of which I was one. Tournament weekend had arrived, and with it, the day and time of my division—adult female purple belt middle heavyweight. The announcement of my name meant it was almost time for me to compete, barring a nervous breakdown, or the earthquake, sandstorm, or other natural disaster I was desperately hoping would happen in the next few minutes. If I ended up being unable to compete due to circumstances beyond my control, I would still get credit for trying, right? Oh well. I was ready to go. I really wanted a piece of her! I guess I will have to sublimate with ice cream. Or road rage.

No diversion of any kind materialized. I was in it.

I had already fought two matches that day, and I was now preparing to compete in the finals of my division. You would think I would have been relaxed by this stage of the game. You would be wrong. This one was for all the marbles, and I could not stop thinking about that fact. Someone had come up with this vercackte plan, and I was not happy with her.

The mat coordinator and I were standing in the bullpen, an area at one end of the gymnasium inside the Walter Pyramid, a huge blue structure on the Long Beach campus of California State University. The bullpen had been fenced off with waist-high barriers made of white PVC pipe and was populated by dozens of BJJ practitioners who were listening to headphones, jumping up and down or running in place to warm up their muscles and break a light sweat or to keep them that way, and giving off the aroma of, well, let's call it excellence. Like me, they were waiting for their turn to compete, to test what they knew about BJJ by applying it to an unknown quantity—fully resisting opponents from other academies. Most of them were wearing hooded sweatshirts, wool skull caps, and sneakers and socks to help them retain their body heat, though all of these would be stripped away when it was time to compete, leaving them in their gis.

If I had tried to explain with a straight face to kindly mat coordinator number 8 that in a former life I had been known in some circles as Dr. Worthington, had been all about business casual, and had regularly said things like "operationalize" and "return on investment," he would probably have stared at me blankly before asking me to step to the side so other competitors could get by on their way to their own mats. At the moment, Dr. Worthington was perspiring through her gi, trying to put on some semblance of a game face, and starting to smell the familiar bouquet of flop sweat.

In a matter of minutes, I would step onto mat 8, which from my vantage point looked huge and imposing, an endless square of slightly spongy blue punctuated by a yellow border. I would be out in the middle of it with only my opponent, who would be trying to rip my head off, and a referee, himself (and in recent years more frequently herself) required to be a black belt in Brazilian Jiu-Jitsu. Referees are well-versed in the competition rules, clad in black from head to sock—remember, no shoes on the mat, please—and responsible for monitoring the action and ensuring the safety of the competitors. When the ref gave the signal, my opponent and I would go to work.

My heart was hammering so hard I could see my gi top move. I had dry mouth and, paradoxically, the almost uncontrollable urge to "go to the euphemism," as Dr. Seuss, I think it was, would say. As I had learned through my tournament preparation, BJJ competition can be very intense, completely exhausting, and utterly fraught with sensory overload. Plus, I was hardly a seasoned competitor, though I had gotten a crash course during the time I had spent at New Breed.

In BJJ, successful competitors have training partners, coaches, sponsors, and other supporters helping them along the way. Preparing a grappler for competition can truly be described as a team effort, and Johnny, John, Vince, and many others had helped me immeasurably with my preparation. Johnny and John were going to be at the edge of the mat, behind more PVC pipe barriers, to coach me, but when it came time to throw down, the only person who was going to step into the fray was me. Me. Oh crap. I looked around. Not even a single locust?

Instead: "You're Valerie? Okay, come with me." I followed mat coordinator number 8 to the scale, where another tournament worker made sure I was within the weight requirement for my division. Competitors are separated into divisions by gender, weight, belt level, and age, though, as with this tournament, I was frequently in the position of having to compete against women who were young enough to be my daughters. I was then led to the gi-checker, who asked me to put my arms straight out in front of me and then to either side, forming my body into a lowercase T, albeit a lowercase T that was close to losing its tenuous grasp on sanity.

The gi checker confirmed that my gi was acceptable for competition, not too tight or too short in the sleeves or pants, and sporting team and sponsor patches only on the IBJJF-approved locations. I noticed that my opponent was being put through the same paces, a step behind me. When we were both approved, we stood awkwardly near each other so mat coordinator number 8 could find us when he needed us, but far enough removed so we did not have to interact. Some competitors like to chat with their opponents before competing.

I am not one of those competitors and had been forced on one or two occasions to request that the person I was getting ready to compete against zip it and save the questions about where I was from and where I trained until after we had finished trying to kill each other. This opponent was not a problem in that way, though she was making me nervous for other, obvious reasons. By and by, mat coordinator number 8 came in to break the tension and lead us to the edge of our mat.

There was a white plastic folding table at mat 8, as there was by each of the tournament mats, each occupied by two people. One of the people was keeping score on two numbered flip charts, a red one for one opponent and a green one for the other. More recently, scores are kept electronically and flashed on a computer monitor, but back then, it was analog.

The scorekeeper kept his or her eyes on the referee, who wore red and green wristbands and signaled points with the corresponding hand to help ensure the proper number of points went to the correct competitor. The other person kept time with a stopwatch, stopping the countdown whenever the referee signaled a timeout for any reason—for instance, when the competitors rolled out of bounds or when a competitor's foot became stuck in the opponent's gi jacket—and restarted it when the referee restarted the action. Again, nowadays the time is projected on a computer screen, but not so back then. The timekeeper was also responsible for signaling the end of matches by throwing a folded-up belt onto the mat in the referee's line of sight when the regulation time ended. At that point, the referee would stop the action, sometimes finding it necessary to physically separate the competitors with his or her hands or body, if the action was particularly intense and the competitors were unaware of the time.

"All right, you stand here, and you stand here," said mat coordinator number 8, placing us on either side of the table. "After this match, there will be one more, and then you two are up. Okay?"

Not okay. Not even a little bit okay, but okay. I examined my fingernails and tried to blur my peripheral vision so I could not see my opponent pacing back and forth on her side of the mat edge. She looked like she knew what she was doing, like this was second nature to her. I did the only thing I could think of to do, and the thing I have noticed people often do when they step onto a grappling mat in an academy and are waiting for class to start but do not know how to occupy themselves: I sat down and did a butterfly stretch. This had the added benefit of putting more of me in contact with the ground, which helped to mask the fact that I was shaking and made it far less likely that I would take a header into the floor due to the vertigo I imagined I was feeling.

I also looked behind me and saw Johnny, John, Vince, and a group of other New Breeders leaning against the PVC pipe barrier that sat a few feet behind the table. They smiled and flashed the thumbs up. I waved and nodded. I did not smile.

With a toss of the belt, the match on mat 8 before mine ended, and the ref raised the hand of the victor. The two competitors stepped off the mat, and this time the table worker yelled my name and that of my opponent. "You two are up!"

I heard Johnny, John, and Vince clap and say, "Let's go, Val!"

I heard my opponent's corner people say something similar to my opponent. I stepped to the edge of the mat, bowed, and walked onto that blue sheet, staying on top rather than sinking into it and emerging in mainland China like I would have preferred. In keeping with the tradition of respect associated with martial arts of all kinds, I bowed to the referee and shook his hand. Then I bowed to my opponent and shook her hand. Then I clenched and unclenched my fists and swallowed, tasting dry mouth, anxiety, and a little bit of bile. My opponent and I faced each other, waiting for instructions from the ref, who stood between us. He asked if we were ready, and when we both said yes, he dropped his hand in a chopping motion to signal it was time to compete. And away we went.

When I get caught in a good blood choke, which is a choke that cuts off the blood to the brain, as opposed to a windpipe choke, which cuts off oxygen, certain things happen to me as I journey toward unconsciousness. In addition to feeling pressure behind my eyes that makes me feel like my head is going to pop off like the top of a dandelion, one of the most notable is that my vision starts to tunnel, similar to the iris wipe effect on a cartoon or old-timey silent movie.

If a grappler, or anyone, for that matter, gets caught in a choke, there are several possible outcomes. One is that the person tries to defend the choke and succeeds, either causing the aggressor to let go and try something else, or continue to insist, unsuccessfully, on keeping the grips and trying for the finish until the buzzer. Another possible outcome is that the person feels him- or herself losing consciousness and taps, at which point the attacker should let go, the blood should rush back into its proper places, and the person being choked should be none the worse for wear. The third is that the person tries to defend the choke and fails, which results in him or her going night-night.

My experience at the tournament felt like I was being caught in a choke, only the tunneling of my vision extended to the other four senses as well. In each match, I felt like I went completely to my hindbrain, acting and reacting in response to only the most immediate stimuli, which were basically the ones I was feeling with my sense of touch due to my close physical proximity to my opponent. Over the years, as I have gained more experience and skill at competing, the tunnels have widened and I can take in more information to help me perform effectively. In that match, though, I was only able to process as much sense information as you might get through a cardboard paper towel tube, and truthfully, that is probably being generous. For instance, I know I was surrounded by noise: cheering (not all for me, but maybe some), refs yelling commands, coaches yelling different commands, announcements over the intercom. I do not remember hearing any of it.

After my opponent and I shook hands, we squared off. She and I closed the distance between each other, and I worked to get good grips on her sleeve and lapel and prevent her from doing the same. I had learned my lessons from my competition practice with James. From there, I pulled guard on my opponent like Kevin had on me during our competition training. In this way, I could connect myself to her but keep her at enough of a distance so I could move strategically.

I knew she herself was a guard puller, someone who liked to sit to the mat and initiate the action from there, so by doing it first, I forced her to play her top game. I hoped this was not as comfortable for her. She ended up in my closed guard, which involved her sitting on her knees while I lay on my back with my legs wrapped around her hips. She focused on keeping her spine straight and her head up, which is known as maintaining posture. I was using my hands and legs to try to break down that posture, pulling on her lapels and bringing my knees toward my chest, and her along with them. Essentially, I was trying to yank her head down into my B-cups.

I climbed my legs higher on her back so more of my body weight would weigh her down and make her top-heavy, keeping that posture broken and her face close to the girls. I put my right hand inside her opposite lapel, in a cross-collar grip, and the back of my left knee came in front of her shoulder. I clamped that leg down on her back, bringing my right leg up under her left armpit and my right foot on top of my left. In this position, I had good control of her posture, and, if I had been so inclined, could have whispered a giggly, girly secret right in her ear, like, "When we're done here, win or lose, I'm going to eat a giant cupcake. You with me?"

For about two months before the tournament, as part of my stepped-up competition preparation, I had spent hours at New Breed drilling a specific movement sequence from just this position, and the match played directly into this sequence. This has not often happened in my tournament experiences. Rather, I am usually uber-prepared for situations that do not arise and less prepared for the ones that do. In this match, for the first and so far only time in my jiu-jitsu competition experience, I felt like I was Neo, easily dodging bullets in the Matrix because they were coming at me in slo-mo. The sequence I had spent time drilling had a Plan A, a Plan B, and a Plan C built into it.

I made it as far as Plan B, when I executed an arm bar from the guard, hyperextending her elbow by using my hips and legs to isolate her arm from the rest of her body and her head. I apparently did it right enough, because my opponent tapped, signaling her inability to escape, which prompted the referee to quickly pull us apart and end the match before I did her any actual bodily harm. Not that I would have intended to, but a cardinal rule of tournament play is that you make the referee end the match rather than letting go of a submission, as some competitors have been known to tap and then deny it. For some, winning at any cost is preferable to losing with integrity.

Still on my back, I immediately looked around for Johnny, John, and Vince, who I am sure had been yelling all this time, giving me useful commands, though that old tunneling effect meant I was barely able to make my relevant body parts do what they were supposed to, let alone hear, process, and act upon such information. No matter. They were happy and proud, as evidenced by their vigorous applause and ear-to-ear grins.

Breathing heavily, I stood up, tried to smooth my disheveled appearance (retying my belt, fixing my hair, which had come out of the ponytail holder, pulling my rash guard down to cover my navel), and went to stand next to the referee. My opponent stood on the other side of him.

The referee grabbed my wrist and my opponent's wrist. Then he raised my hand and kept my opponent's hand down, presenting us to the audience members who were in the bleachers and lining the competition space on one side of the venue, and then turning us 180 degrees to do the same on the other side, signaling my victory in that match, and with that match, my victory in my division. At the precise moment my opponent tapped to my arm bar, I became an adult female purple belt gold medalist at the Mundial of Brazilian Jiu-Jitsu. In other words, I was the best in the world. In those moments,
I realize now, I had found what I was looking for. Contentment. Flow to the nth degree. Accomplishment. Presence. Maybe even a smidgeon of that elusive transcendence. The sense that I did not need to be anywhere else, and I did not need to be anything else. The feeling in my brain, body, and heart that who and what I was were just exactly enough.

EPILOGUE

Before I started writing it, I am sure I fantasized that this book would speak to readers. I am sure I imagined who would play me in the movie version and what songs the soundtrack would have on it, and in what order. Whether the song would be a cover or the original artist. A live or a studio recording. Regardless, it would be uplifting. Inspirational. With the book itself, I think I fully expected to end with the characters, particularly me, living happily ever after. Anticipating only good things, like the ending of *Good Will Hunting*, which shows Will driving toward California "to see about a girl." That ending is satisfying, and it allows the audience to believe that only good things await Will and Skylar. The ending freezes us in a permanent state of happy anticipation.

After I won purple belt worlds, I, too, lived happily ever after, for probably two whole weeks. The moment I stepped off the mat after I won and hugged Johnny, John, and Vince was pretty amazing. I collected my driver's license from the table worker, who also congratulated me, and I went back toward the bullpen where some of my friends and teammates were waiting. Everyone loves a winner. You have accomplished your goal, you are happy, and you have a fun story to tell, so you are enjoyable to be around. Plus, it is much less awkward to congratulate someone than it is to figure out what combination of sympathetic facial expression and sentiment to convey to a loser—and oh, man, what if losing is contagious? Maybe there are no definitive studies positing a causal link between casual contact with a loser and one's own ability to perform in life, but who wants to risk it?

On this occasion, in addition to the people who would have been waiting even if I had lost, there was also a good number of more distant acquaintances. Even some people passing by that I did not know made a point of smiling and flashing the thumbs up when they deduced what had happened. I felt validated that the work I had put in had paid off and that maybe I did not completely suck at jiu-jitsu.

I had serious dry-mouth, the kind that causes you to make a gross, sucking sound when you talk. When I got onto the podium to receive my gold medal, from a perch that was higher than the silver medalist's and higher still than the bronze medalist's, and labeled with a "1" to the silver and bronze medalists' "2" and "3," so everyone knew who was who, Johnny, John, and Vince joined in the applause and photo snapping and video recording along with the rest of my friends and teammates. Then, there in the bustling venue, as countless other matches began and ended, spectators cheered, and athletes milled about on their way to throw down or rest up, Johnny pulled out a brown belt, adding the polar opposite of insult to whatever is diametrically opposed to injury, tying it around my waist before all the other good stuff even had a chance to sink in. I competed on a Friday morning, so there were still more than two days left for me to enjoy the spectacle of the tournament, fielding congratulations, watching amazing grappling, eating acai, which is a Brazilian frozen treat, and secretly rejoicing that I had become ineligible to compete in the purple belt open division. It really was a perfect coda.

The afterglow persisted into the next couple of weeks, as I saw people at the academy who had not been at the tournament but who took one look at my new belt and knew what had happened. My parents had pestered our family and friends with the news, so emails and messages came in fast and furiously. For the next week or so, every time I reached into my gym bag and pulled out my belt, I stopped short, because I was not yet used to the new color. Then I remembered. I got to relive the day and the emotions and what I had accomplished. I had legitimized myself in my own mind by putting it on the line and being able to do what it took to win, literally fighting through tears.

This is where the movies usually stop, right? With the fist raised in victory and the appreciation of the people who understand the significance of what the protagonist managed to do. What happens after the movie is over is implied to be perfection, a lengthening to forever of this climactic moment, or, more realistically but still unrealistically, a settling into a perfect life.

In my version of happily ever after, I am reunited with Jake from Talkeetna, and the initial connection we shared turns out to be the foundation of something worthwhile and sustainable. He, as it happens, is a prince of some kind—an available, interested prince with a comfortable but modest kingdom—not flashy, but substantial. Maintaining my perfect health and my perfect physique—of course I have a perfect physique—requires a steady diet of peanut butter cups. Being a good person means blaming others for my shortcomings and having them concede that I am right to do it. The people I love will live forever, and although many of them are scattered throughout the country and the world, I can see them whenever I want to because the transporter popularized in the *Star Trek* television and movie franchise has become a reality. (Hey, if we are really going to do this, let's do it.)

I would like to be able to tell you that all of the above came to pass, but of course it did not, and will not anytime soon. For one thing, doctors are still working out the exact number of peanut butter cups any individual needs to consume for maximal health. Even though it is not zero, given that mental health is important too, it is probably also not my ideal number.

I would be satisfied with being able to say that farther along on my journey, the experiences I had with jiu-jitsu enabled me to make all the right decisions for myself all the time, and that I never had another moment's doubt or fear about those decisions. I would like to be able to say that trusting that the next lighted square will be there to catch me before I fall is now easy, and that I lose nary a moment's sleep now that I have more practice living this way. That I never feel depressed or intimidated anymore, and that I always feel like training and it always goes effortlessly. That I have everything I ever wanted in my life and no regrets, no what-ifs and no stones unturned. Even if we do not get the physically and scientifically impossible, we should be able to expect something pretty amazing from our happily ever after. That is what it implies.

Yet at an almost imperceptible pace, the stresses, exasperations, second-guesses, and unexpected tremors of everyday life, even an everyday grappling life, started to rise again to my conscious awareness as more days passed. These moved closer to center stage as my accomplishment slowly receded to the "happy memory" section of my brain before taking up permanent residence in "That's nice. What have you done lately?" and dropping off everyone else's radar completely. Life resumed, and days passed. The persistent challenges of making a living and identifying priorities did not go away, though they did get tabled more often than not as I continued to focus on jiu-jitsu, and though I do not recall giving explicit permission for them to do this, the days turned into weeks, which turned into months, which turned into years.

In those years, I went on to earn my black belt from Johnny and John. I continued to compete, with varying levels of success. I have taken on more leadership in my corner of the jiu-jitsu world—teaching, writing, and running events with business partners that reflect what we believe about how jiu-jitsu can be used as a force for good. I am wiser now about the long-term cumulative effects of my countless micro-decisions to pursue jiu-jitsu, or maybe it is just that enough time has passed for me to be experiencing them. Some days I feel I am doing justice to one of the quotes that inspires me, a line from the title character in the movie *Breaker Morant*: "Live each day as if it's your last, and one day you'll be right." Other times I hope I will live to see another day, because the one I am currently living consists only of equal parts self-pity and chocolate Riesen, and I would rather not have to explain that to St. Peter, or Lucifer, or even Charon.

In short, I am living my life. I hope I am doing it justice, and I fear I am not. Today I feel I am in the driver's seat on a straightaway, but yesterday I felt I was at the mercy of the roller coaster operator. I do regular gut checks on whether I am making my choices out of love rather than living my life in fear. Sometimes I catch myself doing the latter, and then I agonize over how to get to the former.

I am ever so slightly better equipped to appreciate virtuosity wherever I see it—not just the observation of it in action, but the understanding of what it takes to achieve it. I see the beauty a little bit better because I have experienced a little bit of the sacrifice. I respect the process and commiserate about the fact that the work is never done. I have never arrived, though perhaps I have moved a step closer, fit one more piece of the puzzle.

I say goodbye to people a tiny bit more easily because I am more likely to see them again.

I have spent some time on jiu-jitsu's D list, garnering a bit of celebrity.

I suspect I am on some kind of IRS watch list, because my address of record changes like the seasons, as do my jobs. I always have some disparate constellation of W2s, 1099s, and multiple state residence declarations in any given tax year. Similarly, every year, my friends and extended family have to reach out to me for my current snail mail address so they can send a holiday card and be sure it will reach me, because it changes like I am on the lam.

Sometimes I feel sad or scared about something, some issue in my life that looms large. Then I go to train, and I come back feeling much better. The question always haunts me, though: Is that a remedy or an escape, and does it matter, as long as the rest of my act is reasonably together?

One of the popular t-shirts that has made the rounds in grappling circles in recent years features the quote "Jiu-Jitsu

Saved My Life." There is even a group bearing that name that provides a lot of information and inspiration on its eponymous website. While I understand the sentiment, I take exception to the wording. Jiu-Jitsu saves no one's life. It *changes* no one's life, as a variation of the above described t-shirt would have you believe. It does not even make me a better person, which is something I used to say, though now I realize the error of my ways. It does nothing but be jiu-jitsu.

What saves, changes or improves a person are the decisions that person makes for him or herself about how to live. Jiu-jitsu may have a significant influence on these decisions, and in that way it can serve as a mechanism through which good things can happen, but in different hands, or in conjunction with a different choice, it can also serve as a mechanism through which bad things can happen. The benefits and consequences of those choices belong solely to the person who makes them. I may have felt inspired to quit my job because of how I felt when I trained and how different—how much better—that was compared to how I felt when I was working, for instance, but I was the one who did the quitting, not jiu-jitsu.

I am the one who got to enjoy the fruits of that labor, through increased happiness and an increased sense of well-being.

For me, it is about doing what is right and best for me, not for some noble purpose, but because, when all is said and done, even though sometimes it is the most difficult thing to do and I would rather do anything else, I can't not.

ACKNOWLEDGEMENTS

At first blush, BJJ and writing might not appear to have much in common, but in my experience, they share some striking similarities. Both are physical, mental, psychological, and emotional processes that challenge, tire, frighten, and exhilarate every particle of my being. Both require me to scrape myself raw and then expose those vulnerable, delicate parts to the sting of oxygen and/or judgment, in the interest of improved performance and self-awareness. Both make me feel at times that they are more trouble than they are worth, but this feeling is always temporary.

Another similarity between BJJ and writing is that while they can sometimes feel like lonely endeavors in that my output is mine alone to contend with, they are inherently social and interpersonally rich. Without the veritable army of people who have supported me as a martial artist, as a writer, as a person, as some combination of these, I shudder to think where I might be now, both in my life and in my mind. Here is my opportunity to thank those people who have played a significant role in helping me at this stage, in no particular order:

JW, FW, DF, and Tim Greenberg, thank you for being some of the first people who not only saw a "there" there, but who provided material assistance in helping me pursue it.

Team Kwok/Hurtado, thank you for unconditional love

and acceptance, and for giving me a home.

Team Macauley, thank you for well over a decade of friendship, levity, and unflagging support. They say friends are the family you choose. If that is true, then you are proof that I chose wisely.

Marshal Carper of Artechoke Media, my editor, my publisher, my sometime therapist, thank you for seeing the possible in my story, for slogging through drafts no one should be made to read, and for helping me construct a "finished" product that is far more readable. Thank you also for talking me down from more than one ledge.

Julie Gordon Willis, who has come to know me better than I know myself and who loves me anyway, thank you for being the kindest, gentlest, and yet tough love-iest mirror a person could ask for.

Adamarie Bell, whose intelligence and strategic mind would terrify me if they were not so often used for my direct benefit and if they were not always tempered with love and support, thank you for helping me see the light, even and especially when it exposes more work for me to do on myself.

Lisa Ivy and Greg Anderson, thank you for helping me see not only that I could, but that I basically had to, and for creating the perfect scenario for me to try—apparently through telepathy, as I sat in your presence and watched my life change for the better before my eyes. And to Sprocket and Dewey for reminding me that sometimes all we need to make it better is a good belly rub.

Everyone at Princeton Brazilian Jiu-Jitsu, especially Art Keintz, thank you for laughter, camaraderie, and, of course, jiu-jitsu.

Rich Fitzgerald, you are a kind and decent person and a good friend, but don't worry: Your secret is safe with me.

David Jacobs and Steve Bowers, you are wonderful ambassadors for jiu-jitsu and walking instruction manuals for how to be a good person.

Sam Faulhaber, you fix all the aches and pains I inflict on myself, help me restore them on the mat, and then repeat.

Hillary Witt and Nelson Puentes of Inverted Gear and Bill

Thomas of Q5, who were friends first and colleagues/sponsors later, thank you for providing valuable services to the jiu-jitsu community, for schooling me on the mat, and for being so ding-dang fun to be around.

Hannette Staack, I so admire your jiu jitsu accomplishments, and I so value your friendship. Thank you for sharing your wisdom about both.

Lola Newsom, you've helped me grow, in jiu jitsu and in life. I am a better person because of it, and I thank you.

Jennifer* Thomas, Pat Burtis, Bryher, and Mimi, I do not have the words to express how much I love and appreciate your presence in my life, though that is probably not something a would-be writer should admit.

Christopher Walker, Natalie Adler, and Lucy, you are stuck with me, but I will always do my best to make it worth your while.

Thank you to Team 1 BJJ and The Academy for hospitality and butt-kickings.

Rodrigo Ranieri de Faria, I would train with you on either coast or anywhere in between.

Rick Webber, thank you for training, perspective, and a more sophisticated appreciation of Star Wars.

Anna Miller, Leigh Doran, Claire Dufort, and Ana Lowry, thank you for bringing me into your fold as if you had always known me.

Tori Garten, you are smart and funny and positive in the realest way, and you are my friend, for which I am forever grateful.

Becca Borawski Jenkins and the staff and readers of *Breaking Muscle*, thank you for not laughing when I called myself a writer and instead taking me at my word since 2011.

Eric Stafford, thank you for capturing moments of community and badassery in equal measure at GGC events, and for being insightful, positive, and fun to be around.

To all the jiu-jitsu academies, instructors, and fellow students I have had the opportunity to encounter, thank you for helping me improve. Whether once or a thousand times, training with each person and at each place gave me more insight into the kind of grappler—and person—I want to be. Now it is my job to apply those lessons myself.

To Groundswell Grappling Concepts and anyone who has ever supported and/or attended a GGC or Women's Grappling Camp event: While I tout these as a way I can pay forward all I have been given on my jiu-jitsu journey, I gain more from your participation than I could ever repay. For this, I am humbled, grateful, and exhausted.

To family and friends who continue to come along for the ride even as I shed skin after skin, thank you for loving, accepting, and feeding me no matter what. You know who you are, and if you do not, then I am falling down on the job.

ABOUT THE AUTHOR

Valerie Worthington was born and raised in Pennington, New Jersey, save for a year her family spent in Germany while she and her sister were in high school. It was probably then that her wanderlust kicked into overdrive, as her family spent the year taking advantage of the opportunity to have as many adventures as possible. She went on to earn a bachelor's degree in English literature from Dartmouth College in Hanover, New Hampshire, and after a few years in the non-profit world in Washington, DC, completed a doctorate in educational psychology at Michigan State University. It was in graduate school, in 1998, that she was introduced to Brazilian Jiu-Jitsu, a meeting that has reverberated throughout her life to this day. She was awarded her black belt in jiu-jitsu in 2010 at New Breed Academy in Santa Fe Springs, California.

She currently resides in Philadelphia and trains at Princeton BJJ in central New Jersey.

Made in the USA
Middletown, DE
24 April 2016